THE EXPERIENCED RESIDENT ASSISTANT

Readings, Case Studies, and Structured Group Exercises for Advanced Training

Edited by

Gregory S. Blimling, Ph.D.
Louisiana State University

KENDALL/HUNT PUBLISHING COMPANY
2460 Kerper Boulevard   P.O. Box 539   Dubuque, Iowa 52004-0539

Copyright © 1989 Kendall/Hunt Publishing Company

Library of Congress Catalog Card Number: 88–82027

ISBN 0–8403–4492–9

Printed in the United States of America
10 9 8 7 6 5 4 3 2 1

Contents

Contributors

Dr. Kent D. Beeler; Coordinator for Student Services, Indiana University-Purdue University at Columbus, Columbus, Indiana

Dr. Christine Bennett; Associate Professor, Department of Curriculum and Instruction, Indiana University; Bloomington, Indiana

Dr. Gregory S. Blimling; Dean of Students, Louisiana State University; Baton Rouge, Louisiana

Dr. Barbara E. Engram; Director of Health Resources, Hood College; Frederick, Maryland

Dr. Gary G. Gintner; Assistant Professor and Director of Clinical Training, Department of Counselor Education and Supervision, Louisiana State University; Baton Rouge, Louisiana

Dr. Thomas W. Hosie; Associate Professor and Coordinator, Department of Counselor Education and Supervision, Louisiana State University, Baton Rouge, Louisiana

Dr. W. Garry Johnson; Assistant Vice President for Student Affairs and Adjunct Associate Professor, Department of Counselor Education and College Student Personnel, Western Illinois University; Macomb, Illinois

Dr. Joseph K. Kavanaugh; Associate Vice President and Dean of Students; and Adjunct Associate Professor of Management, Lamar University; Beaumont, Texas

Dr. Barbara Y. Keller; Director of Residence Education, Bowling Green State University; Bowling Green, Ohio

Dr. Nancy I. Mathews; Assistant Director of the Student Health Center and Coordinator of Wellness Programs, Louisiana State University; Baton Rouge, Louisiana

Dr. Lawrence J. Miltenberger; Dean for Residence Life, Indiana State University; Terre Haute, Indiana

Mrs. Jan S. Miltenberger, R.N.; Assistant Director for Student Health Promotion, Indiana State University; Terre Haute, Indiana

Dr. Myron G. Mohr; Executive Director, Baton Rouge Crisis Intervention Center, Practicing Clinical Psychologist, and Adjunct Assistant Professor of Psychology, Louisiana State University; Baton Rouge, Louisiana

Dr. Robert F. Rodgers; Associate Professor, Departments of Psychology and Educational Policy and Leadership, and Director of the Student Personnel Assistant Program, The Ohio State University; Columbus, Ohio

Dr. John H. Schuh; Associate Vice President for Student Affairs, Wichita State University; Wichita, Kansas

Dr. Alexander F. Smith; Dean of Student Life and Adjunct Associate Professor of Education, Denison University; Granville, Ohio

Introduction and Overview

Recently, Ernest Boyer, President of the Carnegie Foundation for the Advancement of Teaching (1987),[1] observed that the resident assistant (RA) position was one of the most demanding assignments on a college campus. He explained that "RAs confront daily the realities of dormitory life. Beyond the ordinary, day-to-day hassles, they must deal with accidents, abuse of alcohol, depression, and questions about birth control and abortion. It is a twenty-four-hour a day job, one that involves not just keeping order and finding light bulbs, but becoming deeply involved in shaping the lives of students and helping college accomplish its most fundamental goals" (p. 199). Boyer "strongly urged" colleges and universities to provide RAs with intensive training to insure that they are properly prepared to confront the myriad of problems that they encountered throughout the course of the year.

Boyer has recognized what those of us who have worked in residence halls have acknowledged for many years: that RAs are our most valuable resource. It is through the daily contact these students have with the residents that a large part of the residence hall program is realized. The RA position is among the most difficult on any college campus. It requires people who can manage their own studies, personal growth, and social life while helping other students—as individuals and as members of a living group—manage their studies, personal growth, and social lives. Unlike other work assignments a student might have during college, the RA position is constant. RAs awaken to the responsibilities of their job and retire each evening with these same responsibilities. Most residence hall programs invest considerable time and attention in familiarizing RAs with institutional procedures, and in acquainting them with the basic skills needed to perform the RA job.

What is sometimes lost in this process of training is a recognition that the training needs of first year RAs are different from those of RAs who have a year or more of experience. It is not uncommon to hear the experienced RAs grumble about reviewing some of the same material they reviewed in previous years. First year RAs need to be introduced to a variety of topics, which by its nature limits the depth to which each can be explored within the course of one semester. Experienced RAs need an opportunity to extend their knowledge about working with students, and they need a forum to help them focus their thinking about issues relevant to the student residential situation.

What should not happen is to close the opportunities for RAs to continue to grow and develop in these skill areas. When this happens, RAs can easily lose motivation to continue. The experienced RA needs particular reassurance and motivation as the day-to-day stress of the position takes its toll on his or her enthusiasm for the position. If nothing else, advanced training for the experienced RA serves to renew one's dedication and to provide a forum for sharing ideas and information with other RAs from other residence halls confronted with many of the same problems. Ideally, RA training should be a continuing educational experience that combines analytic inquiry of human relations topics with practical application in working with the students for whom RAs are responsible.

[1]Boyer, E. L. (1987) *College: The Undergraduate Experience in America*. New York: Harper & Row.

One can think of RA training as a three level process. At the first level, new RAs should be introduced to the responsibilities of the position and given basic skills to work with students. This might be considered the level of minimum competence for the position. After RAs gain some experience in the position, they should have the opportunity to extend their skills by developing expertise in some of the areas to which they were originally introduced. At the third level, RAs can be used in a pre-professional capacity as trainers and in-house experts who can assist in teaching the first year RAs and in doing in-service education programs for students and staff. This three level process of training 1) minimum competence level, 2) expert level, and 3) instructor level provides a self-renewing training cycle that benefits both the residence hall program and the individual student.

The educational medium for teaching RA skills can take many forms. The traditional classroom situation with academic credit is a method that has been adopted by many institutions and is one that rewards RAs with academic credit for the mastery of valuable human relations skills. Short courses or seminars on special RA topics, workshops, retreats, and in-service educational programs all offer opportunities to extend RAs' training.

The demands of such a position call for a unique temperament, an understanding person, and a variety of skills in working with students growing into adulthood. Little that is said in this book can compensate for the temperament, empathy for others, and motivation that RAs bring with them to their position and refine throughout their experience in the position. What this book offers is the opportunity for RAs to learn from experts about critical issues that college students confront, and the opportunity to apply this information through the use of case studies and structured group experiences.

This book is written for the RA who has had a year or more of experience in the position. It is intended to build upon topics presented in other texts commonly used in introductory RA courses. In each chapter, students are introduced to the most recent information on the topic. At the end of each chapter is a working section made up of a case study and one or more group and individual exercises. The case studies are designed to illustrate the material discussed in the text and to provide opportunities for students to apply the material to realistic situations. They will also be able to utilize the skills that they have already developed through their work and to draw upon their experiences.

Following the case studies are structured group and individual exercises that give RAs opportunities to apply the chapter material, learn from interaction with other RAs, and receive feedback from the course instructor. This structure reflects our belief that learning takes place best in situations where there is an opportunity to apply new information, demonstrate the skill, and receive feedback on how well one has mastered the skill. The feedback an RA receives should help him or her develop greater confidence and insight in working with their residents.

Ideally, the text and working materials would be used in a course setting similar to that used to introduce entree level RAs to the position. However, the material can also be used in an in-service education program or as topics for a series of special workshops or retreats.

Unit 1: The Resident as a Member of a Living Group

The fourteen chapters of this book are presented in four units. Unit One considers the residents as members of a living group. Dr. Schuh's chapter begins this unit, examining the issue of community and how it can be created in a residence hall. The case studies and exercises give the RA specific tasks and examples on how to shape this environment. Dr. Kavanaugh's chapter focuses on how RAs can assert leadership in a living unit by understanding and shaping the unit's subculture. This new approach to leadership utilizes the dynamics of the living group's formative history to enhance the RA's influence in the living unit. Professor Bennett's chapter concludes this first unit. It addresses the very important issue of the cultural and racial differences that students confront in adjusting to others in a new living environment. She gives a new perspective on the adjustments students make, and gives RAs the opportunity to consider the perceptions of people from different cultural backgrounds.

Unit 2: The Resident as an Individual

The second unit of the book examines the individual student and the skills the RA needs to enhance work with students on an individual basis. The first chapter, by Professor Rodgers, introduces RAs to some of the theories underlying the developmental process of students in college and to the influence the environment plays in a student's growth and adjustment in college. He is careful to acknowledge the differing needs that students, professional staff, and scholars have for in-depth information on this topic.

Professor Hosie's chapter examines how to break through some of the barriers people create when they are trying to communicate their feelings. Specific techniques are given for enriching RAs' ability to communicate with others at a more intimate, personal level. The final chapter in this unit is by Dr. Johnson. In it he reviews skills associated with peer counseling and advising in the RA position. In the working section, he provides case studies and exercises designed to give RAs practical experience in the peer counseling process.

Unit 3: Educating Your Residents

The third unit shows RAs several ways they can enrich the educational environment of their living unit through educational programming, by maintaining a living environment that ensures the rights of all students, and by teaching students the skills required to resolve personal conflicts through mediation. Dr. Keller's chapter begins this unit by showing how to structure educational programs for residence students and how these can be woven together into themes to offer opportunities for students to work on developmental issues they are confronting in college.

No living group that does not share standards of reasonable behavior can be expected to accomplish an environment that supports the development, growth, and maturation of the students who live there. Unfortunately, not all residents share the same standard of conduct, and it is often left to the RA, as the respresentative of the university, to ensure that a positive living environment is maintained. In chapter eight, Dr. Smith explores the RA's responsibilities for maintaining a positive living environment for residents and how best the RA can confront situations when residents present disciplinary problems.

Chapter nine, by Dr. Engram, provides an approach to dealing with conflicts that arise between roommates and among the other residents in a living unit. Residents all too often run to the RA with every human relations conflict, expecting that the RA will immediately resolve the conflict. Dr. Engram's chapter presents an approach that can be used to help RAs remove themselves as decision-makers. The basic technique uses these conflicts as opportunities to teach students skills in conflict management. To do this, Dr. Engram explains the process of conflict mediation and negotiation. She gives specific steps in these processes and examples of how they can be used.

Unit 4: Insuring the Well-Being of Your Residents

The final unit covers a variety of issues, all of which focus on methods of insuring the physical, emotional, and psychological well-being of residents. Dr. Beeler begins the unit by introducing the concept of wellness as a multifaceted approach to helping people realize their full potential. He shows how wellness concepts can be used in the residence hall through hall and floor programs and by the personal example set by the RA.

College presents many stresses for both RAs and residents. Professor Gintner, in chapter eleven, examines the signs of stress, its sources, and the behaviors associated with stress. He then presents new and useful coping strategies for approaching stressful situations, modifying the stress-producing environments, and controlling stress.

Dr. Mathews explores another dimension of wellness—the absence of substance abuse. Her chapter critically examines the issues of alcohol, drug, and food abuse. These three substances are among those most abused by college students. Each is analyzed, and specific approaches to confronting these problems with college students in residence halls are given.

Dr. and Mrs. Miltenberger review the most recent research and information on human sexuality, including sexually transmitted diseases, AIDS, contraceptives, abortion, and the implications these issues have within a college living group. They provide information that RAs need in advising residents and give practical suggestions on how to approach some very sensitive issues in sexual relationships.

In the last chapter, Dr. Mohr examines one of the leading causes of death among college students: suicide. His focus is on helping the RA learn the signs of a person considering suicide and on giving RAs some approaches they can use to intervene in this process. Dr. Mohr also discusses the often overlooked issue of post-vention—the issues to be considered in helping residents adjust should a member of their living group or family commit suicide.

Gregory S. Blimling, Ph.D.
Louisiana State University

The Resident as a Member of a Living Group

1

CHAPTER 1

Community Development

Dr. John H. Schuh,
Wichita State University

Developing community is one of the most crucial aspects of a resident assistant's work. Yet, the concept of a community and the ways to develop it in the residence unit can be a little difficult to understand. In this chapter we will identify some of the common elements of community, discuss several aspects of the residential environment that influence community development, and provide you with some specific ways in which you can develop community in your unit.

So that we can operate from a common frame of reference, community will be defined as ". . . a group of individuals engaged in social interaction, possessing common interests and goals, who show concern for and are sensitive to the needs of other members, and are primarily interested in furthering the group's goals over all others" (Blimling & Miltenberger, citing Hillery, 1981, p. 201).

When we speak of a residence unit in this chapter, we are referring to the basic unit of organization in a residence hall. This is the group of students for which a resident assistant (RA) is responsible, usually ranging from thirty to seventy-five students. Commonly, RAs are responsible for approximately fifty students who live together on a common floor or corridor.

Zander (1985) pointed out that certain conditions promote the formation of a group. If people live in close proximity to one another and if they have a common way of life, a group is more likely to form. Over forty-five years ago Barnard (1938) observed that groups come into being when individuals are able to communicate with each other, be willing to contribute to joint action, and have a common purpose (cited in Zander, 1985). Since these elements are very much a part of a residence unit, your work potentially is less difficult than, say, if you were trying to develop community among students who lived in off-campus housing.

Common Elements of a Residential Community

Mable, Terry, and Duvall (1980) identified three basic ingredients of community that constitute an important point of departure for this discussion: sharing goals, sharing responsibilities, and sharing communication. Without these ingredients, it is nearly impossible to develop a sense of community in a residence unit.

Sharing Goals

Presumably, all students come to college with the same goal: to graduate. How students get from matriculation to graduation can be a circuitous route, and, as you know from your college experience, not every student approaches academic work, extracurricular activities, or social life in the same way. What happens on a residence hall floor if some students begin the year hoping to win election into the campus's most prestigious honor societies, while others just want to avoid academic probation? In terms of study conditions and academic support programs, what these disparate groups of students need may differ. How will you as a resident assistant respond to complaints that one group is dominating the floor and that the other group feels uncomfortable?

Clearly, this is a dualistic example and perhaps is more antiseptic than anything you will encounter in the course of your work. But the point remains: students need to agree on a common set of goals in order for the community to develop. And, one should never forget that your college or university also will have a set of goals to which you are expected to adhere. These goals for campus living may not always be congruent with what the residents in your unit want. So, your job, among other things, will be to articulate the university's goals for residential living and to develop appropriate mechanisms that will enlist your residents' support or tolerance of these goals. You must do this early in the semester, or individual goals will fill the void that results from the absence of group goals. Effective goals will serve to guide the floor while providing a sense of mutual purpose (Ender, Kane, Mable and Strohm, 1980). Later in this chapter, you will find an exercise you might conduct at your first unit meeting to encourage members to talk about their goals.

Sharing Responsibilities

Shared responsibilities in a unit grow out of the special nature of a college residence unit. First, when students come to college, they will find that they alone are held responsible for their actions. Generally speaking, parents are not contacted and asked to intervene when their son or daughter does something at variance with the institution's policies or procedures.

In the residential setting, each member of the community has the potential to contribute something to the group, and, conversely, the group has something to teach to and share with each member. The relationship between the individual and the group becomes transactional; that is, each gives and each takes. Your role as a resident assistant among other things is that of institutional representative to the floor. But since your work is part-time and you have responsibilities as a student yourself, you cannot be expected to supervise the floor at all times. At this point the concept of shared responsibilities takes over.

The residence unit should become one where the individual members supervise themselves, take action against those whose behavior is at variance with the group's goals, and enforce community standards. Research conducted at Indiana University (Schuh, Kuh, Gable, Friedman, Stipanovich, and Wegryn, 1981) indicates that this is what occurs over the course of the year. Students should ask less of the resident assistant as the academic year unfolds and assume more responsibilities themselves.

In your work as a resident assistant, you need to challenge students to take responsibilities for their actions and for enforcing the unit's standards. There will be some resistance, no doubt, because it is easier for students to let the RA do it. But, students will grow and develop if they are put in a situation where they assume more responsibilities over time.

Sharing Communication

Sharing goals and responsibilities is great, but if your residents do not communicate well with each other, major problems will develop. You should not assume that your residents have well-developed communications skills. From what we know of college students (Miller and Prince, 1976), developing new and useful patterns of expression and control are challenges for them.

Your role, therefore, is one of facilitating communication between individual residents and the others in the group. The problems that you may encounter can be as simple as one roommate wanting to study with the stereo on and the other wanting it off, to more complex issues, such as how the lounge might be used on a weekend evening (one group wanting to have a record party and another to show movies) or—perhaps the most difficult—how the unit's goals are to be achieved. You probably will assume various roles in fostering communication, including facilitator, consultant, collaborator, and teacher. Early in the semester, do not hesitate to plan programs that are designed to facilitate communication among group members.

Environmental Factors

Hennessy (1981), in his discussion of the development of an ideal environment, listed three aspects of the residential environment that are critical in the development of community. These three aspects include the physical environment, the interpersonal environment, and the normative environment. They will form the basis for the next portion of this discussion on community development.

The Physical Environment

Most residence hall structures in this country were built before many of our current residents were born. The buildings were developed in response to a baby boom, to fulfill the need to house as many students as possible as cheaply as possible. As a result, residence hall structures were not designed with many factors that we would take into consideration if we were building residential facilities today, such as students coming from smaller families and often not having to share a room. Facilities built today might include many more single rooms and would certainly increase the amount of insulation to absorb noise from amplified electronic sound systems and musical instruments.

How students form acquaintances and friendships will depend to a great extent on who their roommates and neighbors are. Those in close proximity with one another are likely to become closer friends than those who are assigned to rooms at opposite ends of the floor (Case, 1981; Menne and Sinnett, 1971). As a result, you will need to make extra efforts to make sure that floor membership does not become divided into geographically proximate groups of residents. One way to prevent this is to encourage unit members to work as a group to modify their physical environment.

Students can influence some aspects of the physical environment, given appropriate policies and directions set by housing officers. Often students are permitted, even encouraged, to paint their rooms and decorate them in ways that personalize their space. They may build lofts or bunk beds, decorate lounges and hallways to suit their tastes, or develop utility rooms into exercise and weight training rooms, dark rooms, or conference rooms. By encouraging students to decorate their facilities, colleges and universities are asking that students become partners in the responsibility for their physical environment. Not only are students asked to develop plans to personalize their rooms and common spaces, they also are asked to supervise the areas and keep vandalism to a minimum. By doing so, students agree on the goals and objectives for their living environment, thus taking a major step toward developing community.

In one study, students who were active participants in a specific redesign project perceived their unit as a friendly place to live, expressed concern about the welfare of others, and were willing to assist each other with academic and personal concerns; non-participants were much more negative about their living situation, even though they lived in the same unit (Werring, Winston, & McCaffrey, 1981). You, as a resident assistant, will deal with this issue in several ways. Students will seek your advice about personalizing their rooms, and you should encourage them to do so as a means of enhancing their sense of ownership and community while remaining within the guidelines established by your college or university.

Students also may be interested in developing plans for decorating their lounge or hallways. Schroeder (1981) suggests that hallways and lounges be decorated or marked so that unit ownership is apparent. "When secondary territory . . . is adequately marked and becomes the common property of a group, attitudes in the group change. Residents begin to take care of the space and share concern for maintaining it" (Schroeder, 1981, p. 46). There is no question that ownership results after students have taken on such projects (Schroeder, 1981), and that students respect their physical environment much more. Not only does respect for the physical environment result from these projects, but they engender cohesiveness among those who participate in the project. In a sense, community is the result. So, do not overlook these excellent opportunities to modify the physical environment and develop community simultaneously.

The Interpersonal Environment

The earlier discussion about developing communications skills among the residents fits with the interpersonal environment. This element of community is defined here to mean how citizenship and regard for others can be fostered in the residence unit.

Colleges and universities encourage student government for many reasons, but none is more important than providing students with training opportunities for citizenship responsibilities they will face after graduation. We want students to develop concern about their community, leadership and organizational skills, the ability to draw up budgets, and to understand a host of other by-products of involvement in student government. You probably will serve as the advisor to your floor government and perhaps to other governmental units within your residence hall. Community will be engendered when students believe that they have an effective governmental structure. Do what you can to see that such happens. And, advising can be a very active process. Don't wait for your student government officers to come to you with questions. It is entirely appropriate for you to take a vigorous role in the advising process, from planning training sessions with the officers to actively critiquing meetings and activities (McKaig and Policello, 1985).

We would hope that students, if they have not already developed this concern, will learn to care for others as a result of their residential experience. Often they will interact with types of individuals they have never met before, be they individuals of different races, national origins, or political or religious orientations. Nonetheless, all students share a common ground. Students begin college from essentially the same position: no credit earned and high hopes. People are successful or unsuccessful based on how they apply themselves and how they make use of the services and resources available. Students can provide excellent assistance and support for each other in times of need, developing friendships that will last a lifetime. You can tell that community is developing when students express concern and care for each other, or when they compromise their positions to assist others. When students start to tutor each other or form study groups, community is developing.

The Normative Environment

The normative environment, as referred to here, is made up of standards for behavior that govern the community. They include state and federal laws, institutional regulations and policies, and rules that the residents set for themselves. Students have no control over some of these standards, such as the federal constitution; the students have limited influence over others, such as institutional policies; students can set their own limits over a few. Included in the latter group are the rules they set for themselves.

Without rules and regulations, residence halls quickly would resemble anarchy. On most campuses that would be antithetical to the mission established for residential living. On the other hand, few of today's students would volunteer to live in an environment so burdened with rules that it resembles a prison. In the final analysis, the rules that the community sets for itself should be tied to the goals that the group has established. Rules should facilitate the process of achieving goals. If one of the unit's goals is to win the scholarship trophy at the end of the first term, then rules should be established to accomplish this goal.

Hennessy (1981) identifies five criteria for establishing rules. They include the following:

1. The rules need to be associated with the common good.
2. The rules should represent consensus.
3. The rules need to be limited in number.
4. There should be adequate promulgation of the rules.
5. There should be provision for reform. (pp. 20–21).

In your role as an RA you will need to make sure that the residents understand what rules they can set for themselves and what cannot be changed. You need to identify channels for reform for students and establish provisions for rethinking the rules that they set for themselves.

Students clearly need to understand the rules of the environment and to know what will happen if the rules are violated. You should set these out early in the semester, and students should realize that, in the final anaysis, they need play active roles in the development of this aspect of their community.

Characteristics of Community

Now that we have looked at some of the common elements of a community and discussed some environmental factors, how do you tell if your residence unit is developing into a community? At least four factors are important characteristics of a community: acquaintance, goals, expectations, and communication. The balance of this chapter will address them.

Acquaintance

Perhaps the initial building block in developing community is to make sure that the students on the floor know each other. That seems pretty obvious, but very early in the term you will find that students will begin to adopt their own routines and will not see other members of the floor for protracted periods of time, unless you do something. Besides making sure that each floor member introduces himself or herself at the first floor meeting, you might do such things as taking snap shots of each person and putting them on the bulletin board or the door of each room, having floor dinners, organizing outings to explore the campus or the community, or planning other activities that put the members of the floor in touch with one another early in the academic term.

Goals

Goals for the floor should be established early in the term. Student government can play a crucial role in this process, but the floor should decide the kinds of activities that it wishes to plan, the academic support activities that it intends to sponsor, the charitable endeavors that it will support, and so on. You can facilitate this process, but it is important that the students take the lead, doing much of the work themselves. For example, at the first floor meeting, you might ask each student to list the five goals that she or he has for the living unit. You can collect these goals and then lead a consensus building exercise for the group membership. You can also introduce the goals the university has for residential living and work with the group to integrate its goals with those of the institution.

Expectations

As with goals, expectations about behavior need to be established early in the academic term. This concept governs everything from the college's or university's expectations of students to what the students expect from each other. Some things are not negotiable, but other things are. Again, you can play a facilitative role, but student government will need to provide some leadership. Ultimately, it may be helpful to put them in writing, have each floor member sign them, and then distribute copies to every floor member and post them in conspicuous places.

Communication

Not every floor member will like everything that every other floor member does. Some roommates will have conflicts. Student government will not please everyone, and almost certainly, everything you do as a resident assistant will not be met with applause. You need to develop mechanisms whereby students can communicate with each other and with you in an easy, informal manner. Will you have a weekly newsletter? Will you hold gripe sessions? Will students be able to voice their concerns about each other without fear of being ostracized, or worse, retaliated against or intimidated? What will you do to encourage communication among members of the floor having different racial, ethnic, and religious backgrounds? You need to develop mechanisms, some of which are listed above, to deal with such problems early in the semester and sustain them.

A Final Thought

We have given you some thoughts about establishing community in your residence unit. The ideas are not unique or magical. We hope they will give a solid conceptual base from which to begin building community on your floor. The following case study and exercises will give you some additional ideas to contemplate as you begin to develop community on your floor.

Case Studies and Structured Group Experiences for Community Development

Case Study: Robert's Floor

Instructions: Read the case study and respond to the questions which follow. First work alone. When you are finished, share your answers with other RAs in small group discussions or as the basis for a classroom discussion.

Robert is a resident assistant on the fifth floor of Jones Hall at Central University. Central, which has grown from a teacher training institution to a comprehensive university since World War II, has an enrollment of 15,000 students and is located in a city of 100,000. Nearly 4,500 of Central's students live in the campus residence halls, and the preponderance of those residents are freshmen and sophomores. Fifty men were assigned to Robert's floor for the academic year.

Over the past several years, Central has made vigorous efforts to improve the quality of programming in the residence halls. Consultants to the director of residence halls have recommended that resident assistants offer programs in the halls to foster student growth and development. To that end, the pre-school training workshop was focused primarily on assessing student interests and needs and developing programs in the residence halls.

Robert took the pre-school workshop to heart. At the very first floor meeting his presentation focused on the programs that he planned to offer during the upcoming year. He took great pains to make sure that each resident introduced himself and told the others about his home town, his intended major, and a little bit about what he had done in high school. Then, Robert handed out 3 × 5 cards. On one side he had the residents write two or three things they would like to learn this year; on the other they wrote two things that they could teach someone else. This formed the basis of individual sharing on the floor, and things got off to a smooth start.

Within the first two weeks of school Robert was happy with how things were progressing on the floor. The men shared meals together, and he could tell from the good-natured horseplay, water fights, and pranks that the men played on each other that they really seemed to enjoy each other's company. The men were learning from each other, and in fact, they rarely indicated that they had nothing to do or were bored. There were plans for ordering floor t-shirts. Robert felt like he had things off to an excellent start.

After the first home football game, which occurred on Saturday afternoon at the end of the third week of classes, someone broke into the fire fighting equipment cabinet on the floor and turned on the water hose. The damage was minor, and although no one came forward when Robert asked if anyone knew who was responsible, he was not worried. These kinds of things happen, he thought, in the aftermath of an exciting football game. It won't happen again, because these guys know better.

Note: Some of the concepts introduced in the case study and exercises were drawn from uncopyrighted staff development publications produced at Michigan State University, Indiana University and the University of Wisconsin–Madison.

About five weeks into the semester, several of the residents came to visit Robert in his room. They indicated that all the programming that he had planned was oriented around sports. That was true. Robert was an enthusiastic sports fan, and he had planned programs with sports themes, including such activities as having an assistant football coach come to the floor to explain strategy, organizing the intramural soccer and football teams, and throwing a pre-World Series party on the floor. Attendance was very good. The residents indicated that they would like some programs in other areas and asked Robert to help them with the planning. Robert said he would think about it and get back to them. After they left he was puzzled, because he was trying hard to provide programs for the residents, and he always enjoyed sports programs.

Elections for floor officers had been scheduled during the second week of classes. Robert called a floor meeting in the lounge a few nights before the election and indicated that the floor should elect officers. He reported that student government on his floor the year before had not been very successful and that most students did not take it too seriously. Nonetheless, being a floor officer was something to list on a resume, and he would help the floor officers if they asked. There was some programming money for them to work with, and Robert said he would be glad to provide suggestions about how to spend it. The election was held, and each of the offices was contested. Most of the residents voted. After the election Robert congratulated the winners (all of whom were freshmen), consoled the losers, and indicated to the officers that if they needed help just to contact him. Also, he said they ought to begin holding meetings in the next few weeks. Surprisingly, no meetings were held for the next month.

The first altercation on the floor occurred just before mid-term exams. It was one of those typical roommate conflicts, in which one resident got tired of his roommate getting up each morning at the crack of dawn to go running and waking him up. The two of them then had a shouting and pushing match, but nobody was hurt. Robert worked with the roommates to help them gain a better understanding of each other's problems. They agreed on a compromise and signed a roommate contract that specified their behavior. The incident was settled amiably.

Mid-term grades came out in early November, and Robert was shocked to learn that many of his students were doing poorly. He thought things were going so well. Students seemed to enjoy each other's company, and they continued to play pranks and jokes on each other. Water fights were common, but Robert thought that they were just a part of college life. And, although some residents had come back to the floor from off-campus parties having had too much to drink, that's part of growing up, he thought. Some additional damages occurred to the fire fighting equipment, but maintenance fixed them quickly. Fewer students stayed on the floor to study, and it was rather noisy during study time. Still, Robert decided, freshmen sometimes need to learn the hard way, and maybe this is a good lesson for them.

Two weeks later students were asked to indicate whether or not they planned to return to the floor for the next semester. About 25 percent indicated that they were going to live elsewhere on campus. When Robert asked many of them why, they simply reported that they weren't comfortable on the floor. At this point Robert had to prepare for his semester evaluation conference with his hall director. He was confident that the conference would go well, but he was beginning to have some doubts as to how well he was doing.

Case Study Questions about Robert's Floor

1. What positive aspects of community did you observe on Robert's floor?

   a. _____

   b. _____

   c. _____

2. What negative things did you observe on Robert's floor?

   a. _____

   b. _____

   c. _____

3. What positive things did Robert do to enhance community on his floor?

   a. _____

   b. _____

   c. _____

4. Identify some things that Robert should have done to enhance community on his floor, but did not.

   a. _____

   b. _____

   c. _____

Exercise: Community Development on the Floor

Goals:

1. To outline a series of characteristics of community of a residence hall floor for resident assistants;
2. To teach participants what to look for in trying to determine whether or not their unit is developing community.

Group Size: Up to 30

Time Required: Approximately 30 minutes

Materials: 1. Pencil or pen; 2. Tablet or hard surface upon which to write

Physical Setting: Conference room or other setting where all participants can be seated comfortably.

Process:

1. The facilitator explains the purpose of the exercise to the participants and then presents a brief discussion on the characteristics of community.
2. The participants complete the exercise form.
3. After the participants have completed the form, the facilitator leads a discussion about the results, and asks the participants for their observations and reactions. If there is difficulty in understanding a particular answer, the facilitator asks the group to help answer the question or help solve the problem.

Community Development on the Floor: Some Observations

The purpose of this exercise is to match your observations of your own residence hall floor with the characteristics of community. Here are seven characteristics of community on the residence hall floor:

1. Residents know each other;
2. Residents support student government;
3. Mutual expectations have been established among the residents;
4. Residents understand and accept hall and university regulations;
5. Personal and group conflicts among floor residents are resolved with staff playing a facilitative role;
6. Programs are developed to meet resident needs;
7. Physical facilities are respected.

Below you will find a number of observations you might make during the course of your work as a resident assistant. In the blank space following each observation, place the number of the aspect of community of which you think the observation is a part. Be prepared to explain why you think the observations fit the characteristic. There are three observations for each characteristic of community.

- Residents participate in floor activities. _____
- Pranks and stunts are kept to a bare minimum. _____
- Programs are held regularly on the floor. _____
- Residents do not depend on staff to resolve all their interpersonal problems. _____
- Residents understand rules and policies. _____
- There are a minimum number of noise problems on the floor. _____
- Residents participate actively in elections. _____
- Residents decide to order floor t-shirts. _____
- Residents follow hall and university regulations. _____

- Floor officers plan and conduct floor meetings. _____
- The amount of damage declines from the previous year. _____
- Residents do not indicate that they are bored. _____
- Residents use proper channels to change policies with which they disagree. _____
- Residents ask how they might run for floor office next year. _____
- Residents have realistic expectations for each other. _____
- Residents eat together frequently. _____
- There is a general atmosphere of ease, compromise, and cooperation on the floor. _____
- Residents follow policies and regulations. _____
- Residents are not afraid to confront each other. _____
- Residents participate in planning, coordinating, and evaluating programs. _____
- Residents express pride in their physical facilities. _____
- Conflicts are resolvled quickly, with the aid of staff if necessary. _____

Are there other things you might observe that would indicate the forming of a community? If so, what are they?

Exercise: RA Activities for Community Development

Goals:

1. To familiarize resident assistants with some of the characteristics of a residence hall community;
2. To teach the participants what they can do to enhance community on their unit.

Group Size: Up to 30

Time Required: Approximately 30 minutes

Materials: 1. Pencil or pen; 2. Tablet or hard surface upon which to write

Physical Setting: Conference room or other setting where all participants can be seated comfortably.

Process:

1. The facilitator explains the purpose of this exercise and briefly reviews the characteristics of community.
2. The participants complete the exercise form.
3. After the forms have been completed, the facilitator leads a discussion about the results, and asks the participants for their observations and reactions. If there is difficulty in understanding a particular answer, the facilitator asks the group to help answer the questions or help solve the problem.

RA Activities

The purpose of this exercise is to have you match your activities with the characteristic of community. Here are seven characteristics of community on the residence hall floor:

1. Residents know each other;
2. Residents support student government;
3. Mutual expectations have been established among the residents;
4. Residents understand and accept hall and university regulations;
5. Personal and group conflicts among floor residents are resolved with staff playing a facilitative role;
6. Programs are developed to meet resident needs;
7. Physical facilities are respected.

Below you will find a number of activities you might undertake during the course of your work as a resident assistant to facilitate community development. In the blank space following each observation, place the number of the aspect of communiy of which you think the activity is a part. Be prepared to explain why you think the activity fits the characteristic. There are three activities for each dimension of community.

- Attend student government meetings. _____
- Report damage to floor members as soon as possible after it occurs. _____
- Encourage students to plan and attend their own programs. _____
- Ask students if they understand policies. _____
- Enforce policies fairly and consistently. _____
- Encourage residents to confront each other with complaints. _____
- Keep your door open. _____
- Offer verbal support for student government. _____
- Stress the positive aspects of policies; explain the rationale for policies and rules. _____
- Discuss the concept of student rights *and* responsibilities at the first floor meeting. _____

DP8 404492RNHD Blimling

- Discuss procedures for reducing individual and group conflicts. _____
- Teach students how to provide adequate publicity for programs. _____
- Encourage residents to report those who misuse physical equipment. _____
- Lead a discussion at the first floor meeting on facilitating study conditions on the floor. _____
- Walk into rooms with open doors and visit with residents. _____
- Report any fire or safety equipment that is not working. _____
- Invite students to share meals with you in the dining hall. _____
- Don't take sides in mediating inter-personal conflicts. _____
- Conduct interest and needs assessments before planning programs. _____
- Serve as an active consultant to floor government. _____
- Follow-up with residents two weeks after a conflict has been resolved to determine if the solution has been working. _____

Are there other things you can do to develop community on your floor? If so, what are they?

Exercise: Brainstorming for Community on the Floor

Goals:

1. To outline a series of characteristics of community of a residence hall floor for resident assistants;
2. To help participants identify programs they can plan to enhance community on their unit.

Group Size: Up to 30

Time Required: 45 minutes

Materials: 1. Pen or pencil; 2. Tablet or hard surface upon which to write; 3. Chalk board or newsprint for group viewing

Physical Setting: Conference room or other setting where all participants can be seated comfortably

Process

1. The facilitator explains the purpose of the exercise to the participants and then presents a brief discussion on the characteristics of community.
2. The participants complete the exercise form.
3. After the participants complete the form, the facilitator lists all the answers to each item on the newsprint or chalk board. Participants are encouraged to make a list of ideas for each characteristic of community besides their own for implementation purposes. Where there are disagreements over the viability of a program, the group is asked to discuss the item and decide whether or not to include it on the total list

Community on the Floor: A Brainstorming Activity

Here are seven characteristics of community on the residence hall floor:

1. Residents know each other;
2. Residents support student government;
3. Mutual expectations have been established among the residents;
4. Residents understand and accept hall and university regulations;
5. Personal and group conflicts among floor residents are resolved with staff playing a facilitative role;
6. Programs are developed to meet resident needs;
7. Physical facilities are respected.

In the spaces available below, try to list at least two things you would do as a resident assistant to facilitate community development. If you can generate more than two ideas per category, that's fine. When the exercise is completed, your discussion leader will provide you with some ideas about various things you can do to facilitate community.

1. Residents know each other:

    a. _____

    b. _____

2. Residents support student government:

    a. _____

    b. _____

3. Mutual expectations have been established among the residents:

    a. _____

    b. _____

4. Residents understand and accept hall and university regulations:

   a. _____

   b. _____

5. Personal and group conflicts among floor residents are resolved with staff playing a facilitative role:

   a. _____

   b. _____

6. Programs are developed to meet resident needs:

   a. _____

   b. _____

7. Physical facilities are respected:

   a. _____

   b. _____

CHAPTER 2

Leadership: The Resident Assistant as a Cultural Leader

Dr. Joseph Kavenaugh,
Lamar University

Schein (1985) distinguishes management from leadership. In exploring this distinction, he asserts "there is a possibility . . . that the *only thing of real importance that leaders do is create and manage culture* and that the unique talent of leaders is their ability to work with culture. If the concept of leadership as distinguished from management and administration is to have any value, we must recognize the centrality of this culture management function in the leadership concept" (pg. 2).

Schein's assertion is a powerful force for reconceptualizing leadership. Presently, the specific functions of a leader in establishing and reinforcing culture are poorly defined. They do, however, transcend those functions that have traditionally defined leader behavior. Culture-forming leadership is not focused on tasks, relationships, decision-making style, communication skills, team-building, or other process skills of leadership, although these are important. Rather, culture-forming leadership is concerned with the values orientation and actions of the organization. It is more concerned with *what* decisions are made than with *how* decisions are made; with *what* is communicated, not *how* it is communicated; with *what* goals are chosen than with *how* goal-directed behavior influences group action. Schein's concept is concerned with the content of leader action more than the processes of leader behavior.

Cultural leadership is transformational leadership (Burns, 1968; Peters & Waterman, 1983). It defines the organization, what is valued and what is not, and what will enable the organization to distinguish itself. Every interaction the leader has with the group either communicates these values or fails to. Cultural leadership presumes that leaders have command of the technical knowledge and personal skills necessary to direct work groups. The issue is not how to lead, but where. Toward what ends should leadership be exercised?

Shaping a culture is a large responsibility. It requires insight, wisdom, and personal courage. Above all else, it requires a vision of the future, an appreciation of the complexity of human interaction, and a certitude that such a future can be nurtured by caring leaders who sense the group's potential long before its members glimpse the possibilities. For such leaders, the rewards are great.

The RA as Cultural Leader

For many residents, the RA is the single most visible symbol of the university community. As an RA, you are a powerful symbol in the residential culture and are frequently perceived as a model of the behaviors and values that constitute high achievement, academically, socially, and personally. This is especially true for resident freshmen. When you serve a floor comprised exclusively of freshmen, the power to influence the lives of new members of the university community is significant.

However, your responsibilities as an RA entail far more than the embodiment and transmission of the academic culture. While your responsibilities certainly include the importance of role modeling, they are broader and richer in their scope and function than the socialization of students. You are also a leader in the definition and formation of the residential sub-culture, a critical environment influencing academic success.

The concept of culture can constitute an integrating perspective for the multiple demands of your job. Culture incorporates all of your behavior, attitudes, values, and beliefs as a counselor, programmer, disciplinarian, clerk, crisis manager, student, friend, and peer. A richer understanding of these relationships will enhance your personal effectiveness in the performance of job duties, permitting you to invest yourself fully in your work, work that influences so many other lives.

To better understand the important nature of your responsibilities, this chapter explores the cultural dimensions of leadership and how they can be used to help change the culture of your residence hall floor. This concept of leadership also provides a framework for understanding your position as an RA and helps unify job functions that initially you may perceive as disjointed or contradictory. The chapter will also focus on how to create a culture and what you can do when the culture evolves contrary to institutional values. First, we will briefly consider what a culture is. Realizing that cultures arise from groups, we will next consider developments in group life that aid in this transformation. An important responsibility of leaders is to communicate qualities of the culture to new members. To do so effectively, leaders must understand how group members learn and realize which leader actions influence culture formation. Finally, we will briefly discuss destructive cultures and possible ways to reshape them.

What is Culture?

Culture is a complex concept that is somewhat ill-defined. Every day we encounter groups and organizations that are different from one another. The men on John's floor are different from the guys who live on Al's floor. The women in Smith Hall are socialites, while the women in Barton Hall are social workers. The Sigma Nu's are bookworms, while the Betas are party animals. What is it that makes these groups distinctive? The element is culture.

Every group or organization has its own culture. Some are bland, nondescript. Others are strong, bold, distinctive. Management studies of successful large organizations suggest that those that excel are those that have strong, distinctive cultures (Peters & Waterman, 1982). The same is true for smaller organizations, such as those found on campuses, and for groups. Strong, distinctive cultures produce performances that are the hallmark of success for that culture. Such performances manifest the distinctiveness of the group. They are, in that sense, symbolic.

Culture embodies a group's deeply embedded values and is represented by the group's mission, goals, and operating practices. It is comprised of the attitudes, beliefs, and normative assumptions that govern decision-making and behavior. Culture is explicit when it is translated into rules and procedures and implicit when it is generally understood but not articulated. It is "the way we do things around here." Culture is symbolized in the group's activities and artifacts, the selection of members, and the deployment of the group's resources. The undergirding values, choice of mission, attitudes, activities, artifacts and outcomes—and the symbolic value of each—contribute to the way both members and non-members perceive the group's culture. They constitute the defining characteristics of the culture.

The concept of culture is different from, and subsumes, the community development perspective of residence living. Historically, the community model has emphasized as its dominant values the development of the group, member participation, democratic decision processes, and personal assumption of responsibility to give rise to the quality of life within the residence community. The culture perspective also emphasizes group development but places greater responsibility on the group and its designated leadership to define quite deliberately the operating goals, the outcomes sought from community life, significant values that will undergird decision-making, and the formation of a strong, distinctive group identity. The culture's perspective also provides greater latitude for appreciating the dynamics operating on a residential floor, including negative as well as positive phenomena, dysfunctional as well as group-strengthening behavior.

Often, in the desire to establish communities, important elements in the unique life of the floor are discounted or overlooked completely. This is detrimental to a full understanding of the floor's cultural dynamics. As an example, consider noise and rowdiness. From a community perspective, rowdiness may be regarded as inconsiderate, destructive of property, and counter-productive, and indeed it can be. However, the culture perspective insists that it be acknowledged that rowdiness can be a cohesive factor on the floor, contributing to group identity, serving as a rite of passage into the group, and significantly distinguishing the floor's culture from others in the residence hall.

Consider two different residence hall floors. Members of the first greet one another courteously, enjoy athletics, like good parties and ribald jokes, study when needed, have four different floor t-shirts to promote their identity, and almost always have their doors open when they are on the floor. Members of the second floor study diligently, prefer strict quiet hours, enjoy classical and jazz music, visit museums, and generally keep their doors closed. Both floors are functioning communities; the culture of each is clearly distinct from the other.

Forming Cultures

The evolution of culture is a product of group formation and development. However, its formation lags behind the formation of the group. The presence of culture presupposes the group has a history and has existed long enough to develop a sense of tradition. This phenomena is perhaps best understood by appreciating the importance of sagas, folk heroes, and myths as symbols in the creation of culture.

As a group develops, shared experiences generate notable events in the group's life. For its members, these events represent special moments or highlights in the group's history. The events are prized because, most often, they signify for the members a moment when the group was "at its best," when the group was truly achieving one of its goals, fulfilling the group's highest potential by enacting one of its values. The events are recounted over time, first among founding members, and later to new members joining the group.

In their retelling, such highlighted events become the group's sagas, important means of transmitting the group's values to others. Sagas are often employed in the socialization of new members or those aspiring to membership in the group. They are the organization's stories. Remember your first rush party, or the first meeting of the University Chorale you attended. Undoubtedly, during the social hour one or more members took the opportunity to tell you about the organization and the great times its members had. This immediately led to "remember when we. . ." recollections of the more outstanding events in the group's life, whether it was an unforgettable party or the tremendous experience of the chorale's latest European tour. These are the organization's stories, its sagas, and prospective members should listen to them carefully. They communicate, in succinct form, the organization's greatest achievements and, by extension, its values.

A similar phenomenon often occurs with the acts of individual members. In this case, the particular act often involves dramatic, contra-conventional behavior that graphically represents the acting out of a core value of the group. Such individuals become the folk heroes of the group. The acts of folk heroes represent the personification of the group's values and, as such, are recounted with enthusiasm. They become models of behavior that each group member, in his or her own way, hopes to emulate.

Not all folk heroes become elevated on the basis of a single, dramatic gesture. Others assume their place in the organization's pantheon of heroes because of consistent, sustained, tenacious adherence to a principle or value critical to the group's core identity. The injured athlete who never missed a practice, the 4.0 student who never missed a class, the fraternity chugger who was never bested in four straight years of beer barrel competition—each represents the embodiment of a value at the core of his or her culture's definition of success.

Over the course of time, sagas and folk heroes become larger than life. The exploits and persona of Paul Bunyon and his Blue Ox Babe in the lumberman's culture or Pecos Bill in the culture of the Southwest are examples of sagas and folk heroes who surpass the capabilities of normal group members. They become mythic in proportion, and their amplified achievements become their culture's myths.

Another form of myth is more contrived, and it evolves to serve the group's needs. As with other fables, it may have germinated in truth, but it now transcends the realm of normal endeavor. It may, in fact, have no basis in truth whatsoever, but is a story fabricated to represent a core value of the group because no real-life drama conveniently exists to illustrate the point. Nonetheless, its function is the same, and it serves as a valuable tool in the definition and transmision of culture (Deal & Kennedy, 1982).

The establishment of a group culture, then, is a product of the group's life over extended periods of time, during which the group's activities have been purposeful for its members, and during which members have made significant contributions that shaped the group, gave it direction, and enhanced its distinctive purpose. From the richness of this group life evolve the symbols that represent the group and its unique character.

Communicating Culture

Transmitting culture is critical to survival of a group. The proper enculturation of members is largely a product of ways in which members are socialized to the group and its values. Wanous (1980) identifies a four-stage entry model for organizational socialization that is fitting for use in the context of new students entering the residence environment or for members moving from one residential sub-culture to another. All four suggest tasks each new member must manage. These stages include 1) confronting and accepting organizational reality, 2) achieving clarity in task and interpersonal roles, 3) locating oneself in the context of the organization, and 4) achieving success in socialization to the group.

The entering student must go through these stages of socialization in order to succeed in the residence hall. First, the student must come to terms with residence hall living and accept its realities. Roommates, limited personal space, different hours, personal independence and accountability, cultural differences, special rules, housing procedures, and the fact that an individual's wants are secondary to the group's interests—each requires the student to confront prior assumptions about other people and one's own lifestyle and to initiate adjustments that will enable him or her to succeed.

In doing so, the student must next learn what tasks he or she must do to live successfully on the floor and how he or she will relate to others in the community. This phase is often painful and filled with uncertainty as the student "tries out" different behavior, tentatively establishes relationships, and generally seeks to understand what is required and expected. As the RA, you can be an extraordinary aid in easing this transition. Eventually, through such testing and exploration, the student will "find a place" within the floor group, establish friendship networks that solidify this position, and assume a special identity within the group, reflecting how the student's unique abilities and contributions serve the group's interests. Having assumed a meaningful role within the floor group, the student is successfully socialized to the group, understands its goals, and adopts behavior supportive of these objectives.

The enculturation process requires that those responsible for the proper socialization of new members be attentive to their needs and accurately represent the context of the group. The distinction between socialization and enculturation must be clear. Socialization identifies specific stages, tasks, and issues that the new member of the group must resolve. Enculturation is the process through which the context and specific value orientations of the organization are articulated and communicated, either explicitly or implicitly, to new members. Culture constitutes the framework within which socialization occurs.

For example, when a student enters the university, he or she learns that certain behavior is rewarded and other behavior is punished. Speaking in class when called upon is rewarded. Speaking during an examination is not. Learning this reality is part of the socialization process. Understanding why this is so, accepting it, and appreciating the values that undergird the decision to reward one behavior and punish the other is enculturation. It is a growing awareness of the *raison d'etre* of the organization, its justification for existence. It is culture that provides a context within which the organization's leadership and its members judge right from wrong.

Learning Culture

The new member in the group must be an active social learner. Social learning is a reciprocal process between cognitive, behavioral, and environmental factors, each of which interacts with the other (Bandura, 1977). Social learning can be experiential, vicarious, or both and is interactive with the environment that the new member engages. The individual can learn by direct involvement with the environment, by observing others in the environment, or both. One need not always experience something directly in order to learn. For example, it is not necessary to cease attending classes and fail to prepare for exams to learn that the failure to attend class and study for an exam yields low grades. One can learn this vicariously, from the experiences of others. The capacity to learn vicariously empowers role modeling as a critical element in the socialization of group members and the transmission of culture.

Role Modeling

It is difficult to overstate your importance as a role model in the socialization of floor members. It is also important to realize that you perform critical functions in the transmission of cultural values beyond those embodied in your own role performance as an RA.

As an RA, you perform many roles in which you model specific attitudes, behavior, and values, as well as transmitting additional cultural information. For example, consider your own performance as a student. As a student role model, your daily behavior can demonstrate to others effective study methods, appropriate time management, approaches to exam preparation, establishing solid working relationships with faculty, a positive attitude toward learning, and an active intellectual curiosity about the subject matter in your courses.

However, additional values and behavior may be critical to success in some academic programs, even though they are not demanded specifically of you in your major. In certain curriculums, academic success depends upon long hours in the library or the laboratory, intensive involvement with the subject matter, extended field trips, participation in the co-curricular life of the department, or the active pursuit of research. While these values may not be significant in your course of study, they may be important for the proper socialization of some students on your floor. In conversation with these students, when you explain *why* such behavior is important, you are transmitting basic elements of their specific culture.

Through teaching and coaching, you can affirm these values for your students, even though you cannot model them. Your students learn vicariously both from observing your behavior and hearing your testimony about what behavior is valued and leads to academic success. You are clearly communicating behavior valued within the university and serve as a symbol of its culture.

When you fail to communicate success-yielding behavior, or when you model behavior associated with poor academic performance, you teach those who have chosen you as a role model values that are counterproductive to their academic success. You become a poor symbol of the university culture.

While this discussion has focused on role-modeling, teaching and coaching are also valuable means of communicating cultural values. Conducting the first floor meeting, advising your floor's representative to the Residence Halls Association, or following up on a disciplinary hearing are each important opportunities to instruct your students on the values and operating style of the residence hall culture.

Establishing a Culture

As an RA, you also have great influence on the shape of the specific sub-culture that is established on your hall, floor or wing of the residence hall. The residential sub-culture is where the RA can assume major leadership responsibilities. You can bring to bear all of the tools of socialization and enculturation in defining and shaping this sub-culture's qualities. The seasoned RA understands this sub-culture and knows how to shape it to realize the educational objectives of the residence hall program.

Schein (1985) identifies several means leaders use to establish and reinforce culture within a group. Among these are:

1. what leaders pay attention to, measure, and control;
2. how the leader reacts in critical incidents;
3. deliberate role modeling, teaching, and coaching; and
4. criteria for allocating rewards and status.

Having already considered the culture-reinforcing value of role modeling, teaching, and coaching, let us examine the importance of Schein's other means. The first two are particularly important, especially in shaping the sub-culture's values and communicating the leader's beliefs. No clearer example exists than your leadership in establishing and maintaining standards within the residential sub-culture.

Inevitably, the decisions you must make are culture-forming. Consider the following:

1. Which policies and procedures will be rigorously enforced? Which will receive lesser attention? Visitation, alcohol, quiet hours, and property damage are each fundamental decision areas. The level of enforcement chosen on each policy will have differing effects in defining the nature of the culture.

2. Quality of life issues (such as the expected nature of relationships between roommates, student participation in decision-making that affects the floor, the level of interaction fostered, and student involvement in unit governance) each help establish certain values that further define qualities of the culture.

3. The issues that you elect to discuss with residents, your personal integrity, the number and types of programs you sponsor, and the quality of your relationship with each resident are venues where you model what you value, what is prized within the residential culture, and what is expected of students.

Through a series of decisions that you and others make daily as the group forms, the sub-culture is defined. As the group solidifies, the life of the group reinforces and perpetuates the culture. What the group values comes to dominate the group's life and make that life distinctive. The group projects a distinctive character and becomes known by its symbols, such as a name, motto, style of dress, qualities of speech, or dominant behavior. All the while, you, through interaction with members of the group, are in the process of helping define and refine the group's character or personality. At the same time, in the role of group leader, you are establishing boundaries and expressing preferences for valued behavior that influence the formation process.

Members bond with the group, continuing interaction yields greater cohesiveness, and the group becomes a community with a clear, distinctive identity. The group's attractiveness to the individual is based upon the values, attitudes, beliefs, practices, and behavior demonstrated by group members. Your actions as the leader are critical in aiding the group to identify those qualities that will make the group distinctive.

Crisis is the litmus test for a culture leader. Here, in highly dramatic circumstances, you enact those values that are the core of the culture or, by failure to do so, you undercut prior efforts to establish the group's desired, distinctive values. In a disciplinary confrontation, a death in a student's family, or a failed exam, the RA chooses the behavior, attitude, and values he or she will employ to address the demands of the situation. Those choices, and how they are enacted, communciate the nature of the culture.

Culture leaders must be cautious not to send mixed messages. It is counterproductive for you as an RA to speak of a caring community centered on openness in personal relationships and then handle disciplinary responsibilities in a clandestine, deceitful manner. Your style and message must correspond highly; they must convey the same values and beliefs and be acted upon with consistency.

Finally, how you and the group respectively choose to distribute rewards and recognition among members is a strong indicator of the values operating within the culture. In student cultures especially, respect among one's peers is often the highest standard of recognition. It is reserved for those members of the group who, by their beliefs and actions, both influence and enact the group's values. Such individuals often become the group's leaders.

The power to recognize and reward valued behavior is perhaps the single strongest tool available to leaders seeking to build strong cultures. Praise, private recognition, public commendation, giving greater responsibility, enhancing another's self-esteem, inclusion in decision-making, seeking out another for consultation, sharing personal confidences, and elevating another's status within the group—all these are vital means for recognizing and rewarding those whose efforts further establish a culture having the qualities and characteristics you desire. Resident assistants should not be hesitant to utilize these means to reinforce valued behavior. In fact, strong leadership demands it.

To build a strong culture, you must be able to state clearly what is valued and what is not. For those in the group, these expectations are vital to a clear understanding of one's responsibilities. A leader owes it to group members to be clear about what behavior is expected, what is not, and his or her capacity to respond to both. Finally, you must be prepared to reward expected behavior that strengthens the culture. Surprisingly, leaders all too often hope for one set of behavior and reward another. (Kerr, 1975).

For the RA who is shaping the culture of a residence floor, the lessons of strong leadership are clear. Know what is valued and what is not, communicate this clearly to residents, and reward that which is valued. Most importantly, do not reward behavior that is contradictory to the values of the culture you seek to build.

Managing Changes within a Culture

Given the importance of culture in defining the student's environment, during the formation process it is vital to establish values broadly supportive of academic arrangement, thereby encouraging the group to participate fully in the larger university culture. Once these values are embedded in the group's social structure, the character of the group is extraordinarily difficult to change.

Cultures occasionally do change course, some for the better, others for the worse. What do you do when the culture of the floor begins to change in ways that are not acceptable?

First, critically analyze where you have lost control of the culture. This should involve a careful review of the values that are sought, the values that are currently dominant, and the particular actions, behavior, and practices that are not acceptable.

Second, examine the floor's evolving leadership structure. Who currently dominates the group? What are this individual's sources of influence, and how are they employed to affect the conduct of others? Indeed, is there a leader, or has the social structure of the floor collapsed completely?

Third, working with the new leaders, insist that they evaluate the impact of their goals on the lives and academic well-being of the residents. Will these goals support students' academic success?

Fourth, aid current leaders in realigning their goals to correspond with the objective of the residence environment.

Fifth, establish new normative conditions within the residence culture. In consultation with the new leadership, reestablish your importance as the RA, your influence as a factor in shaping the culture, and again assert the values necessary for a successful residence experience and the students' academic success.

While this analysis has focused on values with the residence culture, be mindful that culture and values are not synonomous terms. Culture is more encompassing; it is based upon more than values alone. Culture also incorporates the group's network of social relationships, decision-making style, operating rules, activities, rituals and traditions, patterns of leadership, dominant behavior, and reward structure.

In established cultures, destroying the dominant cultural characteristics is almost impossible. The single most challenging organizational problem is to materially change a culture while maintaining the group intact. For this reason, in residence cultures in particular, it may be more expeditious to destroy the group, reassign its members to new floors, or evict its leaders than attempt to re-shape the group. This becomes increasingly true the stronger the culture and the more it deviates from acceptable residence hall standards.

Conclusion

This chapter has sought to explore culture as a new perspective on residence hall living. Particular emphasis has been placed on equipping you as an RA with the tools necessary to see, analyze and understand the cultural dimensions of the residence experience. The task is not easy. Yet, by now the value of the culture perspective should be clear. It allows you to see and interpret life on the floor from a different, perhaps more distanced, vantage point. It enables you to see the floor as a whole unit, a complete social system, not just a collection of unrelated parts.

A second objective has been to detail your unique responsibilities as a culture leader and to highlight some of the means you can use to actively shape the culture of the floor. The discussion emphasized understanding the values that govern group life, but values are not the sole constituent of culture. Rather, they are like telltales for a sailor. Although the wind cannot be seen, the sailor can feel it, and the telltale indicates its direction. Operating values on the residence floor are telltales for you and point the way to the underlying culture. As an active culture leader, you can read these signs and shape the group's goals and characteristics in a direction that supports academic success and a positive residential experience.

The challenges of leadership in the residential culture are demanding. They require the best of every RA as a leader. In many ways, the RA symbolizes the best of this culture, and it should be so. The full development of students in our residence halls requires no less.

Case Studies and Structured Group Experiences for The Resident Assistant as a Cultural Leader

Case Study: Ed Fox

Instructions: Read the case study and respond to the questions which follow. First work alone. When you are finished, share your answers with other RAs in small group discussions or as the basis for a class-room discussion.

This case study presents an opportunity for you to examine the essential elements of culture formation and management. The attitudes, beliefs, values, and behavior of the RA Ed Fox communicate the qualities of the culture Ed seeks to create and maintain. Sometimes, those qualities inadvertently work against achieving the goals Ed seeks. Culture provides a unique perspective for understanding the complexity and dynamics of the residential environment. It enables you as an RA to appreciate more fully the interrelationships between all areas of job responsibility and your personal qualities as a valued member of the residence staff.

Ed Fox is a resident assistant on a freshmen floor in Landsdown Hall. There are forty freshmen on the floor, matched according to preferences for smoking, whether they are early or late night people, and possible majors. Students are housed two to a room, with common bath facilities on the floor. The halls are long and straight, ten rooms on each side, tile walls and floors. The resident assistant's room is opposite the showers.

Ed Fox is the drill sergeant type, with a heart as big as Texas (where he is from) but a no-nonsense guy, nonetheless. For Ed, there are priorities in life and work. Getting the job done is the goal every day. Ed is a campus leader, has a girlfriend, is not in a fraternity, but is active in Army ROTC, which he hopes will put him through law school.

As freshmen arrive the first day, Ed is there to meet and greet them, introduce himself, and introduce them to their roommates. At the first floor meeting, Ed lays down the law. There are rules, he has tough standards, and the first six weeks everyone on the floor plays by his rules. After that, once they are through mid-term examinations, Ed will see about their having something to say about how the floor is run.

The first six weeks pass quickly. The floor is rowdy and highly interactive, people are not sleeping much, and it is noisy. After two weeks, Ed calls a floor meeting and chews the residents out; Quiet hours, 8:00 P.M. every night, no exceptions. The first guy who breaks it goes to the judicial board.

During this time the floor forms an intramural football team named *The Commandos*. "No Prisoners" is their motto. Ed is quietly pleased that they adopted this slogan from a poster on his wall.

The second weekend on campus, two guys on Ed's floor come in early Sunday morning heavily intoxicated. The next weekend, Ed is awakened at 2:00 A.M. Sunday by yelping, cat calls, and laughter coming from the showers across the hall. When Ed enters the shower room, twelve of his freshmen are in the gang showers, hot water steaming, crawling all over one another on the floor of the shower, fully-clothed, yelping like coyotes. With great forebearance, Ed helps them all to bed. By 3:30 A.M., it is again quiet on the floor. At 8:30 A.M. Sunday, Ed rises, wakes all twelve, drags them out of bed and makes them clean the showers and the hall. He then makes them sign a note of apology to all the other members on the floor for being rude and disruptive. At 10:00 A.M. Ed lets them all go back to bed.

Tuesday of the fourth week, crisis hit the floor. John Dover's parents are both killed in an automobile accident. Ed intervenes, arranges an emergency loan for John, takes John to the bus station, and secures home numbers where John might be reached. He also gives John his number and other campus contact numbers. The guys on the hall take up a collection to send flowers.

At the end of mid-term exams, sixty-five percent of Ed's guys are in academic trouble. Ed learns of this during the weekly informal bull sessions held in his room every Wednesday night—10:30 P.M., popcorn provided, bring your own soda. Ed thinks hard about what he might do and possible programs on time management, study skills, or examination strategies he might sponsor. Then, inspiration: a floor meeting where Ed turns the problem over to the members of the floor. He challenges them to take on the problem. The goal is for everyone to succeed. In the next twenty-four hours, he wants a plan from the floor on what they will do to help everyone pass all of their courses.

The floor responds with a plan for study groups, tutoring, help from professors, and an "invite a prof" night where a faculty member is invited to come and discuss his course with students on the floor. (The day before, Ed had planted the seeds for these ideas in a discussion with two of the informal leaders on the hall.) The floor moves into action at a special floor meeting two nights later. The plan is shared, study groups formed, team leaders identified, and individual assignments made for follow-through on "prof nights" and other activities. Two weeks into the program, Ed throws a special Wednesday night "pizza party" to reward the group and let them know explicitly how proud he is of the guys' performances in meeting the challenge of helping everyone succeed academically.

As a whole, the floor is a boistrous, fun-loving, athletic group who love to play hard and compete aggressively. One important outcome of the study groups is that they give the quieter, more studious students on the floor a role to play in group life.

As Thanksgiving approaches, the guys in the two rooms at the end of the hall suggest holding a Thanksgiving Day dinner for the floor. They can cook in the residence hall kitchen, and everyone would enjoy a great meal and a day filled with football and fellowship. The guys agree, and Ed promotes the proposal, being sure to praise the guys highly for their idea and their willingness to do it.

The Thanksgiving Day banquet is a feast. At the beginning of the meal, each participant takes a moment to share with the floor what he is thankful for. Almost all are thankful for not having to eat cafeteria food on Thanksgiving.

The banquet highlights fall term. Later, some participants will recall it fondly and recollect how much it helped them, since they were away from home on Thanksgiving for the first time. For several, it marks the first time that they really feel a part of the floor.

The rest of the fall semester progresses smoothly. The intramural football team wins the championship, and the guys playing volleyball finish second in a tense championship game (they maintain they won; it was lousy officiating). Only eight of the guys on the floor are placed on academic probation at the end of the semester. John Dover does not return to school after his parents' deaths, and one other guy, Robert, drops out.

Robert is an interesting story. The Thursday night after mid-terms he decided suddenly to quit school. Friday afternoon Robert packed his bags and stopped in Ed's room to drop off his keys. Ed was getting ready to leave for an ROTC bivouac. Robert spoke briefly with Ed, mumbled something about homesickness and not being happy with his classes, and said good bye. Ed spoke with him briefly, tried to encourage him to stay, but couldn't talk long because he was running late. Ed took Robert's keys and said he would convey Robert's good byes to others on the floor. Robert and Ed went down the elevator together, Robert going home and Ed to bivouac. Over the weekend, Ed thought occasionally about Robert and wondered if he had missed something. Was there something else he could have done?

The culture of Ed's floor continues to strengthen during the spring term. Among the highlights, Ed counts the following:

- The floor forms two intramural basketball teams; one plays in the championship and wins by a point at the buzzer.
- The study groups are disbanded, but "Profs nights" continue every second or third week. These are well received and help greatly in understanding what faculty expect.
- Ed lightens up on the enforcement of rules, reasoning that a little roof-raising now and again isn't wrong as long as nothing is damaged and no one gets hurt.
- Ed continues to insist that people try to work through their own problems, resolve their own issues with the world, and not wear their hearts on their sleeves.
- Spring fraternity rush does some damage to floor morale, but Ed's demand that it not disrupt respect for one another on the floor minimizes the impact.
- Before mid-terms, Ed meets individually with each student, reviewing his progress and his preparation for exams.
- Mid-term grades show that four of the six on academic probation achieved passing grades. Ed takes major credit for their improved performance, throws a party in their honor, and recognizes each achiever for his improved performance. In doing so, he highlights for others the changes each student made that led to better performance.

To close the semester, Ed feels one more thing is necessary to solidify the floor, an end-of-year banquet. Ed chooses five guys to serve as a nominating committee to create floor awards and decide on recipients; some awards can be serious, some humorous, one or two off-color, but the emphasis of the awards is to be on athletics, scholarship, and floor unity. Everyone is to receive something.

The nominating committee goes crazy. Not only do they create an award for everyone, they put together a formal program and a booklet of the award winners. For each guy they list his name, nickname, award received, a photo if they could get one, and one or two remembrances of his contributions to the floor. One of the floor's favorite professors who had attended several of the "Profs nights" is invited to be the honored speaker.

The banquet is a sterling success. The awards are a highlight, and contain moments of great laughter. A few somber moments are recalled too as those who had distinguished themselves at those times are recognized.

The floor gives a special award to Ed—the "Big as Texas" Award. They recognize Ed's spirit, his concern for them, and his willingness to keep them on track. Most of all, they recognize his efforts to keep the floor together. The award they present is a carved wood desk plaque, stained and varnished, which two of the guys have made with a scroll saw in the Industrial Arts building. The plaque reads, in bold letters, "NO PRISONERS".

Ten days later, the floor is empty. Everyone, including Ed, is gone for the summer.

Case Study Questions

1. What did Ed value? _____

_____

_____

_____

_____

_____

2. What were the qualities that made Ed's floor a distinctive culture? _____

_____

_____

_____

_____

_____

3. What actions did Ed take to build culture on his floor? What actions did he take that worked against establishing a strong culture? _____

_____

_____

_____

_____

_____

_____

4. How was the culture sustained when threatened by outside forces? What were the threats? How were they managed? _____

_____

_____

_____

_____

_____

5. What characteristics of the leader emerged under crisis? How did these work for or against establishing the culture? _____

_____

_____

_____

_____

_____

6. Do you believe Ed had a definite culture formation plan in mind, or did the culture evolve on its own? Would this culture have developed its distinctiveness without Ed's leadership? _____

_____

_____

_____

_____

_____

7. What stories, myths, folk tales, and rituals might have evolved from this culture? What rituals were in the formative stages? What are the symbols of this culture? _____

_____

_____

_____

_____

_____

_____

_____

8. As a freshmen floor, Ed's group dissolved at the end of the year. Should it have? What would be the implications of allowing the group to continue for a second year? What would be the strengths and weaknesses of continuing this culture in the residence halls? _____

_____

_____

_____

_____

_____

_____

9. What distinctive characteristics represent the culture on your floor? In your building? What actions can you take to strengthen these components? Which do you wish to change, and how might you do it? _____

_____

_____

_____

_____

_____

_____

_____

_____

_____

Exercise: The Culture Game

Goals:

1. To explore the characteristics of residential cultures;
2. To identify those qualities or characteristics that enhance culture distinctiveness;
3. To consider actions leaders can take to build strong cultures.

Group Size: 6 to 8 people per group; any number of groups can operate at the same time.

Time Required: Approximately 60 to 75 minutes for each exercise. Time frame can be expanded depending upon the number of groups, the reporting time allowed, and the length of full discussion desired upon completion of the task.

Physical Setting: Separate tables or circle of chairs for each group. The setting should enable participants to write comfortably and encourage discussion.

Materials: Newsprint, markers for each group; pens or pencils and worksheets for each group member.

Objective: The Culture Game is designed to expose new RA's to the complexities of designing cultures and to appreciate how their skills and programming activities can shape and reinforce those qualities desired in residential cultures.

Task: Each work group will receive cards that define the floor's physical space, characteristics of the residents, and the dominant values desired in the culture to be formed. In the time allowed, each group is challenged to identify ways to create the desired culture in the physical setting assigned among residents with the characteristics described.

Instructions to the Facilitator:

1. Prepare separate 3×5 cards for each category in the game. You will have: Physical space (3 cards); Description of Residents (12 cards; 3 each for class year, ethnicity, sex, and option); and Dominant Culture Values (3 cards). These are sufficient for three groups to operate simultaneously. If more than three groups are necessary, create additional sets. You may wish to substitute cards or create additional cards that better represent specific characteristics of your campus.
2. Once work groups are formed, have each group select a recorder. This person will record the group's ideas and report the group's recommendations at the conclusion of the game.
3. To initiate the game, the recorders from each group randomly draw cards from each deck so that each receives a card for physical space, class year, ethnicity, sex, option, and dominant values. Each recorder also receives a Culture Game Instructions Sheet.
4. Recorders return to their groups, review the instructions and content of the culture description cards, and initiate the activity.
5. Allow groups to work 30 to 45 minutes, providing five to ten minutes at the end for each group to present their results, and five to ten minutes for additional processing and summary comments.

Culture Game Instructions Sheet

Select a recorder, who will log the ideas of your group and report your recommendations. Your recorder will then receive several cards defining different elements of the culture to be created. Your group's tasks are as follow:

1. From your Options Card, quickly decide on the additional characteristics you desire to define the members of your floor.

2. Now that the definition of the culture you seek to create is complete, you will have 30 to 45 minutes to identify ways to bring this culture alive, given your particular physical setting and residents. Keep in mind the means identified by Schein (1985) for establishing and reinforcing culture within a group: *a.* what leaders pay attention to, measure, and control; *b.* how the leader reacts to critical incidents; *c.* deliberate role modeling, teaching and coaching; and *d.* criteria for the allocation of rewards and status. Design your culture, identifying programs, formal and informal activities, and RA attitudes and behavior that will aid in culture development. Pay particular attention to the following dimensions of the RA position: *a.* quality of relationship with residents; *b.* disciplinary posture; enforcement of rules; *c.* informal activity on the floor; and *d.* formal programming conducted on the floor. Brainstorm ways in which these dimensions can be employed to create the culture described by the Dominant Values card.

3. At the conclusion of the game, the recorder will have 5 to 10 minutes to report to the full group on the following:
   a. A description of the culture. This is a quick review of the content of your culture cards, including optional characteristics of residents.
   b. Specific actions, programs, activities, or events the RA can use to facilitate the creation and implementation of this culture.
   c. Any observations your group has about the strengths or weaknesses of this particular culture, difficulties encountered, and particular strategies of which you are especially proud.

Culture Definition Cards

Directions: Type each item on a separate 3×5 card.

Physical Space Cards:

1. Four-person apartments with bath, kitchenettes, and living room.
2. Two-person rooms; 20 rooms on each floor, with community bath, straight hallway.
3. Four-person suites with attached bath; 8 suites on each floor.

OPTION: Use descriptions of your own residence hall space.

Description of Residents Cards:

1. Class Year
   a. all upperclassmen
   b. all freshmen
   c. mixed floor, 40% upperclassmen and 60% freshmen
2. Ethnicity
   a. 5% minority populations
   b. 10% minority populations
   c. 20% minority populations
3. Sex
   a. all men
   b. all women
   c. coeducational by room, apartment, or suite
4. Option: As a group, identify and include in your description the following number of additional defining characteristics for residents on this floor: preferred hobbies, personal interests, sports, music, level of substance abuse, attitude toward rules, majors, community involvement, etc.
   a. one optional characteristic
   b. two optional characteristics
   c. three optional characteristics

Dominant Values Card:

1. *EGGHEAD:* Academic excellence; strong emphasis on excellence in learning and classroom performance; campus involvement focused on departmental organizations, honoraries, close association with the faculty. Social life and cohesion on the floor are not highly valued. RA makes the decisions that govern group life.

2. *CLUBHOUSE:* Social engagement and strong group cohesion is paramount. This is to be an energized, high-interacting, and supportive group of individuals; participative decision-making; resident are encouraged to join in campus social life, social organizations, and programming groups. Provide leadership for the social aspects of campus life. Academic excellence is not emphasized, but it is important to stay in school.

3. *ALL-AMERICAN:* Well balanced is the catchword here. A broad, distributed engagement with the campus is what is desired. All residents are expected to be engaged with academics, campus activities, recreation, and other dimensions of campus life. Personal independence and striving for personal goals is supported; decision styles are flexible, as is individual participation in group life.

Exercise: Culture Analysis

Goals:
1. To review cultural concepts.
2. To help RAs access the dynamics of culture he or she is helping to develop.

Group Size: Five to eight students per group with any number of groups.

Time Required: 45 minutes

Materials: Exercise sheets and pencils

Physical Setting: Location suitable for multiple small group discussions.

Process:
> Provide 15 minutes for each RA to complete the "Culture Description Worksheet" and at least 30 minutes for group discussion. In the group discussion the following steps are followed:
> 1. The "Culture Description Worksheet" is used by each small group participant to identify the characteristics of his or her residence floor.
> 2. Each participant shares the results of his or her analysis focusing on those qualities that make the culture on his or her floor distinctive from and similar to other RAs floors.
> 3. As a group, discuss actions RAs can take to strengthen culture on a floor.

Variation: This can be expanded to a half-a-day workshop by focusing on each dimension of floor culture and management.

Culture Description Worksheet

This worksheet will assist you in identifying qualities of your residence hall culture. Use it to guide your analysis of your floor and its unique qualities as a culture.

I. In each of the following areas, write down words or phrases which represent your floor. What comes to mind? What qualities distinguish your floor from others?

Physical Space: _____

_____

_____

Personal Relationships: _____

_____

_____

Level of Floor Activity: _____

_____

_____

Interaction Between Rooms: _____

_____

_____

Types of Floor Activities:

    Social _____

    Cultural _____

    Athletic _____

    Educational _____

    Other _____

Academic Orientation: _____

_____

_____

Relationship to RA: _____

_____

_____

Dominant Attitudes of Members: _____

_____

_____

Dominant Values of Members: _____

_____

_____

Special Events: _____

_____

_____

Other Qualities That Distinguish Your Floor: _____

_____

_____

II. Identify and describe three events that are typically representative of the floor, but that also present the floor at its best. At its worst.

Event 1 _____

_____

_____

_____

_____

_____

_____

Event 2 _____

_____

_____

_____

_____

_____

_____

Event 3 _____

_____

_____

_____

_____

_____

_____

III. Drawing upon these observations, write a brief, six sentence description of your floor. What part of the floor's culture do you take pride in, and which do you wish to change?

_____

_____

_____

_____

_____

_____

_____

_____

_____

_____

_____

_____

IV. Finally, prepare to highlight for your fellow RA's actions of yours that have shaped the culture you have just described.

CHAPTER 3

Issues of Race and Culture on the College Campus

Dr. Christine Bennett,
Indiana University

Lena's Pandora's Box

Lena Jones sagged back into her blue corduroy bed chair and sighed. What had she gotten into!? A stack of anonymous notes from fourth floor residents rested on the bed next to her innocent looking "suggestion box." Whose idea *was* it anyway—a suggestion box where students could express thoughts or concerns, or make suggestions. What was she going to do? She had to think of something before her next floor meeting. Slowly, relentlessly, the students' written comments chugged through her consciousness. All were addressed to Lena Jones, fourth floor RA.

- Something should be done about loud music on this floor. It's always the black students.
- You let the black girls get away with murder. And they do all the talking at meetings. Always interrupting.
- Today is Yom Kippur. I missed an important test and the professor won't let me make it up.
- Why do the Malaysian students have to dress like that. Why don't they try to fit in?
- I feel embarrassed. Out of place. Out of style. My roommate has filled our room with her clothes, TV, stereo, and refrigerator. I came with one suitcase.
- Patsy Lynch is a racist. She won't shower or use the bathroom if black students are in there.
- I'm sick of Asian students. They spend all their time in the library and contribute nothing to this university. Absolutely nothing.
- The black students are racist. They always eat together in the cafeteria.
- The dining room always opens at the worst times; how about later or longer hours?
- Why does the cafeteria serve so much pork? Why can't we get Kosher food around here?
- If Stacey Miller wants to read her Bible every day that's fine. But she doesn't have to try to convert me! Get me a new roommate before I go crazy!
- Did you hear about those Arab students who hung a dead sheep or goat or something in the laundry room? Weird.
- If Sonya don't stop messin' with the brothers she's in for big trouble.
- My professor wrote me last week: "One problem with you Latinos is that you write *bullshit*—a lot of words without any information being given. It is a cultural difference, no doubt."
- I'm really afraid whenever I'm alone on the elevator (or anywhere) with a bunch of blacks or Latins. Can't we have separate dorms?
- I'm shocked at the students on this campus. Especially on our floor. Too much sex, too many drugs, too little religion, and too little studying. Am I the weird one? Can I survive here?
- Last Sunday night my friend Sonny and I got chased by a bunch of "red necks" who told us "niggers" shouldn't be off campus after dark.

Feeling dazed, Lena let the stack of notes slip from her hand. How could these problems have been avoided? Was it too late for change?

The problems and concerns expressed by the students who happened to be assigned to Lena Jones are typical of students in most colleges and universities across the country. Naturally, not every RA faces such an array of problems related to cultural or racial differences, because not all college student populations are as diverse as this example. Yet, chances are that the reader can identify with at least one of Lena's students. What can be done to help deal with their concerns? The purpose of this chapter is to provide some answers.

We begin with an overview of some key social science concepts that help illuminate and resolve misunderstandings and conflicts linked to racial and cultural differences. We will then reconsider the case of Lena Jones and will conclude with some instructional activities designed for RAs on culturally pluralistic campuses.

Racial Differences

Why should race make a difference on campus? Not only have our colleges and universities inherited the society's legacy of racism, they also have become an arena for mixing ethnically encapsulated people in close proximity. Before elaborating on these points, we need to clarify what we mean by "race."

The term "race" is a concept anthropologists created to categorize humans according to physical attributes such as skin color, size and shape of the head, eyes, ears, lips and nose, and hair texture. J. F. Blumenback, the eighteenth century scientist, identified five racial types still widely accepted today: Negroid, Caucasoid, Mongoloid, Malayan, and American Indian. Many scientists, including Charles Darwin, have suggested that we abandon the term race, both because it has not led to useful knowledge in understanding human behavior and because it leads to the dangerous myth of racial superiority. Reknowned anthropologist Ashley Montagu has written that

> "[I]t is not possible to make the sort of racial classifications which some anthropologists and others have attempted. The fact is that all human beings are so mixed with regard to origin that between different groups of individuals . . . overlapping of physical traits is the rule" (1974, p. 7).

Montagu's point was illustrated recently at a Big Ten University. The newly elected Homecoming Queen, a green-eyed beauty with dark straight hair and slender features, was perceived to be white by the general campus community. Most classmates discovered her black identity only after newspaper photographers interviewed her family members at home.

What's important to keep in mind is that, despite its lack of scientific validity, the concept of race persists and remains a primary basis for categorizing self and others within our society. People often confuse the concepts of culture, which is one's acquired way of life, and race, which is genetically determined. (It may be helpful to remember that over 90 percent of our genetic makeup is identical to that of all humans, 3 percent determines sexual attributes, and only 2 percent determines our racial characteristics. The remainder shapes individual attributes.) It is essential to realize that race and culture are not synonymous. As Bennett points out,

> There are Whites who act Black and vice versa, and tremendous racial diversity exists within the Puerto Rican and other Hispanic communities. It is true, however, that racial isolation has been a fact of history for large segments of the population; as a result, cultural differences that can be associated with race have survived. The fact that cultural differences are associated with racial differences confirms myths and stereotypes associated with race. Blacks, for example, are often perceived as having more "rhythm" and as being natural athletes. Jews are often perceived as being miserly and more intelligent. These perceptions are usually based on the belief that genetic racial factors, rather than cultural factors, explain what is perceived. The concept of race has lead to the development of racist ideologies such as the Nazi ideology, which argued for the distinction between Aryans and Jews and led to the extermination of over six million European Jews during the 1930s and 1940s. (1986, p. 31)

The terms *race* and *racism* are also often confused. Many people, particularly whites who have had little contact with non-whites, fear that simply recognizing a person's race is being racist. Many campus programs aimed at improving interracial understanding have failed because this barrier has not been addressed. During "awareness" discussions, for example, many encapsulated white students feel tense and fearful of appearing prejudiced; unaware black and Latino students may feel frustrated and impatient with whites who appear dishonest and prejudiced, or at best naive. It is helpful to recognize that, given our social reality, it is natural and honest to recognize a person's race. We notice whether a person's eyes are brown or blue and whether the person is male or female. True, we cannot always know if a person is black or white or Indian, but when race is obvious, the fact should be recognized. Recognition of physical racial differences is racist if and only if we lower our expectations, accept stereotypes, or discriminate.

Legacy of Racism

Let us now consider the legacy of racism. We have a national history shaped by the doctrine of white supremacy, which resulted in the overall suppression of dark-skinned citizens. This doctrine was used to justify slavery in the past and, more recently, to rationalize inferior schools, substandard homes, low-paying jobs, and segregated restaurants, restrooms, and transportation. Some scholars have written that

> To justify the treatment of the Afro-American citizen, white society encouraged an army of propagandists to "scientifically" prove the inferiority of Black people. While this ideology of racism was applied to all people of color with whom Euro-American society came into contact, its severest application was against Afro-Americans. Because they were the most physically different from whites, because their numbers were the second largest to whites, and because of their geographical and social proximity to whites, Black people have been perceived as the greatest threat.
>
> White supremacist ideology has infected every level of national life. Government officials, social scientists, ministers, teachers, journalists and doctors have all played a part, as new and more sophisticated revisions of the myths and rationalizations of white supremacy keep reappearing. Whether it is religious leaders in colonial days pointing to Biblical passages damning Ham; biologists of a hundred years ago "studying" cranial structures; Social Darwinists utilizing theories of evolution and survival of the fittest; geneticists of the 1920's "proving" inborn moral inferiority; Moynihan-like theories of Black "pathology"; recent genetic pronouncements of Shockley and Jensen about Black IQ—all serve as pseudo-scientific apologies for the ongoing oppression directed against Black people. (Council on Interracial Books, 1977, p. 16).

Racism has always operated on two levels: individual and institutional. Individual racism is the belief that one's own race is superior to another and is based upon the erroneous assumption that biological racial attributes *determine* the psychological and intellectual characteristics of a racially identifiable group, as well as its social behavior. Sometimes racist beliefs remain submerged as hidden racial prejudice, but usually the racist believes this inferiority justifies inferior social treatment, or discrimination.

Institutional racism also means overt discrimination, but it is more difficult to identify the source, which is hidden in laws, policies, and institutional practices. Some of the most blatant evidence of our legacy of racism is the policy of genocide aimed at American Indians, the oppression of Black Americans under slavery, the internment of Japanese-Americans during World War II, and the era of Jim Crowism.

For sixty years after the U.S. Supreme Court decision in Plessy v. Ferguson in 1896, separate but equal facilities for blacks were legal. The extreme dual system pervaded all aspects of life in the Southern states, including separate schools, public transportation, restaurants, theatres, baseball leagues, public bathrooms, swimming pools, hospitals, doctors' offices, and so on. Interracial marriage was banned in thirty-eight states until the mid twentieth century, and blacks were denied the right to vote through grandfather clauses, poll taxes, and outrageous literacy tests until the voting rights legislation between 1964 and 1970. Today, gerrymandering (the division of ethnic minority neighborhoods into separate voting districts attached to predominantly white districts) is still used to divide black communities in order to dilute their voting power. Many Hispanics, particularly darker-skinned individuals, have experienced similar segregation and suppression.

Even though the period of Jim Crow has ended, the legacy lives on openly in white supremacist organizations such as the Ku Klux Klan and in more subtle ways such as textbook errors and omissions, teacher expectations, election practices rooted in gerrymandering and division of potential voting blocks of ethnic minorities, and a legal system that favors people with the money needed to hire good lawyers, plea bargain, and meet bail. As late as 1980, U.S. census data showed that on the average black males with four or more years of college education earned approximately $8,000.00 less than white males with equivalent education (U.S. Bureau of Labor Statistics, 1984.)

The legacy of racism also exists in the memories of the parents and grandparents of most college students today. Both those socialized to become oppressors and those who were the oppressed are victims of white racism (Dennis, 1981). Black, Indian and Latino college students are far more likely than white students to come from backgrounds where their families have been denied equal access to educational, economic, and political power. Now on campus, they are likely to have fewer role models and systems of academic and social support. White students are also the victims of white racism. For example, many whites are ignorant of "the many-sidedness of the black population" and therefore accept racial stereotypes. Many whites have developed a dual consciousness by being taught to hate or fear blacks and to conform to racial etiquette on the one hand, while being taught Christian love on the other (Dennis, 1981).

Racism has kept the races apart to a large degree in this society. Separation breeds myths, stereotypes, and fears. Those whites who do not accept racial prejudices are likely to be perceived as racist simply because they are white. Black, Latino and Indian students are often wrongly perceived to be less intelligent, immoral, and violent. For many students, college offers the first opportunity to personally experience racial differences.

Racism and University Life

Now let us consider the importance of the university as an arena where ethnically encapsulated people meet. Whether they are from rural areas, small towns, inner cities, or suburbs, most students have been isolated from one or more of the ethnic groups present on campus. These students often hold fears, myths, and stereotypes about members of the unfamiliar groups. College life does not necessarily afford opportunities to erode these negative prejudices and misunderstandings. Casual observation of campus life shows that ethnic encapsulation typically continues for many students. While it may be true that much separatism is voluntary or unconscious, it is also true that there are few institutionalized efforts to foster positive interracial contact experiences. In white-predominated schools such as Big Ten Universities, where over 90 percent of the faculty and the students are white, it is possible for white students to go through their college career having had little contact with racially different students. This is not true for the black, Asian, Latino or Indian students on campus.

This does not mean that all white college students have led encapsulated lives. Many have not. Individual differences in past interracial contact experiences must be considered in campus programs aimed at increased interracial understanding. Students arrive on campus with differing levels of readiness for interracial contact experiences. Blanket programs that ignore these psychological differences are likely to fail. Some students, for example, are struggling with the fear they feel when in close proximity with members of another race, while other students are dealing with the pressures of interracial dating.

Research into stages of ethnic identity offers one promising way of understanding a person's openness to ethnic diversity. Several interesting typologies of ethnic self-identity have been developed by black scholars (Banks, 1979, Cross, 1971, and Milleones, 1976). These typologies are similar in that where an individual falls on each indicates his or her level of self identity, self-acceptance, and openness to ethnic or racial diversity. Both Cross and Milleones have focused on the psychological liberation of oppressed groups, particularly black Americans, and have validated measures of ethnic self-identity related to political activism. The Banks typology taps into the individual's degree of openness to human diversity from a multi-ethnic perspective and has been applied to educational settings (Ford, 1979). Because of its applicability to an educational environment, the Banks conception of ethnicity is useful for understanding diversity within ethnic groups on campus.

According to James A. Banks, the following five stages of ethnicity are possible. (Banks has recently added Stage 6, Global Identity.)

Stage 1. Ethnic Psychological Captivity: During this stage the individual has internalized the negative ideologies and beliefs about his or her ethnic group that are institutionalized within the society. An ethnic minority student at this stage rejects his/her ethnic group and feels ashamed of it. Such students try to avoid contact with members of other ethnic groups or strive to become assimilated into the white culture. Examples would be the black student who passes for white, the guilt-ridden white liberal who tries too hard to be accepted into the black student community, or the Polish-American student who anglicizes his or her name out of embarrassment.

Stage 2. Ethnic Encapsulation: Stage 2 is characterized by ethnic encapsulation and ethnic exclusiveness, including voluntary separatism. Stage 2 students interact primarily within student groups of the same ethnic group and believe their ethnic group is superior to others. Contact with members of different ethnic groups is avoided.

Stage 3. Ethnic Identity Clarification: At this stage the individual is able to clarify personal attitudes and ethnic identity, reduce intrapsychic conflict, and develop positive attitudes toward his or her ethnic group. Students at this level have learned to develop a healthy sense of self and ethnic pride (not feelings of superiority), and are therefore able to accept and respond more positively to outside ethnic groups.

Stage 4. Biethnicity: Individuals in this stage have a healthy sense of ethnic identity and the psychological characteristics and skills needed to participate in their own ethnic culture, as well as in another ethnic culture. Ethnic minority students at this stage have a strong desire to function effectively in the predominantly white culture on the college campus, and they are successful. This is accomplished without giving up their traditional culture at home or in their private lives.

Stage 5. Multiethnicity: Stage 5 describes the idealized goal for citizenship identity within an ethnically pluralistic nation. The student "at this stage is able to function, at least at minimal levels, within several ethnic socio-cultural environments and to understand, appreciate, and share the values, symbols, and institutions and several ethnic cultures" (Banks, 1984, p. 56)

Assuming the validity of the Banks typology, students whose ethnicity differs from cultural expectations in the university would need to be at stage 3, 4, or 5 in order to make a successful transition. Individuals in stages 4 or 5 would be most open to ethnic diversity. A person's degree of openness is more important than the stage of ethnicity per se. However, openness to ethnic diversity is believed possible only after an individual has developed a strong sense of self-awareness and acceptance (ie., has reached Stage 3).

One's sense of ethnicity does not necessarily include racial identity, particularly if one is a member of society's racial majority group as are white Americans in the United States. Religion (in the case of groups like American Jews or the Amish), language, or national traditions may be more important variables than race. Where racial differences do exist, as, for example, among blacks, whites, and Latinos, cultural differences are likely but not inevitable. Furthermore, it isn't at all unusual to find students of the same race who misunderstand each other because of their cultural differences. We see this, for example, when college roommates of the same race experience interpersonal conflict and misunderstanding rooted in different socio-economic backgrounds. Racially different roommates may also experience interpersonal conflict and misunderstanding due more to cultural differences associated with socio-economic background than to racial differences. Geographic origins and sense of ethnic identity can be influential, along with socio-economic background. Whether or not cultural differences are associated with racial differences, they are likely to contribute to misunderstanding and conflict on the college campus.

Cultural Differences

How can we better understand cultural differences on the college campus? One of the most promising ways of conceptualizing culture* and avoiding intercultural misunderstanding has been developed by Edward T. Hall. His influential books, such as *Beyond Culture, The Silent Language* and *The Hidden Dimension,* vividly describe how humans are unknowing captives of their culture. People from different cultures perceive the world differently, unaware that there are legitimate alternative ways of perceiving, behaving, and judging. Particularly significant are the unconscious assumptions we make about personal space, time, interpersonal relations, and ways of knowing. These cultural differences exist to varying degrees among microcultures within our society (for example, the Hopi, Navajo, blacks, Mexican Americans, Puerto Ricans, Jews, Chinese Americans and rural Appalachians), as well as among different nations.

Cultural differences and misunderstandings often become evident when people from different cultures try to communicate. Often they assume erroneously that they *are* communicating. This is why Hall's simple but elegant theory of culture can be so helpful to us. He focuses on interpersonal communication styles as a key for illuminating basic culture differences and similarities.

Hall distinguishes among different cultures in terms of what he calls high or low context (Hall, 1959, 1966, 1976, and 1983). In low context cultures, such as much of the United States, Germany and Scandanavia, meaning is gleaned from the verbal message itself, for example a spoken explanation, a memo, or a computer program. *What* is said is more important than who said it—in fact, often we don't even know the author. Members of the university community for example, often communicate by phone or memo over a period of years or even decades without ever meeting each other personally. High context cultures, such as those of the Japanese, Arabs, southern Europe, American Indian, Mexican, and portions of the rural United States, are the opposite. Meaning must be understood in terms of the situation or setting in which communication takes place. A classic example is written Chinese language, where one character may be pronounced in several different ways. An overview of some key characteristics of high and low context cultures are summarized in Figure 1 (Bennett, 1986a).

	HIGH CONTEXT	**LOW CONTEXT**
Time	POLYCHRONIC Loose schedules, flux, multiple simultaneous activities. Last minute changes of important plans Time is less tangible	MONOCHRONIC Tight schedules One event at a time, linear Importance of being on time Time is more tangible (eg. is spent, wasted, is money, etc.)
Space & Tempo	HIGH-SYNC Synchrony, moving in harmony with others, is consciously valued (people and nature) Social rhythm has meaning	LOW-SYNC Synchrony is less noticeable Social underdeveloped rhythming
Reasoning	COMPREHENSIVE LOGIC Knowledge is gained through intuition, spiral logic and contemplation. Importance of feelings	LINEAR LOGIC Knowledge is gained through analytical reasoning, eg. Socrates Importance of words

Figure 1. E. T. Hall's conception of Culture according to context. Source: Christine Bennett. "Teaching Intercultural Competence and Informed Citizenship." Paper presented at the Annual Conference of the National Council of the Social Studies (NCSS) New York City, November 17, 1986.

*Culture may be defined as the way of life of a people, the sum of their learned behavior patterns, attitudes, and material things (Hall, 1973, p. 20).

Figure 1. *Continued.*

	HIGH CONTEXT	LOW CONTEXT
Verbal Messages	RESTRICTED CODES "Shorthand speech," reliance on non-verbal and contextual cues. Overall emotional quality more important than meaning of particular words. Economical, fast, efficient communication that is satisfying and slow to change; fosters interpersonal cohesiveness and provides for human need for social stability. Stress on social integration and harmony; being polite.	ELABORATE CODES Verbal amplification through extended talk or writing. Little reliance on nonverbal or contextual cues. Doesn't foster cohesiveness but can change rapidly. Provides for human need to adapt and change. Stress on argument and persuasion; being direct.
Social Roles	TIGHT SOCIAL STRUCTURE Individual's behavior is predictable; conformity to role expectations.	LOOSE SOCIAL STRUCTURE Behavior is unpredictable; role behavior expectations are less clear, less stereotyping.
Interpersonal Relations	GROUP IS PARAMOUNT Clear status distinctions (eg. age, rank, position), strong distinctions between insiders and outsiders. Human interactions are emotionally based, person oriented. Stronger bonds, bending of individual interests for sake of relationships. Cohesive, highly interrelated human relationships, completed action chains. Members of group are first and foremost	INDIVIDUAL IS PARAMOUNT Status is more subtle, distinctions between insiders and outsiders less important. Human interactions are functionally based, approach is specialized. Fragile bonds Fragmented, short term human relationships, broken action chains when relationship is not satisfying. Individuals are first, groups come second.
Socio-Political	PERSONALIZED LAW AND AUTHORITY Customary procedures and who one knows are important. In face of unresponsive bureaucracies, must be an insider or have a "friend" to make things happen. (eg. going through the back door) People in authority are personally and truly responsible for actions of every subordinate. Humanistic	PROCEDURAL LAW AND AUTHORITY Procedures, laws, and policies are more important than who one knows. Policy rules, unresponsive bureaucracy. People in authority try to pass the buck. Impersonal Legal procedures Mechanistic

What does Hall's theory have to do with residence halls on the typical college campus? It contains two essential points. First, the vast majority of this society's colleges and universities are modeled after the low context macroculture. Academic and social events operate according to tight schedules, often printed months in advance. Freshman roommate assignments and residence hall facilities reflect our egalitarianism, material comforts, and conceptions of privacy and personal space. The list could go on.

The second essential point is that, in contrast to the low context culture on campus, many college students have grown up in high context microcultures. Without understanding the conflicting assumptions and expectations of their home and college cultures, they are likely to experience some degree of psychological discomfort, or transitional trauma, as they attempt to adjust to college life. While it is essential to avoid over-generalizations and stereotypes, likely candidates for transitional trauma are students from rural areas, small towns, and farms; students from economically impoverished homes; black, Latino, and American Indian students who have had little personal contact with white society; students who are devout in their religious beliefs; and international students.

Conflicts Arising from Ethnicity

A necessary (though insufficient) condition for reducing transitional trauma on the college campus is to identify the points of possible misunderstanding and conflict. What do we look for? Wilma Longstreet has developed an exceptionally clear and useful scheme for understanding differences in culturally pluralistic settings. Originally conceived for desegregated classrooms, it can be adapted to establish needed guidelines for observing and interpreting human behavior in any setting, in our case residence halls on the college campus.

Longstreet (1978) defines ethnicity as

> that portion of cultural development that occurs before the individual is in complete command of his or her abstract intellectual powers and that is formed primarily through the individual's early contacts with family, neighbors, friends, teachers, and others, as well as with his or her immediate environment of the home and neighborhood. (p. 19)

College students will have gained some intellectual control over their ethnically learned behavior, but even among bicultural adults that control is likely to remain incomplete.

Longstreet goes on to identify five aspects of ethnicity, based to a degree on the work of E. T. Hall and Ray L. Birdwhistell (1976), that are potential sources of intercultural misunderstanding: 1) verbal communication, 2) nonverbal communication, 3) orientation modes (eg. time and space), 4) social values, and 5) intellectual modes.

Verbal Communication

All students on campus can be expected to possess some degree of proficiency in Standard American English. This is the institution's official language. Although special consideration is sometimes given to international students whose mother tongue is not English, important linguistic differences existing within our own national population are often overlooked. Important areas of potential conflict relate to dialect differences, especially grammar, semantics, and discussion modes.

Students who speak "country," or black vernacular, or any non-standard dialect are often perceived as uneducated or less intelligent. Many white students and some upper income black students who have grown up in ethnically encapsulated environments either cannot understand their black or Latino peers or incorrectly assume they do understand. Black use of the term "nigger" for example, is distressing to many whites.

Nonverbal Communication

It is estimated that 90 percent of what humans communicate is nonverbal. That is, most of the messages we send are through unconscious body movements, expressions and gestures (kinesics); our unconscious use and organization of personal space (proxemics); and when, where, and how often we unconsciously physically touch others (haptics).

The literature is loaded with fascinating examples of cultural differences in nonverbal communication. Greetings are one example, and they illustrate how the accepted behaviors of one culture may be seriously misunderstood in another.

Imagine how public hugging and kissing, customary behaviors during greetings and departures among many Westerners is often perceived by non-Westerners. LaBarre (1972) points out, "Kissing is in the Orient an act of private lovemaking, and arouses only disgust when performed publicly: thus, in Japan, it is necessary to censor out the major portion of love scenes in American-made movies" (p. 173). Public displays of affection among college students may be offensive or distressing to international students or students who are recent immigrants from Eastern Asian cultures. Equally disturbing may be the presence of opposite sex students who visit roommates and others living in residences halls with open visitation policies.

Eye aversion (looking down or away) is another potential source of intercultural misunderstanding. Within the macroculture, "good" direct eye contact signifies that one is listening to the speaker, is honest, and is telling the truth. Within some black American communities (particularly when survival often depended upon showing deference to whites), as well as among the Navajo and many Asian nations, eye aversion is a sign of deference and respect accorded to another. Imagine how an RA raised within the white macroculture is likely to perceive a student who looks down or away when questioned about some stolen money or property. Eye signals, and other signals as well, are further complicated by the fact that many college students are bicultural and may give mixed messages.

Styles of walking have been included in studies of black kinesics. According to Kenneth Johnson (1972), "non-verbal communication patterns in Black culture that are not commonly exhibited by other Americans possibly have their origins in African non-verbal communication patterns" (p. 17). Describing the "black walk" in non-conflict situations, he writes:

> Young Black males have their own way of walking. Observing young Black males walking down ghetto streets, one can't help noticing that they are, indeed, in Thoreau's words "marching to the tune of a different drummer." The "different drummer" is a different culture; the non-verbal message of their walk is similar to the non-verbal message of young white males, but not quite the same.
>
> The young white males' walk is usually brisk, and they walk on the balls of their feet with strides of presumed authority. Both arms swing while they walk. The non-verbal message is: "I am a strong man, possessing all the qualities of masculinity, and I stride through the world with masculine authority."
>
> The young Black males' walk is different. First of all, it's much slower—it's more of a stroll. The head is sometimes slightly elevated and casually tipped to the side. Only one arm swings at the side with the hand slightly cupped. The other arm hangs limply to the side or it is tucked in the pocket. The gait is slow, casual and rhythmic. The gait is almost like a walking dance, with all parts of the body moving in rhythmic harmony. This walk is called a "pimp strut," or it is referred to as "walking that walk."
>
> The walk of young Black males communicates the same non-verbal message as that of young white males. In addition, the Black walk communicates that the young Black male is beautiful, and it beckons female attention to the sexual prowess possessed by the walker. Finally, the Black walk communicates that the walker is "cool"; in other words, he is not upset or bothered by the cares of the world and is, in fact, somewhat disdainful and insolent towards the world.
>
> The young Black male walk must be learned, and it is usually learned at quite a young age. Black males of elementary school age can often be seen practicing the walk. By the time they reach junior high school age, the Black walk has been mastered.

. . . each individual must impose a certain amount of originality onto the general pattern. Thus, some young Black males will vary the speed or swing of the head or effect a slight limp or alter any one or a number of the components of the Black walk to achieve originality. The general "plan" of the walk, however, is recognizable even with the imposed originality. This imposed originality also communicates the individualism of each young Black male (Johnson, 1972, p. 20).

Students of any racial background who are unfamiliar with the "black walk" may feel threatened by it, particularly if it occurs in their home away from home, the residence hall.

Proxemics, the way humans use and organize space, is central to Edward T. Hall's (1972) intercultural research. Drawing upon observations of Americans overseas, Hall notes that cultural differences in the handling of space often leads to misunderstanding and intensified cultural shock. For example, when Americans tend to back away to a "comfortable conversational distance" when people stand "too close" during conversation, they may appear cold, aloof, withdrawn, and disinterested in people of their host country. On the other hand, the Americans may feel irritated and uncomfortable with their hosts "pushy" behavior.

In general, it appears that people from high context cultures require less personal space and do more touching than individuals from low context cultures. Compare riding a public bus in China and in the United States. Americans attempt to preserve a layer of personal space around themselves, even in crowded conditions, and are careful to ask for pardon should personal belongings touch another passenger. Chinese, on the other hand, are accustomed to packing people in like sardines; bumping one another or stepping on another's foot seem to pass unrecognized, and certainly require no apology. American libraries are a perfect place to observe proxemics on the college campus. Most students set up their own territory at the study table and feel irritated or uncomfortable when someone else's pencil, paper, books, or even foot invades the space. Students may also establish ownership over certain tables or areas in the dining hall, and these are often identifiable by race or national origin.

Variations in proxemics within a high or a low context culture do exist, however. In China one's gender makes a difference. It is common to see males walking hand in hand (or even with arms intertwined) with males, and females with females. This does not signify homosexuality, as it would in some cultures. Traditionally, heterosexual touching was strictly private, though today this is changing in most uban areas. Despite these changes, deeply rooted cultural expectations related to dating and courtship are likely to cause misunderstandings between Chinese and Americans. A student from Taiwan, for example, might interpret holding hands, a kiss, or even a date as an indication of serious commitment on the part of her or his American date. The American student is likely to interpret such actions much more casually.

Time Orientation

Differences between "black time" and "white time" in this society are common knowledge. "White time" is monochronic time, in which things are accomplished one-at-a-time in a linear fashion familiar to low context Anglo-Western Europeans. Events occur "on time" according to a clearly stated schedule.

Black time, or polychronic time, is the opposite. (The notion of "black time" should be expanded to include people from polychronic cultures more generally, for example, southern European.) In high context cultures, time is polychronic. Many activities take place simultaneously, and schedules are invisible. In fact, these activities each seem to operate on a schedule of their own. A party takes place when people get there and ends when people leave. Business deals are closed only after preliminary exchanges concerning family, friends, and personal nuances that may take days or weeks. Hall explains the differences this way:

Polychronic cultures are by their very nature oriented to people. Any human being who is naturally drawn to other human beings and who lives in a world dominated by human relationships will be either pushed or pulled toward the polychronic end of the time spectrum. If you value people, you must hear them out and cannot cut them off simply because of a schedule (Hall, 1983, p. 50).

Campus life operates according to monochronic time. University schedules and procedures "take on a life of their own without reference to either logic or human needs" (Hall, 1983, p. 50). Classes end at the specified time, even if an exciting discussion is still going on. Cafeterias in the residence halls open and close according to routine, not according to students' hunger. People who know how to organize their time, don't "waste" time, and can meet deadlines are more successful than those who do not have these characteristics.

Social Values

As is evident in many of the comments from Lena's "suggestion box," social values represent a fertile field for intercultural misunderstanding and conflict. Values are beliefs about how one ought or ought not to behave, or about some end state of existence worth or not worth attaining. They are abstract ideals, positive or negative, that represent a person's beliefs about ideal modes of conduct and ideal terminal goals (Rokeach, 1969, p. 124). Values are like a yardstick, used to judge and compare our own attitudes and behaviors and those of others.

How could the social values of our low context colleges and universities be described? A case could be made for competition, individual hard work, individual achievement, good use of time, equalitarianism, honesty (eg. no plagiarism), freedom of expression, useful knowledge (eg. problem solving, careers), the Greek ideal of physical beauty, what Hsu (1969) refers to as "the good life" (good food, drink, and sex), material wealth, being on time, being financially responsible, and "fitting in."

In contrast, students from high context cultures are likely to value family above all else. Important exams can be missed when a close family member falls ill. Money intended for tuition, board, or books may go home if the family breadwinner is laid off work. If they come to campus alone, students from high context cultures are likely to miss the support network of family and friends. Without the help of a knowledgeable friend, protocol in the library, bursar's office, or health center can be intimidating. Good academic counselors and *people* in the financial aids office are more helpful than written brochures. People are more important than things.

For students from high context cultures, where friendships are initiated carefully but then last a lifetime, strangers living in close proximity seem to ask personal questions too soon, seem friendly to the point of being pushy, and then seem superficial as they move on to others or don't follow through on a promise. When the student does develop a close friend, classes or meetings are willingly missed when the friend falls sick or is in trouble. With perceived superiors and acquaintances who are not close friends, politeness may be valued over honesty (ie., being indirect rather than direct) in order to avoid hurt feelings or group conflict.

Intellectual Modes

Intellectual modes refer both to the types of knowledge that are valued most and to learning styles, or how an individual learns. Although intellectual modes are only indirectly important to the RA, they may be central to the academic success of many students.

Students who value spiritual or religious knowledge may experience transitional trauma when their religious beliefs are challenged or when courses seem to overemphasize science and technology. Students who seek knowledge related to practical living may feel frustrated when their coursework seems too theoretical. Because students do have choices among schools and majors, even more important than what types of knowledge is offered is the way students are expected to learn. On the average college campus those students learn best who are competitive, work well independently, use linear logic rather than intuition, emphasize rational thought over feeling (and can separate the two), prefer abstract thinking over the senses, and require little physical mobility. All these characteristics refer to aspects of learning style.

A variety of instruments currently exist to help educators measure students' learning style, and a growing body of research shows no relationship between basic intelligence and style. Brilliant people can be polar opposites on a single learning style measure.

Keefe and Languis (1983) define learning styles as

> that consistent pattern of behavior and performance by which an individual approaches educational experiences. It is the composite of characteristic cognitive, affective and physiological behaviors that serve as relatively stable indicators of how a learner perceives, interacts with, and responds to the learning environment. It is formed in the deep structure of neural organization and personality which molds and is molded by human development and the cultural experiences of home, school and society. (p. 1)

It is clear from this definition that both genetic and cultural factors help shape learning styles.

Current research suggests that certain learning styles are associated with specific ethnic groups in this society. For example, in her article "Afro-American Cognitive Style: A Variable in School Success?" Barbara Shade (1982) makes a strong case that many black Americans have learning styles that conflict with our low context colleges and universities. And according to Asa Hilliard, authority on race and intelligence, black Americans who have grown up outside the macroculture process information differently than the pattern typically found in our schools. He suggests that many Afro-Americans

1. view their environment holistically rather than in isolated parts,
2. prefer intuitive rather than deductive or inductive reasoning,
3. approximate concepts of space, number, and time rather than aiming at exactness or complete accuracy,
4. prefer people stimuli rather than nonsocial or object stimuli, and
5. rely heavily on nonverbal as well as verbal communication.

Other research suggest that many Hispanics and American Indians, indeed anyone from a high context culture, faces comparable cultural conflicts related to intellectual modes.

The notion that certain learning styles are associated with different ethnic groups is both promising and dangerous. Promise lies in the realization that low academic achievement among some ethnic minorities may sometimes be attributed to conflicts between styles of teaching and learning, not low intelligence. This leads to the possibility that college educators will expand their own instructional styles to be more responsive to the learning needs of students. Danger lies in the possibility that new ethnic stereotypes will develop while old ones are reinforced, as in "Blacks learn aurally," "Asians excel in math," "Latino males can't learn from female peer tutors," and "Navajos won't ask a question or discuss."

Conclusions

While both cultural and racial differences are an important source of transitional trauma misunderstanding, and conflict on the college campus, racial issues are often more serious. With the exception of historically black colleges and universities in this society, most post-secondary public schools are white. This means not only that white American culture rooted in Anglo-European traditions predominates, it also means that white people are in control of campus life.

We find evidence of this in the growing body of literature on college student attrition that shows alarmingly high rates of dropping out among black, Latino and American Indian college students compared with higher rates of persistence among Asian American and white college students (eg. Allen, 1982; Fleming, 1985; Bennett and Bean, 1984, Nettles, 1986, Nora, 1986). The fact that Asian Americans and international students tend to persist does not mediate the importance of race on campus. Research on black college students over the past fifteen years, for example, consistently reports that black students feel more alienated and isolated and experience more negative interracial contact than do their non-black peers. Black students with high entry level skills, as measured by SAT and high school rank, are as likely as those with low entry-level skills to feel unsatisfied with campus life. This affects their desire to remain and complete an undergraduate degree.

Assuming that we value racially and culturally diverse student populations on our college campuses, steps must be taken to create more campus programs that help create a warm and supportive interracial environment. How do positive racial attitudes and behaviors develop among previously encapsulated individuals who hold negative myths and stereotypes?

According to Gordon Allport (1979), noted authority on the nature of human prejudice, unless our prejudices are deeply rooted within the structure of our character, they are likely to be reduced through positive intergroup contact experiences. Contact is most likely to be positive when four conditions are in place:

1. equal status for minority and majority group members;
2. a social climate that supports interracial association, or institutional support from authorities;
3. contacts that are sufficiently intimate to foster mutual knowledge and understanding; and
4. cooperative interaction aimed at achieving shared goals.

Social contact theorists now refer to Allport's conditions as the conditions of positive intergroup contact and have amassed a good deal of supportive evidence in desegregated schools, residences, and work places (Cohen, 1979; Pettigrew, 1973; Amir, 1976; Schofield, 1978; Byrne, 1961; Devries and Edwards, 1974; Wiser, 1971). Clearly, interracial contact alone does not guarantee positive results. In fact, such contact may instead confirm negative myths, stereotypes, and conflict. The key lies in Allport's four necessary conditions. Furthermore, Allport asserts that while humans do tend to prefer the familiar, this is because of "the principles of ease, least effort, congeniality, and pride in our own culture," not prejudice. He disagrees with the frequently heard notion that "everyone is prejudiced." This is not a constructive approach to improve intergroup relations; the critical differences between prejudices and predilections must be clearly understood.

Residence halls on our college campuses provide one of the best arenas for fostering positive racial attitudes and behaviors that students will carry with them long after they leave the campus. Interracial contacts, close contacts, occur there every day. Whether or not these contacts are positive depends upon the degree to which the conditions of positive intergroup contact exist. The pairing of college roommates from different racial backgrounds, for example, is more likely to be successful when guided by these conditions. Do racially different students hold equal status? (Status could be measured by special talents and abilities as well as socio-economic background.) Do they have an opportunity to develop an understanding of their basic human similarities? Where cultural differences are a factor, do students learn about them in order to avoid cultural conflicts and misunderstandings? Do role models and authorities in the residence halls clearly support good race relations and intercultural understanding? (For example, are multi-racial groups of RAs visable as work teams and in informal social settings?) Do students of different racial and cultural backgrounds have opportunities to work together on resident hall projects and problems that are important to them?

This chapter is designed to provide background knowledge for understanding some of the key issues of race and culture on the college campus. Clear definitions of race and racism and the theories of cultural context and positive intergroup contact are helpful in the development of informed practices designed to improve human relationships in many college and university resident halls. The following case study and exercises are intended to help you clarify your own thinking on these issues, as well as translate the background concepts and theories into successful practices in your own particular residence hall.

Case Studies and Structured Group Experiences for Issues of Race and Culture on the College Campus

Case Study: Lena Jones Reconsidered

Instructions: Read the case study and respond to the questions which follow. First work alone. When you are finished, share your answers with other RAs in small group discussions or as the basis for a class-room discussion.

Introduction

Consider the student suggestions Lena faces and assume that you, like Lena, will attempt to act upon them. Some issues are obviously beyond your control, some issues deal with significant behaviors, and others deal with insignificant behaviors. Where intervention is possible, you need to decide when to intervene. Some concerns need immediate action, while others require a long range plan. This decision-making sheet is designed to help guide your judgements.

Read the Case of Lena's Pandora's Box below. Then sort the student's comments into the categories that follow.

Lena Jones sagged back into her blue corduroy bed chair and sighed. What had she gotten into!? A stack of anonymous notes from fourth floor residents rested on the bed next to her innocent looking "suggestion box." Whose idea *was* it anyway—a suggestion box where students could express thoughts or concerns, or make suggestions. What was she going to do? She had to think of something before her next floor meeting. Slowly, relentlessly, the students' written comments chugged through her consciousness. All were addressed to Lena Jones, fourth floor RA.

[1] Something should be done about loud music on this floor. It's always the black students.

[2] You let the black girls get away with murder. And they do all the talking at meetings. Always interrupting.

[3] Today is Yom Kippur. I missed an important test and the professor won't let me make it up.

[4] Why do the Malaysian students have to dress like that. Why don't they try to fit in?

[5] I feel embarrassed. Out of place. Out of style. My roommate has filled our room with her clothes, TV, stereo, and refrigerator. I came with one suitcase.

[6] Patsy Lynch is a racist. She won't shower or use the bathroom if black students are in there.

[7] I'm sick of Asian students. They spent all their time in the library and contribute nothing to this university. Absolutely nothing.

[8] The black students are racist. They always eat together in the cafeteria.

[9] The dining room always opens at the worst times; how about later or longer hours?

[10] Why does the cafeteria serve so much pork? Why can't we get Kosher food around here?

[11] If Stacey Miller wants to read her Bible every day that's fine. But she doesn't have to try to convert me! Get me a new roommate before I go crazy!

[12] Did you hear about those Arab students who hung a dead sheep or goat or something in the laundry room? Weird.

[13] If Sonya don't stop messin' with the brothers she's in for big trouble.

[14] My professor wrote me last week: "One problem with you Latinos is that you write *bullshit*— a lot of words without any information being given. It is a cultural difference, no doubt."

[15] I'm really afraid whenever I'm alone on the elevator (or anywhere) with a bunch of blacks or Latins. Can't we have separate dorms?

[16] I'm shocked at the students on this campus. Especially on our floor. Too much sex, too many drugs, too little religion, and too little studying. Am I the weird one? Can I survive here?

[17] Last Sunday night my friend Sonny and I got chased by a bunch of "red necks" who told us "niggers" shouldn't be off campus after dark.

Categories

Now divide the statements into the five categories below, explaining your rationale in detail.

A. Issues beyond your control   Reasons

_____   _____

_____   _____

_____   _____

_____   _____

_____   _____

_____   _____

_____   _____

B. Issues that require action on a personal level   Possible sources of conflict   Possible actions to resolve the problem

_____   _____   _____

_____   _____   _____

_____   _____   _____

_____   _____   _____

_____   _____   _____

_____   _____   _____

_____   _____   _____

C. Issues based in intergroup dynamics

Possible sources of conflict

Possible actions to resolve the conflict

_____

_____

_____

_____

_____

_____

_____

D. Issues based upon conflict between individuals and institutions

Possible resources of conflict

Possible actions to resolve the conflict

_____

_____

_____

_____

_____

_____

_____

_____

E. Issues based in society in general

Possible sources of conflict

Possible actions to resolve the conflict

_____

_____

_____

_____

_____

_____

_____

Case Study Questions

1. What race is Lena? Does it make a difference? _____
_____
_____

2. How should she structure her interventions at different times of the semester? _____
_____
_____

3. If this were a men's residence hall what would be the similarities? differences?_____
_____
_____

4. Using the list of concerns as a springboard for comparisons with your own environment, what
are the similarities? differences? What would you add to the list? _____
_____
_____

5. Is it always necessary that members of an ethnic minority group "trade off" some aspects of
their traditional culture? _____
_____
_____

6. When might racially segregated residence halls be better than integrated ones? _____
_____
_____

Case Study Questions

Exercise: Can You Recognize Racism

Goals: To develop a better understanding of racism.

Group Size: Small groups of eight to ten or classroom discussion format with up to thirty.

Time Required: Fifty minutes

Materials: Pencils, and racism statements placed on 4″ × 6″ index cards—one statement per card.

Physical Setting: Room with movable chairs for small groups.

Process: Students are asked first to work alone and to read and decide which, if any, of the nine statements are racist. When the students have finished they should be divided into small groups and asked to decide as a group which, if any, of the statements are racist. One member of the small group should then report to the whole group the small groups decisions.

Variation: The statements can be used as a basis for class discussion by having the students work individually and then discuss each statement. Students, after adequate discussion, may rate on whether or not the statement is racist.

Exercise: Can You Recognize Racism?*

Basic Terms to Know Before Follow Up Exercises are Implemented

Culture, race, individual and institutional racism, ethnic group and minority group, Jim Crow, cultural assimilation and cultural pluralism, stereotype, prejudice and predilection, ethnic encapsulation and ethnic identity clarification, high and low context culture.

A. **Instructions:**

First work alone. Put a check before each statement you think is an example of racism. Then work with your small group and try to agree on the examples of racism. To make the task easier, each statement can be placed on a 4″ × 6″ card. The group can then sort the cards into racist and non-racist statements.

B. **Analysis:**

Which of the following quotations or descriptive statements are examples of racism? Indicate these with a check (✓).

1. _____ "A black family moved into our neighborhood this week."

2. _____ The university interviewed two equally outstanding faculty candidates, one black and the other Latino. The search committee selected the black professor because the campus had several Latino faculty members but no black faculty.

3. _____ In 1882 immigration laws excluded the Chinese, and the Japanese were excluded in 1908.

4. _____ During the 1960's Civil Rights movement, Mrs. Viola Liuzzo, a white civil rights worker from Michigan, was shot by white southern segregationists.

5. _____ Between 1892 and 1921 nearly 2,400 black Americans were lynched by vigilante mobs that were never brought to justice.

6. _____ "The best basketball players on our college team this year are black."

7. _____ The band director discouraged black students from playing the flute or piccolo because he believed it was too difficult for them to excel on these instruments.

8. _____ When Mrs. Wallace, a black woman from Detroit, visited a predominantly white university in northern Michigan to see her son play basketball, she was seriously injured in a car accident. She refused a blood transfusion because she was afraid of being contaminated by white blood.

9. _____ When Stacey Russell, a black undergraduate went through rush, the girls of an all-white sorority decided not to pledge her because several members threatened to move out if they did.

10. _____ The geography textbook described the peoples of Nigeria as primitive and underdeveloped.

11. _____ The children who attended an elementary school in southwest Texas spoke only Spanish at home. When they came to school, all the books and intelligence tests were in English. Nearly all of the children were placed in remedial classes or in classes for the mentally retarded.

12. _____ The U.S. Constitution defined slaves as 3/5ths of a man.

13. _____ The student newspaper reported that "Toni Morrison is a brilliant writer who accurately portrays much of the black experience in America."

* © Christine Bennett, 1986. (From *Comprehensive Multicultural Education*.)

14. _____ When John brought home his college roommate, his father was shocked and angry. Peter, the roommate, was of Japanese origins and John's father had been seriously wounded by the Japanese in World War II. John's father refused to allow Peter to visit again.

15. _____ In 1896, the Supreme Court rules that separate facilities for the races were legal as long as they were equal. This resulted in separate schools, churches, restaurants, restrooms, swimming pools, theatres, doctor's offices, neighborhoods, Bibles used in court, etc.

16. _____ When Mary Adams wanted to find a place in the residence hall cafeteria, the only vacant chair was at a table seating five black girls. Mary, who is white, was afraid to join them.

17. _____ In California today, approximately 10% of the population is black, while 41% of those in prison are black.

18. _____ Other examples you can think of? _____

C. **Small Group Decision Sheet:**
    Select one member of your group to write your group's decisions below and another person to share the results with the rest of us. Be prepared to explain your reasons, if necessary.
    1. The following statements are examples of either individual or institutional racism: (Write numbers and a word or two for description, and arrange them according to those which refer to racist individuals, and which refer to racist policies and institutions.)

Individual Racism   *Institutional Racism*

2. Our group's definition of racism is: _____

_____

_____

_____

_____

_____

_____

_____

_____

_____

3. The main difference between individual and institutional racism is: _____

_____

_____

_____

_____

_____

_____

_____

_____

_____

_____

4. Examples of individual and institutional racism that we know about on campus are:

Individual Racism _____

_____

_____

_____

_____

_____

_____

_____

_____

_____

Institutional Racism _____

_____

_____

_____

_____

_____

_____

_____

_____

_____

5. Steps we could take to reduce racism on campus are the following: _____

_____

_____

_____

_____

_____

_____

_____

6. Discuss how likely it is that you will take these steps. Explain. _____

_____

_____

_____

_____

_____

_____

_____

_____

Exercise: Creating Conditions of Positive Interracial Contact in the Residence Halls

Goals:
1. To identify current residence hall practices that impede conditions essential to positive interracial contact experiences among students;
2. To identify current residence hall practices that foster conditions essential to positive interracial contact experiences among students;
3. To identify new practices that in the future could help strengthen positive interracial contacts among students in the residence hall.

Group Size: Up to 45

Time Required: Approximately 60–90 minutes

Materials: 1. "Interracial Contacts in Residence Halls" sheet for each participant; 2. Pens or pencils; 3. Poster showing Allport's four conditions of positive intergroup contact (optional).

Physical Setting: Movable desks with writing surface, or tables and chairs for small groups

Process:
1. The facilitator tells the group that the purpose of this exercise is to identify ways of improving students' interracial contact experiences in residence halls. They will be using Gordon Allport's four conditions for positive intergroup experience as guidelines for identifying practices that hinder/foster interracial contact.
2. The facilitator gives each participant the "Interracial Racial Contacts in Residence Halls" sheet and reads the instructions aloud. Participants work individually for 5 to 10 minutes, then in multiracial groups (if possible) for approximately 30 minutes. (See attached sheet.)
3. Small groups report back to the large group, followed by large group discussion. Before concluding, identify new possibilities to be implemented, and outline the steps to be taken to accomplish this, including a time line and planned progress reports.

Interracial Contact in Residence Halls

Under what conditions can racially diverse students who are unfamiliar with each other and often harbor misconceptions and fears about each other, experience positive intergroup relations in the residence halls on our campus? According to contact theorists, at least four basic conditions are necessary if social contact between different isolated groups is to lessen negative prejudice and lead to friendly attitudes and behaviors. These conditions are listed below. As you read each one, note current practices in your residence hall that would impede the development of that condition (negative practice) as well as practices that would help establish it (positive practices). Finally, note practices not in use that could be implemented to help build this condition in your school or classroom (possibilities).

A. Contact should be sufficiently intimate to engender knowledge and mutual understanding between different ethnic or racial groups that have been isolated from each other.

Negative Practices	Positive Practices	Possibilities
(1) _____	(1) _____	(1) _____
(2) _____	(2) _____	(2) _____
(3) _____	(3) _____	(3) _____

B. Members of the various ethnic groups should share equal status.

Negative Practices	Positive Practices	Possibilities
(1) _____	(1) _____	(1) _____
(2) _____	(2) _____	(2) _____
(3) _____	(3) _____	(3) _____

C. The contact situation leads people to do things together; it requires intergroup cooperation to achieve a common goal.

Negative Practices	Positive Practices	Possibilities
(1) _____	(1) _____	(1) _____
(2) _____	(2) _____	(2) _____
(3) _____	(3) _____	(3) _____

D. There is institutional support—an authority and/or social climate that encourages intergroup contact.

Negative Practices	Positive Practices	Possibilities
(1) _____	(1) _____	(1) _____
(2) _____	(2) _____	(2) _____
(3) _____	(3) _____	(3) _____

The Resident as an Individual

CHAPTER 4

Theories of College Student Development for Resident Advisors

Dr. Robert F. Rodgers,
The Ohio State University

If you as a resident advisor learn developmental theory, will you perform better on the job? As one resident advisor recently asked, "Do I really have to learn this stuff to do my job?" Some residence hall professional staff members assume that the answer is "yes" and proceed to introduce developmental theory to RAs in hopes that it will help them do their jobs. Will it? Answers to this question depend upon 1) what we mean by "teach RAs about college student development theory" and 2) how the RA's job has been designed. In exploring these two issues and ultimately the question of the usefulness of learning about college student development, it will be helpful to distinguish among a scholar, professional and paraprofessional, and to examine the kind and depth of knowledge needed to perform in each of these roles.

Scholars are deeply involved in theoretical knowledge and related research. The very nature of their work is the advancement of theory or the development of new theories. Occasionally, they also may work on applied problems. A professor of developmental psychology or higher education may be such a person.

A professional is primarily a translator between practice and theory or theory and practice. Professionals have in-depth knowledge of the theories and research underlying their practice and know how to use those theories to design environments that help people learn and develop. Professionals know the phenomena covered by a given theory. They know how developmental change supposedly takes place according to that theory. As a consequence, they are able to assess the developmental levels of students, then use the assessment and knowledge of the theory to design environments that (hopefully) help students grow and develop rather than get in their way. One such environment is the RA position, with its functions and roles.

A paraprofessional, such as a resident advisor, does not primarily translate theory into practice or advance new theories. A paraprofessional primarily performs certain roles, functions, and services in ways prescribed by professional supervisors. The parameters of their roles and functions are defined by professionals, and they are usually trained by these same professionals or by scholars. In the strictest sense, therefore, a paraprofessional only needs to know the goals, roles, and function he or she is to perform and to be trained appropriately to do them.

Hence, a resident advisor does not have to know college student development theory in order to do his or her job. A scholar or professional who supervises and trains the resident advisor, however, needs to be intimately familiar with these developmental theories in order to integrate developmental perspectives appropriately into the definition of the roles, functions, and training of the RA. Nevertheless, some knowledge of college student development *may help* a resident advisor in at least two ways: 1) it can help the RA understand both the behavior of their students and the reasons their jobs are defined as they are, and 2) it can help motivate the RA to invest in their role and function as taught and designed rather than amending their role and function based upon tacit personal beliefs about what is best for college students.

The Degree of Theory Needed

We will return to the potential benefits of knowing some developmental theories in a moment. First, however, let us explore the question of "to what degree does an RA need to know developmental theory in order to accrue the potential benefits?" At what depth does the professional staff need to teach RAs about developmental theory, or, stated differently, in what depth do RAs need to learn developmental theories in order to benefit? Rodgers (1983) has abstracted four levels or degrees to which a person might know a theory. Understanding these levels and their relationships to the roles of scholar, professional, and paraprofessional will provide one response to the question of "the degree" to which RAs need to know developmental theory.

Level 1: Amorphous

This level represents an amorphous, almost distinctionless, understanding of a theory or construct. For example, an RA may have heard the terms "managing emotions" (Chickering 1969) and may wonder, "What is that, and how does it relate to my work?" The RA may only recognize the name of this developmental vector but not know its meaning.

Level 2: Basic Understanding

At this level, a theoretical construct such as "managing emotions" has meaning for a person. For example, an RA is able to recognize and give a brief description of the construct: "Managing Emotions is a developmental issue for young adults between ages 17 and 25 in which the control of emotions moves from rigid control by the external rules of one's heritage, through external control by the norms of one's primary peer group, to flexible internal control. With flexible internal control a person can act on his or her own without the need for sanctioning by peers or family."

Level 3: In-Depth Understanding

At this level a person has achieved in-depth and detailed understanding of a theory or construct. For example, the person knows that the concept "managing emotions" focuses on controlling the emotions of *sex* and *aggression* in the 17-to-25 age range and that it involves a process variable (Figure 1).

Managing the emotions of sexual impulses and aggression moves through the following phases:

A. release of rigid controls over emotions by the external rules of one's heritage or peer group;
B. achievement of an awareness and acceptance that these emotions are legitimate and normal;
C. trust in one's feelings as a basis for action—that is, appropriate action is often an integration of logic and these emotions;
D. acting on these emotions both vicariously and realistically and receiving feedback;
E. acting and receiving feedback repeatedly; and
F. reflecting on one's experience with sex and aggression and integrating and internalizing personalized control.

Phases A, B, and C involve awareness, trust, and differentiation tasks, while phases D, E, and F involve both action, feedback, and reflection. As such they are differentiation and integration tasks. Programs which respond to phases A, B, and C should focus on awareness and trust. Programs responsive to phases D, E, and F should reflect support as a person lives through new behaviors and learns their meaning.

Finally, a person at Level 3 knows how to use the theory to develop an interview for estimating a person's location in the process. If the person at Level 3 is a student affairs professional, he or she can design programs for phases A, B, C, D, E, and F of the process. Some of these programs may involve the RA as an active paraprofessional.

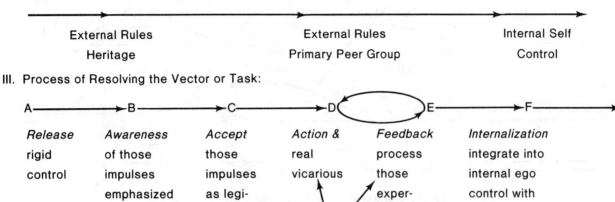

I. Content of Emotions:

     Sexual and aggressive feelings, emotions, impulses

II. Directionality of the Vector or Task:

External Rules	External Rules	Internal Self
Heritage	Primary Peer Group	Control

III. Process of Resolving the Vector or Task:

A———————▶B———————▶C———————▶D⬭E———————▶F———————▶

Release	*Awareness*	*Accept*	*Action &*	*Feedback*	*Internalization*
rigid	of those	those	real	process	integrate into
control	impulses	impulses	vicarious	those	internal ego
	emphasized	as legi-		exper-	control with
		timate		iences	flexibility

    differentiation   recycle   integration
            repeatedly

IV. Developmental Change

 Challenge • What challenges will help a person release rigid control? become aware? facilitate acceptance? What support is needed at the same time?

    • What challenges will facilitate acting on emotions? being open to hearing feedback? provide real and vicarious action? provide processing of the meaning of the experience and feedback?
What support helps a person act, process, and integrate the meaning?

Figure 1. Managing emotions.

Level 4: *Integrated In-Depth Understanding*

At Level 4, a person not only knows "managing emotions" at Level 3, but has in-depth knowledge of the rest of Chickering's Theory and can define the relationships between "managing emotions" and all of the other vectors in the theory (Figure 2). These relationships are known in sufficient depth so that the Level 4 person is able to reconstruct the possible role of managing emotions within the broader developmental issues of values and moral development, developing the capacity for depth of intimacy, definitions of sexuality, and career development. This person can integrate and apply his or her knowledge of several vectors to understand a given student, diagnose a problem, or design an intervention. The person also can critique the theory and knows the limitations of the various means for measuring the theory.

Matching Roles and Levels

Scholars need knowledge of developmental theory at level four. With that knowledge they can advance a given theory or understand a problem in sufficient depth to generate new syntheses of theoretical perspectives. Similarly, professionals need knowledge of developmental theories at level four, or at least three. Such knowledge is needed in order to design environments that one hopes will help students learn and develop rather than get in the way.

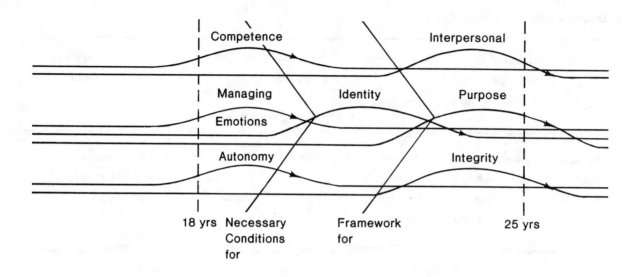

Figure 2. Chickering's (1969) seven vectors in chronological, directional, and age-related order.

Professionals with level four or three knowledge of college student development should use that knowledge to design the RAs' roles and function and plan their training. That training, however, should not attempt to teach in-depth level four or three knowledge of college student development to RAs. Professional staff need these levels of knowledge, not the resident advisor. Level two is sufficient for the RA. However, if professionals do teach resident advisors at level two and then expect the RA to translate theory into practice, then we can usually expect little if any change in job performance. Level two is not sufficient for translating theory to practice.

Hence, professional staff must be careful not to abdicate the responsibility for "what to do with this knowledge" to persons having only level 2 understanding. To do so misplaces professional responsibility from the professional staff to the paraprofessional staff. As a consequence, the goal of this chapter is to help professional staff teach college student development at level two to RAs. The goal is not to teach RAs at level three or four, and it is not to leave the logistics of using this knowledge initially in the hands of the RA. It is important to note that this chapter is not sufficient *per se* for learning any theory, even at level two. Professional staff need to know college student development theory at level three or four, and use their knowledge, teaching ability, and this book to prepare RAs at level two.

Theories of College Student Development

What theories of college student development should RAs learn at level two? Knefelkamp, Widick, and Parker (1978) and Rodgers (1980) have developed similar classifications of theories of college students including psychosocial, cognitive-structural, person-environment, and typological theories. We will examine each type of theory briefly, along with one specific theory in each family. We will then relate this basic knowledge to the RA's paraprofessional roles.

Psychosocial Development of College Students

Psychosocial theories of college student development describe the conscious preoccupations of young adults in the 17-to-24 age range. These preoccupations are called developmental tasks, and in this age range they center on three broad questions:

1. The career question: Who am I? and what do I want to become?
2. The question of sexuality and the capacity for intimacy: Who am I to love? and what does love mean anyway?
3. The values and philosophy of life question: What am I to believe that is really mine? I know what I have been taught, what my family and heritage stands for, but I have to decide what I am really going to believe.

Psychosocial theories such as Chickering's (1969) describe in detail the tasks that make up the developmental substance of these questions. In a residence hall, these descriptions can become a blueprint for evaluating past programming efforts and, it is hoped, planning programs that are developmentally appropriate. For example, if a resident advisor has only freshmen on his or her floor, what programs would the RA encourage the floor government to sponsor in order to facilitate development on career, sexuality, and philosophy of life tasks?

Chickering's theory describes these developmental tasks (vectors) in chronological, directional, and age-related order. His summary of the research on college students indicates that, developmentally, most freshmen are involved in resolving the first four of Chickering's tasks, while many juniors, seniors, and graduate students are involved with the last three tasks. Hence, most traditionally aged college freshmen are developmentally involved with resolving issues of competence, managing emotions, developing autonomy, and establishing identity. Each of these tasks involves a series of contents and processes that takes place over time, often one or more years. A professional residence hall director, therefore, can use Chickering's tasks as a blueprint for designing training for resident advisors on appropriate programming for a freshman floor.

To illustrate, let us examine the vector of developing competence and its implications for an RA with a freshman floor. Developing competence is divided into three areas: intellectual competence, physical manual competence, and social-interpersonal competence.

Intellectual Competence Upon entering college, many freshmen are preoccupied with the question of whether or how well they will survive academically. "What grades will I make? How hard are final exams? How much will we have to read? How hard do they grade? Will I fit in, make it as a student at this university?" If the student knows he or she is bright, the question is a little different. "Will I still be top of the class? I want to make it into medical school, and I can't afford to make any Bs. Can I make it to the top at this school?"

Translated into the roles and functions of a resident advisor, the RA should learn who is doing well after initial midterms, who is doing average, and who is struggling. The RA can also monitor who studies a lot, who studies a moderate amount, and who seldom studies. What kind of support or words of concern or encouragement may be needed by those who are struggling or who seldom study? Hopefully, resident advisors are discussing their perceptions with the professional staff. The best course may be referrals to the counseling center or to a learning skills center. Tutors may be needed. RAs can help set up, administer, and refer a resident to a tutorial service in the hall. In some cases, the resident advisor may make suggestions or offer encouragement. In other cases, the professional staff probably should make referrals after talking with the student.

How might the resident advisor work in preventive ways rather than waiting to learn who is struggling after midterms? Before classes start or early in the quarter, floor or hall programs might be offered on "How to prepare for examinations," "How to Study," or "Career Workshops." In this case, the professional staff or the resident advisors are usually asking other professionals to present outreach efforts to the hall as preventive programming.

Physical Manual Competence Each resident advisor could have the following goal: Involve at least 80 percent of the members of my unit in some form of appropriate physical manual activity. Who are the intercollegiate athletes on the floor? Who could profit from sports clubs athletics, a level of competition just below intercollegiate? How can we get as many as possible on our floor intramural team? How about organized recreation for those who are less endowed with physical prowess? The RA can make these kinds of common-sense distinctions, and the RA also can actively encourage all residents to become involved at least some level of physical/manual activity.

A more professional-level response to this task would have the professional hall staff and professional exercise physiologists and health educators combine their talents in planning and conducting wellness interventions. RAs could play a part in wellness programs; however, the professional staff would determine the design of the assessment, program, and role of the RA.

Social-Interpersonal Competence Just as a given campus has an "academic press," each campus also has a "social press." For the beginning freshman, "social press" may mean something like the following: "What's it really like on the main street social scene?" "I know how to negotiate the social scene at my hometown and at my high school, but will I know how to behave at this college's campus?" In other words, initially many freshmen are preoccupied with *whether* and *how* they will fit socially on their campus. Do they have the social skills to fit the social scene? If not, how can they get them?

There is also a career component to this issue. In how many social contexts is a given freshman competent? Does the freshman know how to negotiate the social scene on campus? Does the freshman from a rural background know how to negotiate the social scene in the inner city? Does the student from the inner city know how to negotiate a rural environment? Does the student have the social and interpersonal skills to present a budget before a faculty, staff, and student committee that allocates funds? Do students who have roommate conflicts have the negotiation and confrontation skills needed to mediate and solve conflicts? Does a student leader know how to behave in a formal reception line introducing the president of the university?

In all of these cases, there is a different social context with associated norms and rules concerning expected social and interpersonal behavior. In how many social contexts is a given student competent? The developmental task is to expand social-interpersonal competence of the student in order for the student to be competent in as many contexts as possible. The difficulty in doing this, however, is that freshmen are often preoccupied only with what's "in" with their peer group, and as a consequence they tend to repeat a single set of competencies over and over. Given this difficulty, how can a resident advisor expand the social-interpersonal competencies of the students who live on his or her floor?

There are a number of possibilities. For example, the resident advisor might try to persuade the floor to sponsor different kinds of social activities, rather than repeat the same activity over and over. How about a ski party, a dance, a formal (really formal) dinner, a play at the theater, or learning to negotiate the social scene of a formal French restaurant? Can the RA influence the norms of the peer group and help them try different social contexts? An RA should at least try to do this. If the RA can model different social or interpersonal competencies and genuinely encourage students to try different social contexts, he or she may well help the freshman student resolve the developmental tasks of social-interpersonal competence.

Cognitive-Structural Development of College Students

Cognitive-structural theories of development describe how college students think or make meaning of their classrooms, hall experiences, career search, love life, and moral choices. Specifically, these theories attempt to describe intellectual (Perry, 1970) moral (Kohlberg, 1974), faith (Fowler, 1981), and ego (Kegan, 1982; Loevinger, 1976) development. These theories are more abstract than psychosocial theories and not as easy to understand or use. Nevertheless, they can aid the professional staff and RAs if translated appropriately.

Cognitive-structural theories are useful especially in helping professional staff and perhaps RAs to understand how students view the proper role of staff members and how students may make meaning of experiences such as roommate conflicts or their search for a career. That is, students who reason or make meaning in different stages of cognitive-structural development apparently make different assumptions about the proper role of authority figures and the nature of answers to questions such as career or moral choices. A brief examination of Perry's theory of intellectual development may be used to illustrate these points.

Perry (1970) found that college students make meaning of their encounters with questions of knowledge and valuation in two broad levels that he calls dualism and relativity. A question of knowledge could come from the classroom (why did we have the Civil War?) or personal areas (what career should I pursue?). In the level of dualism, students assume that there are absolutely correct answers to knowledge questions, whether about the classroom or personal issues. Authorities are mediators to knowledge and should, if they are good authorities, know the answers to a question such as a career choice or solutions to a problem such as a roommate conflict.

In the level of relativity, students make different assumptions about knowledge and the role of authorities. In early relativity, students assume that all questions are "up for grabs." They cannot find bases for knowing anything for sure, whether about history or career choice, for example. They cannot find criteria for making such decisions. Hence, the role of authority figures changes radically. Since there are no criteria for making decisions for sure, there are no authorities. "The only absolute is that there are no absolutes." In such a world of making meaning, people in roles of authority are just people. They have no more wisdom than anyone else, even though they may act as if they have answers. People in authority roles, therefore, often may not even be consulted since the student's opinion on a question (historical or career) or problem (roommate conflict) is just as valid as any staff member's opinion.

In later relativity, students find criteria for making judgments on knowledge questions or problems; however, the criteria are not absolute. They discover criteria for making relative judgments on classroom questions (e.g., they can build a case for a set of factors causing the Civil War) or personal issues (they can explore and narrow career choices and anticipate a specific vocational commitment). Neither judgment, however, is viewed as absolutely correct. Instead, students build a reasonable, probabalistic case for their judgments. In this way of making meaning, therefore, authority is not absolute nor non-existent. Authority is synonymous with competence in a given field or area. Hence, authority is not a question of role (e.g., being the RA), but of being competent as an RA. If the RA is competent, then he or she will be viewed as an authority in that role by advanced relativists. These distinctions in ways of making meaning and viewing authorities are summarized in Table 1.

If RAs or professional staff members understand the basics of these ways of making meaning, then they are better able to understand their students' behavior. For example, some students may come to their RA complaining about their roommate and expecting the RA to speak to their roommate and solve the problem for them. "After all, that's your job isn't it?" Other roommates may work out their differences without ever even speaking with the RA.

In the first example, students in dualism may perceive roommate conflicts as a fairly one-way problem— I am right, and my roommate is the problem. They may appeal to an authority, the RA or the professional staff, for a solution and expect the expert either to solve the problem or to tell them how to solve the problem. On the other hand, students in advanced relativity would have the skills to resolve conflict and be able to perceive conflict situations from a perspective of give-and-take, or mutual causality. They might not need help from the RA, or, if they called upon the RA to assist, they would expect the RA to help facilitate interactions but not actually solve the problem.

TABLE 1
The Voices of Development on Perry's Scheme

Assumptions of help-seekers about the staff from whom they seek help:

DUALISM

1. This staff member knows how to solve my problem (e.g., choice of career or roommate conflict).
2. Good staff members know how to solve my problem (e.g., choice of career), but this particular staff person may or may not be that knowledgeable. S/he is a poor staff person if s/he can't tell me the answer or solve my problem for me.
3. Psychology may or may not be sophisticated enough as yet to know how to solve my problem (e.g., choice of career or resolving roommate conflicts). I'm going to this staff person to find out. If psychology knows enough, the staff member will tell me the answer or solution. If not, this staff member will give me a procedure to work it out on my own.
4. There are no answers to my problem (e.g., choice of career or resolving roommate conflicts); what I think is as valid as what any staff member thinks.

RELATIVITY

5. There are a number of solutions to my problem (e.g., choice of career or resolving roommate conflicts) depending on how you look at it; maybe this staff member can help me see myself and the alternatives more clearly.
6. There are a number of solutions to my problem (e.g., choice of career or resolving roommate conflicts) depending on how I look at it; maybe this staff member can help me determine what I want from a career or a solution to these conflicts.

Concepts like Perry's can help RAs understand why different students act so differently in similar situations and why an RA may need to act differently in response. The professional staff can assist RAs in perceiving these potential differences as the RA faces various situations during the year. These might include discipline problems, roommate conflicts, understanding and discussing campus issues, or helping students with academic problems such as taking essay tests, writing themes, or finding a major.

Person-Environment Interaction Theories and Topological Models

Person-Environment Interaction theories attempt to examine characteristics of college students, college environments, and the nature of their interactions. For example, one might study attrition and retention of college students. What students tend to drop out—and why? What characteristics of the student and/or the college environment may account for dropping out of college? Answers to such questions require one to identify relevant dimensions of students, their campus environment, and whether the interactions between the two are congruent or incongruent.

There are very diverse theoretical alternatives within this family of social science. Some person-environment theories are behavioral in orientation; some are perceptual. Some theories are sociological, and others are psychological. Some focus on group characteristics and some on individuals. Some attempt to measure both the person and the environment; some only the environment. Among these choices milieu management is perhaps the most useful in residence halls.

Milieu management (Schroeder, 1980, 1985) is an applied version of several person-environment perspectives applied to residence halls. It involves marshalling all pertinent resources (including the RA) to create a hall environment that facilitates student maturity, promotes student satisfaction, and attempts to reduce negative, self-defeating behaviors (Schroeder, 1980).

The two points of view for guiding these efforts are territoriality and theories of group cohesiveness. The three kinds of interventions are personalization of space (derived from both territoriality and development of community), social interactions that tend to build cohesiveness (derived from community and group cohesiveness theory), and the creation of four kinds of physical space (derived from territoriality). In order to understand the points of view and recommended interventions, Schroeder's (1985) characterization of the environment of typical residence halls will be informative.

Characterization of Typical Residence Halls Schroeder (1985) describes the typical residence hall as dense, crowded, overly stimulating, noisy, occasionally chaotic, and institutional in atmosphere. Students often complain about an inability to sleep or study, do not like their roommates, and want to be released from their contracts. Rooms are small, rules about decor are rigid, and architecture and furniture are designed to be "destruction proof." In such an environment, students often are not satisfied, may not achieve as well as they could in the classroom, and may not mature as rapidly as possible. Following the recommendations of territoriality and group cohesiveness, Schroeder recommends that residence halls increase social cohesiveness, personalize space, and create four kinds of physical zones in order to mediate the problems.

Social Cohesiveness Milieu management attempts to build close, cohesive groups, or communities, through floor and roommate assignment strategies, controlling group size, and giving as much autonomy and self-direction to these groups as possible. Let us examine each of these strategies.

Roommate matching is usually accomplished by either arranging roommates with the same major or with similar personality types as defined by a typological instrument such as the Myers-Briggs Type Indicator (hereafter MBTI). Similarly, floor communities also are assigned by majors, interests, or MBTI types. The objective is to create relative homogeneity in order to build community but maintain enough diversity for challenge (Schroeder, 1985). Considerable evaluative research supports these strategies. For example, students assigned to MBTI floors and rooms perceive their environment as more supporting, more academically oriented, more student controlled, and more innovative than heterogeneous units (Kalsbeek, Rodgers, Marshall, Denny & Nicholls, 1982; Schroeder, 1985). In addition, students in more homogeneous units make higher grades, form more stable friendships, drink less alcohol, and make fewer visits to remedial mental health services.

Group size is kept at 35 or less. This rule of thumb generates from the research on small group cohesiveness, which indicates that groups larger than 35 often lose significant degrees of cohesiveness in their community. In addition, smaller groups also offer more opportunities for meaningful involvement and participation in group activities (Barker, Gump, 1964). Hence, if a given hall's units numbered over 35, proponents of milieu management would break down these units into smaller groups, each with separate physical territory and identity. The emphasis, therefore, is on units of 35 or less, not on the hall per se. In Schroeder's residence halls, for example, there usually are no all-hall governments, and even floors decide whether or not there will be a floor government. Floors receive all the student activity fees, while in more traditional halls monies are usually divided between hall and floor governments.

Schroeder (1980, 1985) also advocates delegating as much policy-making and procedural authority as possible to the students in these smaller units. To the extent that the college will permit, each smaller unit decides what its rules will be; that is, whether there will be pets; when and whether there will be quiet hours, liquor, and visitation; and who is permitted to move onto their floor. RAs support such things as rites of passage, special unit tee shirts, and unit names and colors. Professional staff offer cash prizes for the most creative remodeling of room and/or floor physical space. In short, self-directed groups are given as much authority as possible over their physical space, rules, group membership, and activities. RAs act as advisors to their floors or units, reinforcing factors that increase cohesiveness.

Personalization of Space and The Creation of Four Kinds of Space Broadly conceived, territorialists (Audrey, 1966) teach that human beings have four basic needs that should find expression in four kinds of physical space. These are summarized in Figure 3.

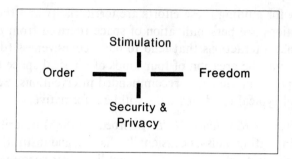

Figure 3. Four kinds of human needs and physical space.

Human beings apparently need stimulation, quiet, and privacy. They also need opportunities for freedom of expression and for order and predictability. Hence, among student rooms, unit space, and hall public areas, an adequate representation of each of these zones needs to be created. Typical halls, however, overemphasize stimulation and order and underemphasize freedom and privacy. As a consequence, milieu management attempts to create a better balance among these kinds of space. In student rooms, for example, freedom is maximized by giving the residents as much free rein as possible to personalize their space. Rooms may be painted in individual ways. Students may decorate as they desire. They can build lofts and can even change furniture and lighting. In secondary space, such as unit hallways and lounges, the group is given control over physical decorations and encouraged to remodel. In public space, stimulation zones such as game rooms, snack bars, physical conditioning rooms, or music lounges need to be developed, while quiet and order needs to characterize study lounges, libraries, and computer terminal rooms in the hall.

Territoriality also emphasizes the need for communities to control, demarcate, and defend their space. Hence, milieu management encourages group control over floor decorations and encourages the group to demarcate their unit with a unit name, symbols, and/or colors. Keys to floor lounges or even to access to the floor itself may be limited to group members only.

In such an environment, the RA's roles need to be carefully defined by the professional staff and the RA needs to be trained to facilitate and support the values and objectives of the milieu management approach to college student housing.

Conclusion

To sum up, in principle RAs can be taught the basics of psychosocial, cognitive-structural, person-environment interaction, or topological theories. Specifically, Chickering (psychosocial), Perry (cognitive-structural), milieu management (person-environment interaction), and Myers-Briggs (typological) are among several reasonable alternatives within each family of theory that may be useful to the RA. Teaching the basics means level two understanding of the theory selected, it does not mean level three or four. Basic knowledge should help RAs both to better understand their students and their jobs and increase motivation to do their work. Leadership in these efforts, however, is a professional responsibility. Professionals need to be the translators and designers, not RAs.

Case Studies and Structured Group Experiences for College Student Development

Case Study: Bob Rodgers and Charles Schroeder Go to College

Instructions: Read the case study which follows and consider what developmental issues Bob and Charles are trying to satisfy. Consider also the environment in which they are living and how this may be influencing them. When you have finished reading the case study, respond to the questions which follow with a short answer or essay, then share these answers with other RAs in small groups or as a basis for class discussion.

The Residents

In the autumn two typical 18-year-old freshmen, Bob Rodgers and Charles Schroeder, arrive at Any University, U.S.A. Everything has been done for them—they have been assigned to a nice, clean room on the second floor of their ten-story tower. During orientation, their RA has informed them about various policies and procedures, and they are now ready to embark on their college careers.

Bob, who was raised in a moderate-sized town in west Texas, is a sociable, outgoing, warmly enthusiastic and creative person. Bob is into everything. He pledged a Greek group, joined a student union committee, wants to run for freshman senate, and dates a lot. He tried out for and made the freshman golf team at A.U. Bob works in bursts of energy and postpones a lot of tasks until the last minute. He means to do these tasks ahead of time, but somehow he pulls a lot of last minute "all nighters." Bob always studies with his favorite classical music in the background, and he prefers to have others around him when he studies. He is making good grades but seems more interested in his activities than his studies.

Bob's ACT scores are slightly above average for A.U., and he made very good grades in high school. Nevertheless, Bob can't figure out what he should take as a college major. He figures engineering will bring "big bucks." He did well in math and science courses in high school; however, has he got what it takes to be successful in electrical engineering? He is also deeply committed to religion, and has been a successful salesman in his family's business during the summers. Bob also draws and paints and sometimes considers architecture as a future career. And, how about golf? Could he be good enough to become a professional golfer?

Although Bob dates a lot, he has never had a close, steady relationship. He wants one, however, and wishes he could meet that special, perfect woman. In his fantasies they meet, fall in love, stay committed to each other throughout college, and marry on the day that they graduate. He wants a near perfect marriage, without all the petty bickering and quarreling he sees in his parents. Will princess charming ever appear?

Charles grew up in Dallas, Texas. Charles is a practical, analytical person who can schedule and manage his time, do things according to his schedule, and manage his life in a very orderly fashion. His part of their double room is organized, his books are neatly arranged on the desk, he makes his bed each day, and he keeps to his schedule. Charles wants it quiet when he studies. He has hung a rug between his desk and the rest of the room so it will screen out voices and visual contact. He doesn't like Bob's music disturbing his study time. He insists that it be quiet. He studies religiously at the same time each day and evening.

Charles made average scores on the ACT, and he entered college absolutely sure he had made a career choice. His father is a physician, and his father provides his family with a life style and social status that Charles wants to duplicate. Hence, he is going to be a medical doctor, and he is taking Biology, French, English Composition, Mathematics, and History of Man during his first term. Charles is having difficulty in his classes, however, even though he studies many hours each day. He cannot see the practical value of most of his courses and recently flunked a biology examination after studying 18 hours in preparation.

Just as he has decided on his career, Charles believes that he has already decided on a wife, also. Charles and Barbara started going steady in high school, and he returns to Dallas every weekend in order to be with her. He has not dated anyone at A.U., nor has he gotten involved in any extracurricular activities. In fact, he considers clubs, activities, and student government to be a waste of time.

The Residence Hall Environment
Architectural arrangements

Bob and Charles live in a high-rise, ten-story building that has a large lounge on the main floor and one in the basement. The hall has long and narrow double-loaded corridors, with two centrally located community baths on each floor. All rooms are double occupancy, resulting in 46 students per floor, for a total of 460 residents. Each hallway has a floor lounge located in the middle of the corridor. This lounge is usually used for studying or floor meetings.

Student rooms measure 10' × 14' for a total of 70 square feet of living space per student. The entire building is painted in rather bland, institutional colors—off-white for student rooms and light green for hallways and lounges.

Student characteristics

In this all-male residence hall, the majority of students (approximately 65%) are freshmen. There are also sophomores (20%), juniors (10%) and seniors (5%). The students come from diverse backgrounds, rural and urban, black and white. They perceive their hall atmosphere as highly competitive, very socially oriented, highly ordered, and with few degrees of freedom.

The hall is not academically oriented. Since Greeks do not have houses at A.U., Greeks are scattered throughout the halls. Very few floor residents have similar career aspirations, and few of the freshmen have settled this question. The freshmen residents, in fact, seem more interested in the ten rules for "getting a good sun tan" than in the ten steps in "career planning."

The hall has an RA-to-student ratio of 1/46 and a professional staff-to-student ratio of 1/153. A full-time director and two half-time graduate assistant directors live in the building, as do all 10 RAs.

Administrative policies and procedures

Freshmen roommates are assigned on a random basis, with only two criteria held constant—date of application and smoking/non-smoking preference. Assignments of freshmen to floor living units are totally random. Upperclass students can request roommates and floors. Usually the Hall Director grants these requests. Various rules and regulations limit visitation, room decorating, and the number and size of appliances. Drinking alcoholic beverages in the hall is prohibited and strictly enforced. Only "tropical fish" are permitted as pets.

Each Resident Advisor is required to conduct a minimum of two "developmental" programs each quarter. In addition, RAs are expected to initiate maintenance requests and investigate damages and possible rule violators.

Organizational characteristics

There is a fairly active all-hall government in the building, with social, athletic, and cultural committees. Each floor also has a floor government, which splits activity fee monies with the all-hall government. Most student government programming is done on a floor basis. Most floor governments don't sponsor programs. They use their funds for an end of the term illegal "beer blast."

Case Study Questions:

1. What are the basic vector needs Bob and Charles are trying to satisfy? _____

_____

_____

_____

_____

_____

_____

_____

_____

_____

_____

_____

_____

_____

_____

_____

_____

_____

2. How are the two residents' needs the same? different? What effects do the similarities and differences have on what the RA should do? _____

_____

_____

_____

_____

_____

_____

_____

_____

_____

_____

_____

_____

_____

_____

_____

_____

_____

_____

_____

_____

_____

_____

_____

3. How do Bob and Charles make meaning of their struggles with vector issues? Are they similar or different? How might they view authority figures such as the Director or the RAs? _____

_____

_____

_____

_____

_____

_____

_____

_____

_____

_____

_____

_____

_____

_____

_____

_____

_____

_____

_____

_____

_____

_____

_____

_____

_____

_____

_____

4. How does Bob's and Charles' hall environment compare to the milieu management view on:

   a. Architectural arrangement _____

   _____

   _____

   _____

   _____

   _____

   _____

   _____

   _____

   _____

   _____

   b. Group cohesiveness _____

   _____

   _____

   _____

   _____

   _____

   _____

   _____

   _____

   _____

   _____

   _____

   _____

c. Administrative policies and procedures _____

_____

_____

_____

_____

_____

_____

_____

_____

_____

d. Four kinds of space _____

_____

_____

_____

_____

_____

_____

_____

_____

_____

_____

_____

Exercise: What Programs are Developmentally Appropriate for What Students—and Why?

Goals:

1. To use basic knowledge of Chickering's vectors as criteria for analyzing and classifying residence hall programs;
2. To use basic knowledge of Chickering's vectors to hypothesize about the appropriateness of residence hall programs for different students.

Group Size: Unlimited number of small groups of 4 to 6 persons.

Time Required: Approximately one hour to one hour and thirty minutes.

Materials Needed: Copies of worksheet entitled "What Programs are Developmentally Appropriate for What Students and Why?"

Process

1. Introduction: The facilitator presents the goals and then distributes the worksheets.
2. The facilitator then gives individuals 15 to 20 minutes to analyze the programs on the work sheet and make notes on what vector this program assists and, therefore, for whom might it be appropriate—freshmen, sophomores, juniors, or seniors of traditional college age? The facilitator reminds participants of the "group profile" nature of the hypotheses on appropriateness and reminds the group that the hypotheses may not apply to a given unit's group or individuals.
3. After 15 to 20 minutes, the facilitator forms groups of 4 to 6 and asks members to share their analyses of each program, one program at a time. Then, each group should work toward a consensus on what vectors are involved and, hence, its appropriateness for what students.
4. The facilitator leads the total group in a general discussion of each program. Each group reports, and the facilitator records their conclusions on chalkboard, newsprint, or transparency. Conflicts between groups are identified, discussed, and a consensus reached if possible.

Variations

1. Each small group can select a scribe to represent the group in a discussion among all the selected scribes.
2. The facilitator can reveal a normative analysis prepared by scholars or the professional staff on each program.

What Programs are Developmentally Appropriate for What Students and "Why"?

Please examine the following actual programs sponsored by residence halls at various universities and determine the answers to the following questions. Make your judgments alone, individually at first. Then, along with the rest of your group, develop a group judgment.

1. What vectors does this program attempt to assist? Why is that? What criteria(ion) do you use to support this judgment?
2. For what students—freshmen, sophomores, juniors, seniors, graduate—would the program be appropriate? One of the above? All of the above? Several? Please be specific.

Program I: Study Abroad

Objective: To aid students in learning what to expect in studying abroad and to motivate applications.

Description: A one-hour presentation was given by students who had studied abroad the previous year. Slides were shown and there was a question-answer period. The presentation and slides described living with fellow American students is a hostel, experiences of "culture shock," and language and history classes taught by USA professors who accompanied the group to the host country. The classes were held in a university in the host country. The group of students and professors toured the country at the end of the term.

ANALYSIS

1. What vectors? _____

_____

_____

_____

_____

2. Appropriate for what students? _____

_____

_____

_____

_____

Program 2: Chicano Workshop

Objective: To promote awareness of the Chicano bicultural concept of life and to explore Chicano stereotypes.

Description: This is a four-hour presentation. A short film entitled "I am Joaquin" is shown, followed by a structured discussion and a short lecture on Chicano bicultural way of life. Anglos and Chicanos participate in mixed groups.

ANALYSIS

1. What vectors? _____

_____

_____

_____

_____

2. Appropriate for what students? _____

_____

_____

_____

_____

Program 3: Cross-Cultural Suite

Objective: To promote in-depth relationships, cultural awareness, and appreciation of cultural differences among students.

Description: Sixteen students live together in a suite within a residence hall. Rural whites, rural blacks, suburban whites, and inner-city blacks are represented. Cross-cultural workshops of increasing depth are proposed, in addition to processing daily living encounters. Standards for living together are to be negotiated by the group, under the leadership of a leader appointed by the group. Staff will provide the workshops, but as much as possible the students are asked to take responsibility for their own leadership, processing, and activities.

ANALYSIS

1. What vectors? _____

_____

_____

_____

_____

2. Appropriate for what students? _____

_____

_____

_____

_____

Program 4: Alternatives to Marriage

Objective: To develop an awareness of various adult lifestyles among couples and singles.

Description: This was a panel discussion that included discussion of traditional marriage, living-together, single career women, homosexual pairs, bachelors, and single parents. Each participant talked candidly for 15 minutes; then questions were raised from the audience.

ANALYSIS

1. What vectors? _____

_____

_____

_____

2. Appropriate for what students? _____

_____

_____

_____

_____

Program 5: Dating Game '84

Objective: To promote dating and social mixing among students.

Description: This was a modified version of "The Dating Game," using residence advisors from a male and female residence hall and then residents from each hall. A hall director was the Master of Ceremonies. The program rotated from hall to hall. A two-hall "mixer" with dancing followed each game.

ANALYSIS

1. What vectors? _____

_____

_____

_____

_____

2. Appropriate for what students? _____

_____

_____

_____

_____

Program 6: Pairing Groups

Objective: To explore dating relationships between men and women, the nature of intimacy, the sexual bases of intimacy, how to say "no," and how to set sexual standards of behavior within relationships.

Description: A six-week program designed to have students explore the objectives in a small group setting of 10 persons, half male, half female, with student personnel staff facilitators in each group. Structured group experiences using the real experiences, attitudes, and values of the participants and facilitators were used each week. Lecturettes on the topic of the evening were used to summarize and generalize on the experience.

Week 1: Acquaintance and self-revealing on topics of dating level of experience.

Week 2: The Nature of Intimacy: Self-revealing on values on sexual behavior within dating relationships and discussion of what the capacity for intimacy means? Lecturette on intimacy.

Week 3: Controlling Sexual Emotions: Structured experience and lecturette.

Week 4: What I Want in a Relationship at this Time in my Life: Structure experience and lecturette.

Week 5: Negotiating Sexual Standards in a Relationship: Simulation and lecturette.

Week 6: Feedback to persons and facilitators. Closing.

ANALYSIS

1. What vectors? _____

_____

_____

_____

_____

2. Appropriate for what students? _____

_____

_____

_____

_____

Program 7: Negotiating "Fancy" Restaurants

Objective: To teach students how to make reservations, order from a "foreign menu," order appropriate wine, and negotiate paying the bill and arriving at an appropriate tip.

Description: A head chef, head waiter, and wine steward for a famous restaurant meet with students to make presentations, then discuss the areas outlined in the objectives.

ANALYSIS

1. What vectors? _____

_____

_____

_____

2. Appropriate for what students? _____

_____

_____

_____

Program 8: Career Planning Workshop in the Halls

Objective: To explore the relationships among career choice, lifestyle, and values, and to help participants narrow alternatives and move toward an initial career (vocational) commitment.

Description: This was an 8-week workshop meeting once per week for three hours with a trained student affairs staff member. Roles, relationships, careers, lifestyle, and values of participants were shared and explored. Participants worked hard toward an initial vocational commitment.

ANALYSIS

1. What vectors? _____

_____

_____

_____

_____

2. Appropriate for what students? _____

_____

_____

_____

_____

Sample Analysis of Program 1: Study Abroad

1. What Vectors?

This program primarily involves developing autonomy and developing cultural difference skills as a social competence.

Developing autonomy is made up of three parts as described by Chickering. One of those parts is called "Instrumental Autonomy," that is, developing the skills necessary to be mobile in solving problems, "to deal" with the environment in getting things done, and to be confident to move into a new situation and cope with new demands. The skills needed are coping and problem-solving skills. The awarenesses and experiences needed are to encounter situations (like having to live in another culture) that are new to an individual and demand that he or she adapt. By so doing, one learns to be autonomous and self-confident.

Social competence in this case involves developing awarenesses of cultural differences while not yet having a total or in-depth experience with such differences.

2. Appropriate for what students?

Probably best applicable to freshmen and sophomores. Would be applicable for juniors and seniors only if living with families in the host country were included, as well as serious study with host country professors rather than USA professors, or if the country were a culturally different, developing nation.

This program could help stimulate freshmen and sophomores to spend their next year or one quarter of their next year in another culture. Such experience would stimulate growth in autonomy, if the challenge isn't too difficult. If classes were taught by USA professors, ones fellow students were also from the USA, and one lived with only USA students, the challenge of coping with a new country in all other ways (money, social customs, getting around in the city, etc.) would be appropriate and probably stimulate development.

The challenge would probably be too much for freshmen who are not yet instrumentally autonomous if the program included living with a host family and being taught only by host country professors, or if the host country is under-developed and/or very different in culture.

In contrast, a senior might already have good coping skills and might study abroad more for the "study" and for freeing interpersonal relationships than for autonomy. Seniors or graduate students tend to be more committed to their areas of study per se, and the study part of being abroad would be a serious, important challenge related to "developing purpose." Living in intimate contact with persons culturally different from themselves would be good stimulus for freeing interpersonal relationships. Research shows many freshmen do not profit as much from "family" experiences. Freshmen may see host families as different, or stupid, or wrong, and miss the subtilities of cultural relativity. Many freshmen aren't ready for in-depth relationships with another culture. They are ready, however, to experience another culture in less intimate ways and to cope with solving problems of autonomy.

In short, this program probably should be advertised for freshmen and sophomores and switched to juniors, seniors, and graduate students if classes are taught in the style of the home country by host country professors, if living with host families is involved, and/or if the cultural is radically different from our own.

Exercise: Identifying Appropriate Programming for My Unit or Floor

Goals:

1. To use Chickering's vectors as criteria for defining appropriate programming for a given unit of students;
2. To identify resources at my university/college appropriate for programming on the vectors;
3. To set goals and specific plans for things I will do in my job as an RA on developing competence.

Group Size: Unlimited number of groups of 3 or 4

Time Required: Approximately 2 hours.

Materials Needed: Worksheets; pencils

Process:

1. The facilitator introduces the goals and then gives directions. RAs are instructed to fill out as much of the worksheet as possible as individuals.
2. The facilitator then forms groups of 3 or 4, and the RAs share their pooled answers to the questions, identifying areas where information is missing.
3. Each group takes a few days to collect any missing information about the campus or city environment.
4. When the group reassembles, the collected information is shared.
5. The facilitator then asks individuals to reflect on the information that they now have, then to set specific goals and plans for intellectual, physical/manual, and social-interpersonal competence programs for their unit. RAs are then reformed into their groups, and each RA shares his or her goals and plans.
6. The facilitator asks individuals to reflect on how their fellow group members could help them follow through on their goals. The facilitator models examples of such support. For example, the group could meet once a week to share progress and help each other solve problems. Groups reform; individuals share their thoughts on support and negotiate specific supports from their fellow group members.

Variations: Teach rules for writing specific behavioral goals and objectives along with this experience.

Developing Intellectual Competence

1. Who on my unit is doing poorly on tests, quizzes, and papers this term? _____

_____

_____

_____

_____

2. Who studies a lot? very litte? _____

_____

_____

_____

_____

3. What referral resources exist on my campus for study skills referrals? writing skills? What hours are they open, and how do they operate? _____

_____

_____

_____

4. What tutor resources exist on my campus for mathematics? physical sciences? English? foreign languages? _____

_____

_____

_____

5. If I have freshmen or sophomores on my unit, what preventive programs (e.g., study skills, test taking) might be needed before or just after classes start. Can I bring them to the floor or unit? _____

_____

_____

_____

_____

6. Specifically and realistically, what will I try to do to assist with developing intellectual competence?

_____

_____

_____

_____

Developing Physical/Manual Competence
1. What levels of physical/manual organized activities exist on my campus? What intercollegiate sports?

_____

_____

_____

_____

What sports clubs? _____

_____

_____

_____

_____

What intramural sports? _____

_____

_____

_____

_____

What organized aerobics or recreation, activities? _____

_____

_____

_____

_____

2. What wellness programs such as alcohol abuse, stop smoking, diet and nutrition programs, etc. _____

_____

_____

_____

3. What students might need my support and encouragement to engage in one of these activities? _____

_____

_____

_____

4. Can we achieve a goal of getting 80% of the floor members engaged in some physical/manual activity of their choice? What specifically and realistically will be my goal? Why? _____

_____

_____

_____

Developing Social-Interpersonal Competence

1. What kinds of social activities are "in" with my students at this time. List them and be specific. _____
   _____
   _____
   _____
   _____

2. What social or interpersonal skills are involved in each of these activities? _____
   _____
   _____
   _____
   _____

3. What are this college's traditional social events? When do they occur? What kinds of things take place? How might my floor/unit be involved? _____
   _____
   _____
   _____
   _____

4. What kinds of activities are *not* "in" with my students at this time? List them, e.g., formal dances.
   _____
   _____
   _____
   _____

5. What skills would be needed if these events did occur? Do my students have these skills? _____
   _____
   _____
   _____
   _____

6. What resources on this campus/city could teach my students these skills? _____
   _____
   _____
   _____
   _____

7. What realistically and specifically will I do to try to expand social competence? _____

_____

_____

_____

_____

CHAPTER 5

Enhancing the Interpersonal Communication Skills of Resident Assistants

Dr. Thomas W. Hosie,
Louisiana State University

A major responsibility of resident assistants is to help students adjust to college life and overcome the numerous difficulties encountered in living on campus. The primary means by which RAs attempt to intervene and help students is through verbal communication. The purpose of this chapter is to enhance the interpersonal communication skills of RAs so they can directly assist students in adjustment, personal growth and successful problem solving.

College students are in the latter phase of adolescent development, in which they are learning to become adults. Often being in college is the first time they have been away from home and forced to make their own decisions, without the usually available resources of family and friends. Students must learn to adjust their schedules and living habits, make new friends, and acquire the appropriate academic and social behaviors in a new environment. Students bring to campus different levels of social and academic skills. Each, however, must develop his or her own sense of purpose, establishing attainable goals in both the social and academic areas. College students are continually testing and solidifying their abilities, values, and interests. Most aspire to higher grades and class standing than they will achieve, and many have unrealistic ideas about their participation in leadership roles in extracurricular activities (Davis, 1977).

The methods used to facilitate students' adjustment to the demands of college life must include opportunities for students to adjust their conceptualizations of this new environment. Students need to have a specific and clear understanding of their experiences and how they are using these experiences to create their actions. Knowing what they believe about themselves and what they think about events they are involved in can tell them why they act as they do. When individuals know their thoughts and can directly connect them to their actions, they can more readily modify their behaviors to appropriately attain their goals. A helper uses interpersonal communication skills to clarify another's experiences—the other's thoughts, feelings, and actions. Through the use of interpersonal communication skills the RA can personally intervene, when needed, to help students understand their own thinking and feelings, and to decide objectively on an appropriate course of action.

The purpose of this chapter is to enhance RAs' interpersonal communication skills. The beginning section, the influence of our beliefs, provides a rationale for use of these skills by describing how people formulate their thoughts and actions. Knowing these dynamics will help the RA understand students who are experiencing problems adjusting to college life. The following section, interpersonal communication skills, describes the skills used to communicate with students to facilitate their adjustment. Following this section is an illustrative case using interpersonal communication skills with a student experiencing adjustment problems. The chapter concludes with a group experience for resident assistants to practice communication skills.

The Influence of Our Beliefs on Our Behavior

Self-Concept

People modify their behavior and adjust to new situations by using their past experience in similar situations. Each person, however, has his or her own set of experiences and interpretation of these experiences. Therefore, each person has a different frame of reference for interpreting his or her experiences. The frame of reference we use involving the "I" or "me" beliefs we have of ourselves is called the self-concept. Our self-concept determines how we perceive ourselves in relation to other people and the events we are involved in.

How we think of ourselves is based on the input from others that we have experienced in different situations. When the messages to an individual conflict with how the person thinks of him/herself, that person may try to deny or distort the meaning of the messages. A student, for example, may not understand some material presented in a particular class. This student does not seek help from others and does not take additional time to learn the material. When tested on this and other material within the class, the student may deny that the instructor ever covered or assigned the information. A student who has "D" grades in a course, does not understand much of the material presented, and thus has done poorly may say, "I was not interested anyway." This student could also say that the instructor was incompetent, did not like him or her, or if remotely applicable, that the instructor was racially biased. Not understanding and not learning the material puts the responsibility for that failure on the student's shoulders. In an attempt to shift this responsibility, students may distort their inability to understand the material by blaming their failure on the instructor or on the concept that one must "like" the material to be successful.

Students find themselves in this predicament because they do not wish to include the belief, that they may be incapable within their self-concept. When circumstances threaten the concepts they have of themselves, they defend against changing their views and distort the reasons for their lack of success.

When individuals deny or distort the events around them, they have difficulty being successful. They cannot accurately interpret their experiences. In many cases, they do not know what to do and, needing to do something, act incorrectly. If they are not successful, they again may distort or deny the outcome of their actions. This cycle has individuals continually defending against changing their conceptions about themselves. For example, students who deny or distort the reasons for unsuccessful course work will be unable to make accurate decisions about selecting a college major or elective courses. Oftentimes, students who are unsuccessful in their first choice of a college major will select another solely based on their ability to comprehend the course work. They may move from one extreme to the other, without considering the prospects for employment, salary, or duties of the position they are likely to obtain. RAs can assist students by helping them clarify their self-concepts. This will enable them to make choices that will satisfy their needs over the long term rather than the short term.

Goal Levels

In our society, generally speaking, people are taught that they need to be highly competent, successful, and loved or approved of by virtually everyone they meet (Ellis, 1962). These goals are impossible to attain in all aspects of a person's life. Every human being has specific strengths, capabilities, and limitations. People are not highly competent in all areas and will not be successful in all endeavors. Also, we will not have everyone like or approve of us at all times. Unable to attain these extremes, individuals tend to "cover up" and pretend to others that they are always competent. This type of behavior causes denial and distortion concerning others' reactions. After doing this for some time, the person is unable to accurately perceive his or her interactions with others and thus is not able to behave adequately. Ultimately, many people can give up and not enter into situations they perceive to be difficult for them. Oftentimes they have not established relevant goal levels as a determinant of success.

For example, students who have difficulty making friends and forming interpersonal relationships may make up excuses about why they will not attend a social gathering or party. They do not attend the social because they are unable to act as they think they should. Some students may believe that others will be watching and think them odd or inept. They stay away from the social because they think they will be a failure and do not want to think of themselves this way. Because of their fears of failure and the thoughts about themselves that this may bring, they do not attempt to put themselves in a position to further develop interpersonal relationships.

The problem here may well be one of unrealistic goals. Such a person does not need to be the "life of the party" and could do well by talking to just a few people. By setting this new goal, the individual would then be willing to attend because he or she could be successful. In order to have students enter into situations in which they have difficulty adjusting, you may be called on to help these students adjust their goals to more realistic levels. Entering into new situations and adjusting to them is part of the process leading to eventual success.

Resistance to Evaluation

When people have not been successful in adjusting to new situations, they are usually fearful of evaluation. Evaluating their behavior may show them how they are wrong. In many cases, people interpret "wrong" as meaning incapable. Since they do not wish to think of themselves this way, they tend to stay away from situations in which they may be evaluated. When you first talk to a student who is experiencing a problem in adjustment or making a decision, do not begin by confronting his or her self-beliefs. To continually point out a student's shortcomings will produce a situation that the student would rather avoid. If an RA emphasizes students' inabilities as a primary means to change student behavior, the students whom the RA wishes to help may avoid him or her.

The threat of evaluation also keeps many people from seeking help when they wish to change their behaviors. They believe that seeking help is the same as saying to themselves that they are incompetent or inferior. For individuals to deal with the problems they are experiencing, they must be in a situation in which they are willing to talk about themselves and their problems. The situation must be relatively free of overt attempts to evaluate the individual. Thus, when a student comes to you for assistance, you do not want to confront the student about his or her reasons for seeking help. Early thoughts of being "wrong" or incapable may also cause a person to distort and defend against any attempts aimed at change. If RAs stress a student's lack of knowledge or insight to motivate that student to change, they may only increase the student's resistance to change.

Personal Constructs

Different people have different views about the same subject. They also have different beliefs about how to act and succeed in specific situations. These views of action, which are included in one's self-concept, are based on the individual's personal construct system. Personal constructs are the thoughts that form patterns or relationships on which the individual bases his or her behavior. Constructs are derived from how individuals perceive the events surrounding them and how they use those perceptions to interpret future events. Personal constructs are important because individuals use them to anticipate events and the outcomes of their behavior. Personal constructs are means of creating a frame of reference for an individual so he or she can act in an organized and successful manner. Individuals need to modify their personal constructs when the individuals undergo new experiences. People need to incorporate their perceptions of new experiences within their construct system so that they can adapt when similar situations occur later on. People who do not change their concepts based on new experiences do not adjust well to new situations.

Stereotyping people is an example of creating and using personal constructs. Having a fixed image or view of a group of people to the degree that an individual from that group is assigned all the group's characteristics is an example of a personal construct that stereotypes every individual in the group. The construct that a particular group of people is industrious, rich, kind, intelligent, or lazy enables the construct holder to predict how they act and thus how he or she is to act toward them. Stereotyping, however, does not allow for understanding people's uniqueness, a skill that is necessary for accurate interpersonal communication and establishing social relationships. Knowing that stereotyping is created by personal constructs helps us understand what personal constructs are and how they are used. More importantly, however, is the understanding that people with stereotypic concepts will find it difficult to change these constructs and therefore change their behavior in new and different situations.

For example, a male student who is having difficulty dating women more than once may base his behavior during the dates on inaccurate concepts about women. He may believe all or most women are unable to compete with men in most areas, and, being inferior, they want and expect men to make decisions for them. This student, besides making all the arrangements for the date, tells the woman what her opinions need to be on different topics when they are engaged in conversation. Another male student may have the same type of problem but have a different set of constructs about women. He may see women as highly demanding and interested only in satisfying their own needs. This student then bases his relationships with women on letting the woman make all the decisions and gives no opinions of his own because they may conflict with those of his date. To assist students in modifying their behavior, the RA needs to understand the constructs students are using to formulate their behaviors and convey this information to students. Knowing the constructs they are using and knowing that these constructs are not producing the desired or anticipated outcome provides the students with the opportunity to adjust their constructs.

Thoughts-Feelings-Actions

Almost all behavioral scientists agree that peoples' thoughts determine their actions. However, an individual's feelings are often accepted as the major ingredient of their actions. Albert Ellis (1973) perhaps best outlines the thought-feeling-action process of human beings. Based on their personal constructs, including self-concepts, people perceive and give meaning to an event that occurs in the form of a thought. The thought then produces their feeling, or affect. It is the thought that forms their basis for action, however, not the feeling. Consider a student statement like "I felt so nervous when talking to that professor that I could hardly talk, and I had to leave before I could finish all that I needed to say." The nervousness the student felt did not make him or her leave the professor's presence. Rather, it was the thoughts of the inability to succeed in this situation that caused him or her to leave. People feel nervous or anxious because they think they do not have the ability to be successful. Apparently, this student's doubts about his or her ability to be successful increased while talking with the professor, producing an increased nervousness to the extent that he or she had to leave the situation. Self-doubts, in this case, produced the student's behavior; being nervous was also a product of these doubts.

Knowing how people feel can tell us about their thoughts. People who have difficulty making decisions or solving their problems are experiencing some degree of confusion. Clarifying how people feel, however, gives us insight into what they are thinking. People's thoughts about their behavior relate to their personal constructs and their self-concept. When we wish to increase peoples' understanding of themselves, we must specify their feelings as well as what they may be thinking. Thoughts produce feelings, and understanding how these dynamics are connected gives individuals an awareness of why they act as they do.

Also, when individuals have been unsuccessful and are quizzed about their thoughts, they may become defensive, guarding against any changes in their self-concept system. Talking to a person about his or her feelings does not produce the same level of defensiveness. Including feelings along with the thoughts of individuals facilitates their willingness to talk about their problems. Adjusting to college life requires adjustments in self-concept, personal constructs, and perhaps goal levels. For some students these adjustments will be relatively minor, and they will modify their behavior. Students who are having difficulty adjusting their behavior are also experiencing difficulty modifying their self-concepts, personal constructs, or goals in the college environment. Knowing the basic dynamics of how people formulate their thoughts and, hence, their actions will help you understand students who experience problems adjusting to college. Conveying to students an understanding of their thoughts and how these thoughts influence their behavior and their success provides students the opportunity to adjust in these areas. The following section describes the skills that will help you to communicate effectively with students in order to enhance student self-understanding.

Interpersonal Communication Skills

Through skillfull communication, you can enhance your ability to talk with students about their problems and increase their awareness of their motives and actions. The skills discussed in this section are used together to maintain a conversation and provide clarity in communication. Your overall objective is to clarify the student's messages in order to facilitate their self-understanding.

Attending Behaviors

An important part of interpersonal behavior and communication is the physical aspect of paying attention to another person. Looking at another person and maintaining eye contact communicates that we wish to speak to that person. You must maintain eye contact throughout much of the conversation. In this way we communicate that we are listening and that the other person's messages are important to us. Do not become distracted if the conversation is important to you or the other person. Arrange the situation so that you can be alone with the individual without any distractions. Sit or stand facing the person you are communicating with. Be relaxed, gesture appropriately, smile when appropriate, and express your words in an even and accepting tone of voice. Attending to another person in these ways enables that person to relax and want to be in your company and to talk. Appropriate attending behaviors actually reinforce the other person's willingness to continue to be with you and talk to you.

Empathic Responding

The most important ingredient in helping a person understand himself or herself is the communication of empathy (Carkhuff, 1969). An empathic communication contains both the thoughts and feelings that another person has transmitted to us. The basic format for this type of communicaton is the "You feel _____ because _____ " statement (Sydnor & Parkhill, 1978). Empathic responses communicate to the other person that you understand that individual's thoughts and feelings and that you can connect these dynamics. You show the other person that indeed you understand what has been said to you. The empathic response reinforces the person to continue to talk to you. Thus, not only does this type of response enable people to understand their thoughts and feelings, it also keeps them talking about their problem or situation.

A student talking to you may say, "I don't like the holidays that are coming up, but there'll be so few students on campus that I guess I'll have to go home. That'll be difficult for me. Lately I haven't gotten along well with my parents. All we seem to do is fight, and I never seem to win." An empathic response would be, "You're anxious about having to go home because all you can think about are the arguments you and your parents always seem to have." The student may then reply, "Yes, we always seem to argue about what I'm doing and the grades I get. You would think that I can't do anything right. I just don't look forward to going home anymore." An empathic reply would be, "You feel rather hopeless because you can't seem to meet their expectations for you." The indication given by this student is that he or she may have stopped trying to resolve the problem with the parents and, not knowing what else to do, simply ends up arguing with them. The result is that the student does not want to, or at least does not look forward to, being with his or her parents.

From Ambiguity to Specificity

Enabling individuals to understand their thoughts and feelings involves moving them from a relatively ambiguous awareness of these dynamics to a specific awareness of exactly what they think and feel. The example of the student who does not want to go home shows the beginning of this type of progression. People who accurately perceive their situation and know their thoughts will have little difficulty making accurate decisions. The difficulty arises when they are unsure about what to think, as is the case in the above example. Should the student not go home because he or she is unable to figure out how to act to stop the arguments with his or her parents? Does the student think that he or she has tried all the possible solutions for this problem? Has the student thought of specific goals for his or her interaction with the parents? Having students know their own answers to these questions adds clarity to their thinking and behavior and will also change their feelings about the situation. They will begin to understand why they act as they do.

In helping others through interpersonal communication, the helper clarifies other people's thoughts so that they understand their actions. Clarity or specificity of their thoughts and feelings is given in response to their communications. The intent of the process is to move the individuals from an ambiguous to a specific understanding of their thoughts and feelings about themselves. This is the goal of the interpersonal communications of an individual wishing to help another. Having individuals perceive accurately by thinking clearly and understanding why they have the thoughts they do will enable them to make wise decisions and act in a successful manner.

An RA will have to expend some time and effort in helping a student understand himself or herself. The time and effort involved needs to be viewed as part of the learning process necessary for students to adjust their behavior. At first, some students will resist undergoing changes. They have difficulty realizing that they can be successful by behaving differently. You must not take this resistance as a personal rejection but rather acknowledge that change and adjustment occur over a period of time, not immediately. The case study that follows illustrates the use of interpersonal communication skills to help one male student adjust to college life. Following this case is a group experience exercise in which RAs discuss the students' adjustment problems and practice using interpersonal communication skills in assisting with these problems.

Case Studies and Structured Group Experiences for Enhancing the Interpersonal Communication Skills of Resident Assistants

Case Study: Jack

Instructions: Read the case study which follows. In "response set one" select the best response the RA could give and in "response set two" complete the statement by filling in the blank. When finished, share your answers with other RAs in small groups or as a basis for a classroom discussion.

Jack is an 18-year-old college freshman who lives in one of the campus residence halls. His home is over 750 miles away, and he has no relatives or friends in the area. He is attending this college because his parents think it is an excellent school and believe that Jack will be able to be more successful in obtaining a highly rated job than if he attended a local college. His parents know that he has had few friends at home, yet they believe that this is the time for him to strike out on his own. Seven hundred fifty miles is not that far away, and Jack's parents believe that he will be able to come home on all holidays and a number of weekends.

Jack's few friends at home have been his acquaintances almost all of his life. They live in his neighborhood and attended school with him. Jack was the leader of his small group, and they did what Jack requested of them. They followed him around, and he directed most of their behavior. Jack made no new friends his last three years in high school and was content to lead his small group. He has above average academic abilities and graduated in the upper 25 percent of his high school class. Jack was apprehensive about going away to college and leaving his very tight-knit group of friends. Most of his enjoyment was being with and leading this group.

In college, Jack found that he had difficulty making friends. Some of the students already knew each other because they were friends in high school. Also, many students seemed to make friends easily and enjoy each other's company. Jack felt that very few people would talk to him for any length of time, and that he was never asked to be part of the same group when students went out on different activities. Students would talk to him but they never wanted to spend much time with him. He was not enjoying his experiences at college. He would study most of the time and was able to do fairly well in obtaining As and Bs on his first tests. Yet, he was lonely and angry at the same time. He began to think about leaving this college and returning home to attend the local college in his area.

The resident assistant for the dormitory floor on which Jack lives noticed that Jack studied most of the time and had little interaction with other students on the floor. He thought that perhaps Jack was not doing well in his classes and needed to use his time to study. On observing Jack talking to a group of students in the floor lounge, he saw Jack make an angry face, turn, and abruptly leave. Based on what he had seen, the RA followed Jack down the hall and said to him, "It looks like you feel offended because of what happened in that group." Jack replied, "They are all jerks. I don't like them, and anyway I need to go to my room and study."

How would you reply to Jack? Select one response from each of the following sets of replies to Jack's statements.

I. Response Set One

RA: a. Yes, getting good grades is more important than talking in the lounge.
  b. Don't worry, you will work it out with that group.
  c. You should not get angry, they are all good guys.
  d. Sounds like you feel very angry because of something that was said to you.

Jack: "Well, how would you like it if no one ever listened to you?"
RA: a. You will get over it.
  b. Keep trying; they will eventually listen to you.
  c. You feel resentful because they do not seem to accept what you have to say.
  d. People always listen to me. You need to be more aggressive.

Jack: "I have really tried to make friends here, but they won't listen to me. I tell them what's really great to do, but they won't listen. Even in the beginning when I did go out with them, they wouldn't accept what I had to say on what to do."
RA: a. You sound like you are mad at them.
  b. Don't worry Jack, they really like you. Just give it more time.
  c. You feel angry because you believe they must accept what you have to say and the directions you give them.
  d. You don't need them anyway. Perhaps it is best that you go back to your room and study.

Jack: "Well, why won't they accept what I have to say? I have tried very hard to get them to listen to me. But lately all I do is get in an argument with them. They just won't listen."
RA: a. Well, you will just have to keep after them.
  b. Let me tell you what I would do. I would . . .
  c. Sounds like you need to listen more to them rather than their listening to you.
  d. You feel confused because you think you know how to be friends with them and how to act but what you are doing is not working for you.

II. Response Set Two

For the following sets of replies to Jack's statements, the correct reply will not be in the form "you feel _____ because _____ ". However, the correct statements will specify Jack's feelings and thoughts. This change in communication statements, after the "you feel _____ because _____" model has been learned, allows RAs to vary their replies and not be constrained by having to always use the same format. Choose the correct reply to Jack's communications.

Jack: "No, it is not working; but what do I do?"
RA:
  a. You don't understand what to do at this point; so you get frustrated and angry at them and try to force them to do what you want as proof they like you. That is not working.
  b. You will have to be more friendly.
  c. Don't take it so hard, Jack. You are bound to find someone to be friends with you.
  d. What do you think you should do?

Jack: "But I had friends in the past. I have friends at home, and I just don't understand why it is so difficult here."
RA:
  a. You just don't want to admit it Jack. You are a loser.
  b. Well, you need to go to those fellows and apologize to them for all the arguments you caused, and maybe they will accept you.
  c. You need to take your mind off this. Get some rest.
  d. It is very frustrating to think that you don't know what to do.

Jack: "Well, I will just leave here. I will go back home and attend school, and I know I will feel better."
RA:
  a. If that is what you want to do, go ahead.
  b. You sound angry about the fact that you may have to change some of your thoughts and behavior to make friends with the students here.
  c. No, you are not right. This is a much better place for you.
  d. You should think about it much more before you make such a decision.

Jack: "I don't know what else to do, and I still think they don't like me."
RA:
  a. Thinking that some of this may be your fault makes you very apprehensive, and you would rather blame them.
  b. Sure they like you.
  c. You must have thought of some other things to do.
  d. This situation is your fault, and the quicker you realize it the better off you will be.

Jack: "Well, it's not easy thinking I am at fault. I did have some good friends in the past, but they were the friends I grew up with. Perhaps this is a different situation."
RA:
  a. These people are different from your friends at home.
  b. Go to that group and apologize. It will work.
  c. I knew you would come around.
  d. Changing an opinion you have of yourself makes you anxious.

At this point in the dialogue, Jack begins to change his thoughts about his behavior. This change will lead to his talking about how he must act to gain friends. Realizing that he is part of his own problem will enable him to understand that he has some control in the situation. Changing his behavior will cause others to change their behavior towards him.

The RA in this instance will need to continue to clarify Jack's thoughts about the need to change. If Jack fails in any of his attempts to change and become accepted by the other students, he may again blame them. Jack has not yet changed his behavior, even though he has begun to change some of his thoughts about that behavior. What additional areas of thought-feeling-behavior might the RA cover in talking to Jack to help him understand what must be done to become accepted and make friends?

Decide from the following list what these areas might be, and for each area chosen, determine the thoughts that Jack may have that can conflict with his changing his behavior.

1. Anxiety that comes from being rejected.
2. Anger at not getting one's way.
3. Sometimes being nervous when being with people that are important to us.
4. Being flustered when we don't know exactly what to do.
5. Feeling elation when being successful.
6. Being offended when criticized.
7. Feeling lost when alone.
8. Being washed-out after being with a group of people.
9. Feeling uptight in a large group of people.
10. Seething when others do not give us their full attention.

Changes in Jack's behavior toward others will depend on his having appropriate thoughts concerning many of the above areas. The ideal situation for an RA working with Jack is to be able to observe Jack in social situations and during his attempts to be accepted. The RA's ability to accurately observe Jack's and the others' behaviors can help Jack to understand his own behavior objectively.

Exercise: Group Experience in Interpersonal Communication Skills

Goals:
1. To have group members determine the thoughts of college students that can cause unsuccessful behavior;
2. Have group members experience interpersonal communication skills in clarifying students' thoughts.

Group Size: Eight to ten participants

Time Required: Approximately one and one-half hours

Materials: 1. Copy of Student's Problem Statements; 2. Pencils and note paper

Physical Setting: Chairs placed in a circle

Process:
1. The group leader briefly discusses the session's objectives.
2. Copies of the Student's Problem Statements are distributed to participants.
3. Working individually, the participants choose a problem statement and write out what they believe to be the thoughts of the student expressing his or her problem.
4. Participants read their descriptions, which the group then discusses. Participants accept additional thoughts presented and can modify their original presentation.
5. Other problem behaviors that may be exhibited by the student expressing the problem are discussed and recorded for each case.
6. Time is given for participants to think over the problem statement so they can role play a student expressing that problem.
7. Each participant then takes on the role of his or her student in interpersonal communication with a volunteer member of the group. The group member attempts to clarify the thoughts of the problem student. The communication lasts for five to seven verbal interactions between the pair.
8. After each pair interacts, the other group members discuss the case and make recommendations about other topic areas that would need to be discussed for the problem student eventually to be successful.

Variations:
a. The group leader may wish to start the experience with one- or two-sentence statements of students experiencing a problem. A statement such as, "I'm not going to be able to go home during the holidays because I have too much unfinished work here. I had looked forward to going home so much" could be used. RAs could respond, giving the feelings of the student making such a statement and then the thoughts producing the feeling. Thoughts and feelings would be combined to produce empathic replies as a lead-in to the group experience.
b. The group leader may have participants develop similar case statements to the Student's Problem Statements based on a student they know and have observed.
c. The group experience may be extended to include role plays of students experiencing problems that have been observed by one or more RAs.

3. I wish I was as smart as everyone else here. They seem so content and even happy. I know I'm not going to make it. All I can think about is my next class paper or exam. I take so much time thinking about what I have to do that I can't get much done. How are these other students doing it?

4. I can never find the right roommate. Even when I know the person and we decide to room together, she turns out to be messy. She never seems to care about how she leaves her things. I get so angry that I could shout at her, but I never say anything. Eventually we end up not talking, and then we dislike each other. I've been here three years, and have had a different roommate each year.

5. My girlfriend won't see me anymore. She lives in my hometown and says she was told that I was dating girls here at school. That isn't true. She's the only person I ever dated in my life. I have tried, but she won't have anything to do with me anymore. I feel so low that I can't stand it. Most of the time I feel like I could cry.

6. I like to have a good time, but this beer drinking is starting to get to me. My friends like to enjoy themselves, and each weekend we go out and drink every night. Lately we do the same thing on Wednesday night. We have a great time, but my grades are beginning to slide. I always go along with them, but I can't keep up this pace. I don't know what to do, but I certainly won't sit home alone with no one or nothing to do.

7. Passing calculus means so much to me because if I fail I can't get in the major I want. I get so nervous before the exams that my mind goes blank, and I can't remember any of the answers. I don't know what to do. It's gotten so bad that I have thought about trying to get some pills to calm me down or hiding the answers on me during the exams.

8. I'm really put out by the instructors here. They aren't teachers. They can't teach. They're not prepared. They talk to the board and can hardly speak. Their lectures are boring, and I need to be motivated. I need to be interested to do well, and they don't make me interested. I know that I'm not going to do well here because of these lousy instructors.

9. I don't seem to care about school anymore. There's so little to do here. All I do is study to take up my time. My grades are fine, but that isn't all there is to life. The students here aren't friendly. They don't talk to you. They all seem to have their own groups and aren't interested in anyone else. Sometimes I wish I was back home where I was comfortable and happy.

10. I know I'm loud and fool around a lot, but my friends like it. I'm a big hit with them. So what if the others on the floor think I make too much noise. I don't care if they think I'm wild, and I disturb them. I don't need them. I've got my friends.

CHAPTER 6

Peer Counseling

Dr. W. Garry Johnson,
Western Illinois University

Resident Assistants are expected to play many different roles in college and university residence halls. The helping/counseling role is listed consistently as one of the key roles you are asked to play for students that live on your floor. Several authors have attempted to underscore the importance of your role as a helper. Blimling and Miltenberger (1984) indicated that, "The second role that the RA serves is as a counselor, consultant, or advisor." (p. 7) They explain that while the term "counselor" may be an overstatement, the functions of the role are clearly counseling oriented. Upcraft (1982) indicated very clearly that the role of the RA involves counseling:

> RAs provide personal help and assistance as students come to them with their problems concerning roommates, academic difficulties, parental relationships, career decisions or the opposite sex. Although they are not trained to counsel or provide therapy (nor should they be encouraged to do so), RAs are frequently the first person in the institution to learn about a student's problems. Thus they should be skillful in solving minor problems and referring major ones to professional sources. (p. 10)

Powell, Plyler, Dickson, and McClellan (1969), in their book *The Personnel Assistant in College Residence Halls,* stated that, "Although it is recognized that you are not a professionally trained counselor, the greater portion of your work as an RA may be devoted to a helping relationship similar to counseling. To do this work effectively, you need to understand some basic notions about the counseling process." (p. 24)

It is the working premise of this chapter that you need to develop and improve your helping/counseling skills if you are going to do the kind of job on your floor that will truly be of help and support to your students. Improving ones skill level can best be accomplished through the use of practical experiences such as the ones outlined later in this chapter. Although counseling theories and counseling intervention techniques are important information for the professional counselor, most of what the RA does as a helper can best be learned through structured group exercises and role-playing exercises. The chapter has been organized to give you some basic information and to provide you with a variety of opportunities to practice and receive feedback on your helping skills. The preceding chapter, by Tom Housie, provides you with some additional information on listening skills and interpersonal relationships. You are encouraged to read it before embarking on the exercises in this chapter.

The Helping Role

The task of counseling is to help individuals better learn to solve their own problems. The majority of the students attending colleges and universities are normal, well-adjusted young men and women. At times, however, they may find themselves temporarily unable to cope with the stresses and strains of events in their lives. Stresses confronting students may come from within the educational environment. Such issues as roommate problems, academic concerns, relationship problems, and financial concerns can place considerable stress on the average college student. At times, the stresses students face may come from outside the educational environment. Family problems such as a change in one or both parents' work conditions, divorce, or illness can tax the coping skills of the strongest, most-well adjusted young person.

The goal of counseling is to help individuals develop healthy coping skills and sound decision-making skills so that they can solve their own problems in the future. As a helper/counselor, we do not want students to become dependent on us to solve their problems or to make them feel better. Rather, we want them to become independent and gain control over their lives. For most young adults, counseling is an educational process designed to teach the individual to be a more effective, fully functioning community member.

Research has demonstrated that a student's peer group can have a significant impact on his or her development during the college years (Brown, 1972; Feldman and Newcomb, 1969; Newcomb and Wilson, 1966). As a peer helper you can have a lasting impact on the students you come in contact with in your role as an RA. The more training you have in helping skills, the greater your potential impact.

You may be asking youself "how can I as an RA help students on my floor with their problems? I'm not a counselor!" Many counselor trainers believe that it is not necessary to go through a long period of professional preparation to work as a helping person (Carkhuff and Truax, 1965). With appropriate supervision and training you can be an effective helper.

Guidelines for Helping Skills

There are several guidelines that you need to follow if you are going to be an effective helping person in your role as an RA. First, you must take the time to get to know your residents as well as humanly possible. The better you know and understand them, the better you will be able to anticipate the types of problems they will experience during the course of the year. Establishing rapport is a significant part of the helping/counseling process. The more you can do ahead of time to establish a meaningful relationship with your residents, the easier your job will be later on, when problems arise.

Second, you need to know and recognize your own limits. Don't assume responsibility for the problems of others. Learn to recognize when a resident needs the skills of a professional counselor. One of your key roles as a helper is to refer students to someone who has the knowledge and experience to help them. Once you refer one of your residents, you may not be able to find out how he or she is doing in therapy. Every institution is different, and some Counseling Centers may not be willing to keep you informed on the student's progress. Remember, since you referred the resident in the first place, you can always ask the student how things are going. You may even be asked by the counselor to keep them posted on how the student is acting on the floor.

Third, make sure your supervisor knows who you are working with and the types of problems you are dealing with. You are not a professional counselor. Finally, treat what students tell you in a very special way. Nothing will ruin your credibility faster than to have another resident repeat something to a student that that student told you in confidence. What you hear from students should only be shared with your supervisor or someone else in authority. Appropriate confidentiality and respest for what others have shared with you are building blocks in the helping relationship.

As an RA, you will be asked by residents to help with many unique problems. One of the more challenging will be working with residents who have gotten themselves into difficulty with the institution or other floor or hall members. Often, forced counseling situations are threatening to students since they did not initiate the contact. They may be reluctant to talk with you about the situation or may deny any problem. While these contacts may be the most difficult, they may also be the most fruitful and rewarding. Do not shy away from them. If you work to develop your helping skills, you can turn these contacts into important learning opportunities for your residents and yourself.

There are some basic rules that can make your job as a helper much easier. Active listening is a key component in the helping relationship. Few of us really listen to what others are saying, but effective helpers listen actively. An active listener listens not only to the words but to the messages sent by nonverbal communications such as body language and facial expressions as well. In our everyday conversations with people, we seldom pay close attention to everything that is said by the person with whom we are talking. While this less-than-attentive approach to communication may be acceptable in everyday conversation, it is not appropriate in the helping/counseling situation. Our undivided attention must be focused on the person we are trying to help if we are to understand clearly the depth and breadth of the problem he or she is trying to deal with at that point in life. Active listening takes practice. No one is born a good listener; rather, a person develops good listening skills, generally as a result of hard work and effort.

Asking questions can be a problem at the beginning of the helping relationship. In the early stages of becoming an effective helper, the RA has a tendency to ask the person questions. It is true that if we are going to be helpful, we need some basic information. But questions get in the way if they are poorly stated or timed. When asking questions, it is important that they be open-ended rather than ones that require a simple yes or no response. Asking a resident "How was your weekend at home?" will yield more information than asking "Did you have a good time at home this weekend?" The former question allows the person to tell his or her story, while the latter simply calls for a yes or no response.

Too many distractions can get in the way when you are in a helping situation. When you are trying to help someone, you need to focus your attention on that person exclusively. Turn off the TV or stereo so that you can give the resident your undivided attention. Since you know you will be helping residents with problems as part of your job, set up your room so you can have the best possible helping environment. Two comfortable chairs or a bed and a chair are all that you need to set up your helping environment. Whenever possible, seating should be movable so that you can face the person you are trying to help.

It is important to be available as much as possible. You cannot help your residents unless you are there when they need you. Spending quality time on your floor will increase the likelihood that you will find yourself involved in helping situations.

The RA who is not on the floor much is often viewed as someone who really does not care a great deal about his or her residents. When you spend time on your floor, students will come to you for help. Once they trust you and feel you care about them, they will wait to talk with you, rather than trying to deal with the problem themselves or going elsewhere for help.

Empathy and respect for the individual are key components in the helping relationship. If you intend to help someone, it is important to have a genuine sense of how they feel about the problem. One can never know exactly how another person is feeling; your goal is to try to understand as much as possible what the person is feeling. Our only hope is to come close to the feeling by thinking about experiences in our own lives.

Sometimes when we are busy, we forget that the problem a resident brings to us is the greatest concern in that person's life at that point in time. A problem that seems small to us may cause another person to be unable to function effectively in his or her everyday life. In order to be an effective helper, you must treat your residents with respect at all times and in all circumstances. Showing respect for the resident and his or her problem is important. Saying to a resident, "Hey, that's no big deal" or "Don't worry about it" will probably end your role as a helper for that person and others. Being able to recognize and acknowledge the feelings expressed by your residents is a skill you must develop if you want to be an effective helper.

The following case study is designed to give you a better understanding of the type of situations you may encounter as an RA in a helping role. Following the case study are several structured exercises designed to help you practice your helping skills.

Case Studies and Structured Group Experiences for Peer Counseling

Case Study: Jane and John

Instructions: Read the case study and respond to the questions which follow. First work alone. When you are finished, share your answers with other RAs in small group discussions or as the basis for a classroom discussion.

During the course of the past semester you have been made aware of the fact that one of your residents, has been involved in a relationship with Jack, a resident in the adjacent hall. While this is not unusual, the fact that you have been told that the couple has been observed and heard fighting on several occasions does have you concerned. On one occasion, you noticed that Jane appeared to have a badly blackened right eye. When asked about it, she said that she had walked into her room door. After the black eye incident, you observed that Jane spent more time on the floor with the other residents than she had before the incident. A few weeks later you observed that Jane was once more absent from the floor and that she seemed to be spending a great deal of time with her boyfriend Jack, in the hall next door.

Then, one evening during rounds you hear yelling and shouting coming from Jane's room. As you approach, you see several floor members standing in the hallway close to her door. They tell you that Jane and John have been fighting for the past 30 minutes. A woman that lives next door to Jane indicates that she heard what sounded like someone getting slapped and shoved into the wall in the room. You decide to confront the situation. After getting permission, you use the phone in the next room to call the Hall Director for assistance in the confrontation. The Hall Director knocks on the door and asks Jane to let her in so they can talk. In the background you hear John tell her she had better keep her mouth shut or he will really fix her good. You enter the room and find it in a shambles. Jane is sitting at her desk in tears. John is standing next to her at the desk.

Case Study Questions:

Your first task in this situation is to deal with the residents and the two students involved.

1. What do you say to your residents in the hallway? _____

_____

_____

_____

_____

2. What do you say to the two students? _____

_____

_____

_____

3. What do you do with John? _____

_____

_____

_____

Role Plays

A. Jane and Her RA

Later the same night, after John is gone, Jane comes to your room, crying. (Role play with another RA) What do you say to her? _____

_____

_____

_____

_____

B. John and His RA

Later the same night, John comes to you, upset that Jane's RA and the Hall Director interrupted him and Jane in Jane's room. You have been advised of the earlier situation by Jane's RA. (Role play with another RA)

1. What do you say to John? _____

_____

_____

_____

_____

_____

_____

_____

_____

_____

_____

_____

_____

_____

Exercise: Attending Skills

Goals: To provide practice in attending skills

Group Size: Any number

Time Required: 30 minutes

Materials: pencils

Physical: Room with movable chairs

Process: Students are divided into pairs and asked to follow the directions given in the exercise. Students should perform each exercise and write their answer in the text as indicated.

When all students are finished the instructor should reverse the exercise with the whole group and use it as a source of class discussion. Emphasis should be placed on similarities among answers.

It is important that you pay careful attention to the person you are working with in a helping situation. The purpose of this exercise is to give you an opportunity to practice your attending skills. The first exercise will help you with your physical attending skills which allow you to communicate with the person you are helping using your personal body language. It is important that you feel comfortable in your role as helper. How you sit or stand communicates something to the person you are working with in a helping situation.

Getting Comfortable

For this exercise you will need a partner and two chairs. First, set the chairs side by side. Sit down and talk to each other about how things are going on your floor.

How did this feel, in terms of how well you communicated with each other? _____

_____

_____

Set the same two chairs facing each other and resume your conversation. How did it feel this time? Did you feel like you got more out of the conversation? Did you feel more comfortable than before? _____

_____

_____

It is important that you feel physically comfortable when you talk with someone in a helping situation.

Posture

Using the same two chairs and partner, practice different sitting positions. First, lean back in the chair; next, cross your legs and arms; finally, lean a little forward and square of your body with your partner. Continue to talk with your partner as you try the different positions.

How did the different positions feel for you? Did one feel better than the other? Which one felt most comfortable for you and for your partner? Did you feel you were communicating more effectively in one

position rather than the other? _____

_____

_____

_____

_____

_____

Eye Contact

It is important to attempt to maintain eye contact with the person you are working with in a helping situation. You need to get and maintain comfortable eye contact. You are not trying to make the person feel you are staring at them or attempting to drill a hole in their head with your eyes. Remember, in some cultures it is considered disrespectful to look someone in the eyes, especially if the person is older or in a position of authority.

1. Using the same two chairs and partner, practice getting and maintaining eye contact with the person. Occasionally look away to allow the person some space. You do not want them to feel uncomfortable because of your eye contact. You should continue to practice this skill with other people you come in contact with each day.

Exercise: Your Bubble

Goals: To help students understand the need for personal space between people.

Group Size: Any size

Time Required: 15 minutes

Materials: pencils

Physical Setting: Large room or outside space.

Process: Each student is asked to select a partner. Students stand five feet apart. Follow the instructions given in the exercise.

Students should write the answers in the space provided and the instructor should use these questions to process the exercise with the group.

Everyone has a different size personal bubble, or comfort zone, that they carry around with them. Some people feel uncomfortable when other people get inside their personal space. It is hard to help people if they feel their bubble or space has been violated.

1. Standing about five feet away from your partner, one person should move toward the other one step at a time and then pause. Move forward one step at a time until your partner raises his or her hand indicating discomfort. Move in different directions around your partner using the same hand signal as a show of discomfort. How did you feel about doing this exercise? _____

_____

_____

2. How far away was your comfort zone? _____

3. How far away was your partner's comfort zone? _____

4. Was there a difference in the size of the comfort zone for men and women, and, if so, what was the difference? _____

_____

_____

_____

_____

5. Were there any differences based on culture, and, if so, what were they? _____

_____

_____

_____

_____

_____

Exercise: Referral

Goal: To help RAs identify campus referral sources and specific individuals to contact.

Group Size: Any size.

Time Required: 45 minutes.

Material: Paper and pencils.

Physical Setting: Room with movable chairs.

Process: RAs are asked to complete the "Problem, Resource Service, and Resources Person" list given in the exercise. When completed, the RAs divided into groups of five and this information is shared in the group.

The most frequent problems reported in each small group should be reported to the entire class. A list of the most frequent problems should be identified and the course instructor should facilitate a discussion about campus referral resources and procedure.

One of the pitfalls you must avoid as a peer helper is getting into a situation with a student that is beyond your level of experience and skill. You are not a professional counselor! Your role is to help those you can and refer those you cannot. The secret is to know when to refer a student and to whom the referral can best be made.

Searching Out Professionals

Identify the ten most common problems you feel your students face during the year. Then, identify the referral agency or service you feel could best help the student. Finally, at each agency or service, identify a specific resource person to whom you could send a student for help.

PROBLEM	RESOURCE SERVICE	RESOURCE PERSON
1.		
2.		
3.		
4.		
5.		
6.		
7.		
8.		
9.		
10.		

Comparing Resources

When you have developed your list, you should get together with five other RAs and share your list and compare resource agencies and resource persons.

Exercise: The Helping Interview: Role Plays

Goals: To give RAs practice in helping skills.

Group Size: Small groups of three students each with any number of small groups.

Time Required: One to two hours.

Materials: Role play exercises.

Physical Setting: Room with movable chairs.

Process: RAs are divided into groups of three. One RA plays the role of an RA, one plays the role of the student resident, and one acts as an observer. The persons playing the roles work through one role play exercise and receive feedback from the observer. Roles are rotated among the three RAs on each successive role play so that each RA has an opportunity to serve as the RA, the student resident, and the observer.

Variation: The course instructor selects two students to participate in one of the role plays. The class observes and comments on the role play. The instructor participates by giving feedback to the students and by pointing-out the good helping skills demonstrated. When the feedback is completed, two other students are selected and are asked to participate in a different role play. The process of class observation and feedback is repeated.

Helping skills, like athletic skills, are learned and perfected through practice. There are no good listeners, only people with good listening skills. People are not born good counselors; rather, they learn and perfect the skills necessary. The purpose of this exercise is to provide you with some role plays that you can use to practice your helping skills.

The following exercises require teams of three people. Two people will role play the situation, while the third person observes the interaction and provides the RA playing the helper, with feedback on how he or she performed.

Role Play #1

A student from your floor comes to your room and asks to talk with you. The student begins by telling you that he is not doing very well in school and that his parents are not going to pay tuition if his grades don't improve by the end of the semester. The student indicates that he could not stand to go home a failure, saying "I'd kill myself before I would go home."

Role Play #2

A female student comes to you, obviously very upset. After a few minutes of crying, she begins to talk about the fact that she has just found out that she is pregnant. She seems very confused and unclear as to which way to turn for help. She informs you that the father of the child is someone she dated during the summer while she worked at a resort away from home.

Role Play #3

You are the only staff member in the building. A call comes to the desk from the Campus Security office indicating that one of your student's brothers has been in a serious car accident and that the parents have been unable to locate your student to tell him (or her) about the accident. The parents are at the hospital and can't be reached. You have been asked to inform the student of the accident and tell the student to come home as soon as possible.

Role Play #4

You have noticed that one of your residents seems to be out at the bars almost every night. You have also observed that on at least three occasions the person has missed classes because he or she had too much to drink the night before. You decide to confront the resident about what you have seen happening.

Role Play #5

One of your residents comes to you and indicates that he or she wants to move to another room because he or she can't get along with his or her roommate. You ask the student what the problem is and if it has been discussed with the roommate. The student indicates that there had been no mention of the problem with the roommate. You tell the person that you will check into a room change, but that you feel he or she should talk with the roommate. The student agrees to go back to the room to talk to the roommate. About 15 minutes later a resident runs into your room and tells you that the student you just talked with and his or her roommate are fighting in their room. You go to the room and confront the two students.

Role Play #6

You have noticed that one of your residents seems to be involved in a very negative relationship. You have observed what you considered to be very serious fights, many of them in the cafeteria at mealtimes. You decide to talk with the resident about what you have seen. Your goal is to get one or both students to see a professional counselor.

Role Play #7

You are walking down your hallway coming back from dinner, and as you pass one of your resident's room you smell marijuana. You knock on the door and confront two of your new freshmen. Both students get very angry and start to yell at you. Later, after the situation has been dealt with, you return to your room. About one hour after the incident, one of the residents comes to talk to you. The student is really frightened about what might happen as a result of the incident.

Role Play #8

You are confronted by one of your residents who indicates, that he or she is really concerned about the new resident, who moved from another hall to the room next door. The resident is concerned because some of the floor members have been picking on the new person. It seems that the new resident has a problem with body odor, due to poor hygiene habits. You decide to talk to the person before the situation gets out of hand.

Role Play #9

One of your fellow RAs was supposed to switch duty with you last night to repay you for taking his or her duty earlier in the week. You had an important meeting for a group project for a management class. The RA who was to take your duty left you a note 15 minutes before you were to leave, saying that he or she had decided to go to the show, and that he or she could not take your duty. You couldn't find anyone else, so you could not go to the meeting. This is the second time this semester this RA has done this to you. You decide to confront the RA.

Educating Your Residents

3

CHAPTER 7

Educational Programming

Dr. Barbara Y. Keller,
Bowling Green State University

A student at a residential college or university spends an average of sixteen to eighteen hours in a classroom each week. In terms of time distribution over a week, an average student spends only 10 percent in the classroom, while 40 percent will be spent outside the classroom, engaged in activities and social interaction. The amount of time spent in activities and socializing underscores the importance of intentional, planned activity, or programming. The key words of programming are *intentional* and *planned*. Programming is a deliberate, schematic, and purposeful blueprint applied to the time a student spends outside the classroom. As an integral part of the educational process, programming complements the classroom experience in reaching the goal of helping the student develop as a whole person—a totally educated person.

Meaningful programming in residence halls is intentional and directed with specific goals/objectives designed to enrich the environment and contribute to the educational process for the student—Intentional Student Development.

Programming is a learning tool. Through programming students are exposed to new ideas and new ways of thinking as well as to new perspectives on traditional issues. Programming not only provides the opportunity to learn about new ideas but offers the opportunity to learn about the spectrum of opinions and attitudes held by others related to those ideas. Programming is a learning tool used in the process of helping the student develop as a whole person.

Programming is an important vehicle in building community. Participation in programming activities provides a supportive environment where students can learn together. Programming is a way for students to share common experiences. Involvement in common experiences shared by students living together helps the cohesiveness of the group.

Programming is fun. The opportunity to interact with other students in a positive environment is conducive to learning. Programming is an opportunity to present ideas in new and creative ways. Having fun and enjoying the experience is fundamental to good programming.

Planning and Development

Using a theory or a concept as the basis for program development gives direction to intentional, planned activity. Programming serves a meaningful purpose if planned schematically. Three ways to develop a systematic framework for developing well rounded programs include: 1) the use of student development theory; 2) the use of person-environment interaction theory; and 3) the use of a wellness concept.

Student Development Theory

Arthur Chickering (1969) describes seven vectors of development in young adults. The developmental tasks described by these vectors can provide the basis for meaningful programming. For example, the vector of developing competence describes the students' need to achieve intellectually, physically, and socially. Programming planned to respond to these needs can provide an educational impetus to achieve these competencies positively. Workshops on study skills or time management help address the development of intellectual competence. Recreational programming such as intramurals addresses physical competence. Programming events such as mixers and parties help students develop social competence. Thus, programming provides the challenge or stimulus that can bring about developmental change in students.

Person-Environment Interaction Theory

Kurt Lewin (1950) describes behavior as a function of the interaction of the person and the environment. Programming can create a positive environment in an entire residence hall and on a given floor. Programming that encourages sharing ideas and interaction among residents will be conducive to building a cohesive group and a positive community. In terms of Lewin's theory, programming becomes an important tool for shaping the environment and thus influencing student behavior. Students who participate in activities and have varied experiences are likely to develop their talents and abilities and feel positive about their environment.

Wellness Concept

The concept of wellness offers the opportunity to view development from a holistic perspective. Wellness is a process of proactively making choices and developing a lifestyle. Using wellness as a basis for programming allows students to involve themselves in decision-making about their own lifestyles. For example, using the physiological dimension of wellness as the basis for programming, the RA encourages residents to explore issues such as physical health and fitness and sexual health. Through exposure to these concepts, students can be challenged to make choices about their own wellness.

A Rationale for Programming

Programming can be an integral part of the educational process by being a mechanism to influence the students' total development and to shape the environment where they live. In a very real sense, programming in a residence hall contributes significantly to students' out-of-classroom experience. Students spend the largest percentage of their time engaged in life experiences outside of the classroom. Well planned and interesting programs make learning fun and contribute to a well-rounded education. In this context, programming fosters learning outside the classroom and enhances the quality and content of the collegiate experience through a structured living and learning environment.

Exposure to new ideas, opinions, and information is a desirable experience for students and can be gained through diverse programming. Some programming acquaints students with selfdevelopment and growth-oriented activities. This programming not only encourages creative learning and expression but provides residents with opportunities to teach and learn from each other.

When students live together and learn to share ideas, respect and tolerance for individual differences is a plausible outcome. Interaction among residents builds a sense of community. When students play an active role in planning activities they not only are taking responsibility for building a sense of community but are growing individually as they engage in roles of leadership and followership.

Programming also provides students with informal opportunities to interact with faculty and staff. A wealth of opportunities arise when faculty and staff become involved in the residence halls, creating a learning opportunity for both the residents and for faculty and staff members as well. Involving faculty and staff in resident hall programs exposes them to an important facet of university life—residence halls. Showcasing the positive aspects of student life and utilizing the talents and hobbies of the faculty and staff can be an enjoyable and meaningful experience for everyone.

Programming, then, has many beneficial outcomes that will influence student development and shape the environment. Programming for student development serves these purposes:

- encourages creative learning and expression
- acquaints residents with selfdevelopment and growth oriented activities
- provides opportunities for students to teach and learn from each other
- allows student to experience roles of leadership and followership
- provides informal opportunities to interact with faculty and staff

Programming to shape the environment serves these purposes:

- fosters learning outside of the classroom
- promotes a living/learning environment
- builds a sense of community
- exposes faculty, staff and community members to an important facet of university life—residence halls

Categories of Programming

A well-rounded approach to program development requires balancing the types of activities that you offer. You have four basic categories: social programs, educational/cultural programs, recreational programs, and community service programs.

Social programs offer a wide range of opportunities for groups and individuals to interact in a relaxing, enjoyable activity. Planning social activities is fun, and finding creative ways to socialize usually poses no difficulty for either students or staff. Social programs include dances, ice cream socials, floor parties, and dinners.

Educational/cultural programs offer a spectrum of possibilities to gain new information and ideas, confront issues, develop new skills, acquire an appreciation of the arts and humanities, and express creative talents and thought. The programs themselves can be formatted in many ways, such as workshops, lectures, panel discussions, and field trips. Educational programs can include talent shows, art shows, coffee houses, and discussions. Making arrangements for a group of residents to attend campus-wide activities such as theatre productions, concerts, and guest lectures is an effective use of campus resources.

Recreational programs offer residents the opportunity for personal interaction as well as the chance to engage in team play. Such programs allow residents to use their skills and talents in healthy competition, while at the same time allowing them to "let off steam," thus reducing stress. Recreational programs can include: intramurals, tournaments, canoe trips, ski trips, picnics, races, triathalons, and new games.

Community service projects offer students two main opportunities: they can engage in philanthropic activities for the campus and/or local community, and they can share their talents with others. Involvement in service projects often heightens students awareness of the needs of others. These programs include blood drives, visiting nursing homes, supporting meals-on-wheels or adopt-a-grandparent projects, participating in campus clean-up and food-collection drives.

Using the above four general programming categories to develop programs should not limit the planner. Some programs can combine more than one category. For example, a Halloween party for handicapped children is an event that is social and recreational because it allows students to interact and play games with the children; is educational/cultural because residents learn how to interact with handicapped persons; and is a community service project because it is a philanthropic activity. A well-balanced calendar that includes a variety of experiences will be the end result of utilizing these four basic categories in the planning process.

Programming Resources

Programming can utilize all available human resources, and the RA should consider the campus and community environment that surrounds the student. Anyone is a potential programmer—even the students on each wing or floor. Groups of students living together are the best immediate resource for successful programs. The staff member on the floor is an important catalyst to the process. At the beginning of the year the resident assistant is the one who actively initiates and plans many activities and program ideas. However, this role should gradually shift to that of coordinator of ideas generated by residents as they themselves assume an active leadership role.

Members of the hall council or governing board can also be programming resources. The RA should serve as an advisor to the group. Helping residents organize a hall government that reflects the group's needs and interests is a positive way to develop a strong programming base. When students have input and control over their own environment, their motivation and participation levels are likely to increase. Initially, the RA's role as an advisor will be an active one, offering alternatives and ideas. As student leadership emerges, the role of the advisor will shift toward one of guiding elected/appointed executive officers. The role of the advisor throughout is to help student officers develop and refine their own leadership skills and styles.

Resident assistants can significantly influence programming for both students and staff. Sponsoring and organizing some of the educational programs to augment student social programming is an appropriate role. Programming offers RA's the opportunity to expand their own knowledge base and to develop new skills.

Staff members associated with offices like Greek Life, Student Organizations, and Campus Activities are other sources for programming ideas. Bringing these people or activities into the hall or organizing a group of residents to attend an activity out of the hall are both important ways to help expose a resident to the offerings of the campus.

The student is also a member of a local community by reason of the campus location. The RA can expose students to good program resources and the facilities in the immediate area around the campus. Acquainting students with local organizations, parks and recreation areas and local issues will broaden programming options.

Strategies for Programming

Programming effectively involves the development and implementation of a plan. Having good ideas is not enough. Developing programming strategies will give any activity structure and direction as well as provide a blueprint for the event. Programming strategies include developing a calendar, assessing student needs, and planning, publicizing, and evaluating the program.

Developing a Program Calendar

Two extremely useful calendars to help launch a program plan are a semester/quarter calendar and a specific program timetable. Both are effectively used in conjunction with each other. The semester/quarter calendar gives the planner an overview of significant campus and residence hall events. To begin, develop a rough idea of programs that can be planned over the course of a semester/quarter to dovetail with specific holidays, sports events, campus functions, and exam periods. Balance the activities among social, educational/cultural, recreational, and community service. Consider the timing of events. Utilize holidays as themes for programs. Capitalize on campus events to encourage floor members to attend as a group.

Once the general outline of events is in place, use a program timetable to establish a timeline for specific events. The schedule should include the dates that preparations begin and are to be completed, and dates to begin publicity, to confirm arrangements, and to undertake any follow-up activities.

Assessing Needs

An important aspect of successful programming rests with understanding the interests, needs, and talents of the target population, namely, the residents. Students are more likely to participate in—and attend—programs that appeal to their interests and needs. Such information is readily available. To assess students' needs and generate ideas, use interest inventories/surveys, personal contacts, talking with student leaders, observing, listening and brainstorming.

Interest inventories/surveys can provide useful information about each resident. You can construct the survey not only to allow the student to indicate an interest in participating in a given program but also to indicate interest in organizing and leading the activity. Compiling information from residents gives you a useful profile of the group's collective interests. This data is helpful in calendaring activities for the group.

Individual contact with residents to discuss ideas and solicit opinions is an accurate way to check out their level of interest in a given topic. Asking students directly what programs they would enjoy and would be willing to help plan is a more personal method of getting students involved.

Floor leaders and hall officers are an important group of students to involve in assessing interests. Utilizing the ideas of student leaders and delegating the responsibility to recruit volunteers to implement the program will help ensure greater participation from the group. Students will be more inclined to support programs they help create.

Observation is another useful assessment tool. Being aware of what residents enjoy doing, observing their activities, noting their concerns, and identifying the issues and events that affect their lives can help you to assess quite accurately the kinds of programs that will appeal to students. Noticing which students spend time together can help you learn who would effectively work together in planning an event.

Listening to dinner conversations and "rap sessions" can tell you a great deal about the issues that concern and interest students. Visiting students in their rooms can provide insight into the issues that excite, bore, and concern residents. The RA needs to be aware of the issues that the residents want to know more about and to program activities accordingly.

Brainstorming is a useful technique for gathering program ideas that have the potential to involve all the members of a floor/hall. In this type of session, every resident has the opportunity to contribute ideas, no matter how bizarre. Every suggestion is listed, and no idea is criticized. Brainstorming encourages new ideas and includes the ideas of people who rarely speak up or get involved. After the ideas are generated, the list is narrowed down. Items are prioritized, according to the interests of the group as well as what the group can reasonably accomplish, given costs, people power, and time constraints. When an idea is chosen, develop a plan that includes a specific timeline for the event and fits into the semester/quarter calendar of events.

Planning the Program

A well thought-out program is much more likely to be successful than a last minute effort. Planning ahead is essential. Three phases are important as a program plan is developed: preparation before the program, arrangements during the program, and follow-up after the program.

The preparation before a program should include formulating ideas and establishing goals. Knowing the goals of a program helps give the planners a focus. Utilize the residents in all planning stages of the event. Appointing a resident planning committee will guarantee more support and participation in the event. One of the committee's first tasks is to avoid possible conflicts by checking the campus and hall program calendars. Identify where the event will be held, and reserve the space. Set the date and time for the event. Determine budgetary needs and constraints and prepare a budget before the specific plan gets underway. Understanding the financial parameters for the event will help planners use the budget wisely.

The planners should contact resource people for the program well in advance of the event. Making arrangements to meet the needs of the resource people, including food, lodging, honorarium, and special equipment requirements is an important next step. Planning a publicity schedule and confirming all arrangements at least two days prior to the event concludes the preparation phase of the program. By that time, there should be a specific timetable for the event, one that will incorporate all the preparations necessary to carry out the program.

Arrangements for the program itself are as important as the advanced preparations. Planners should arrive early to set up any equipment and finalize last minute details, making certain that the facility is set up properly and that all the equipment is in working order. Student hosts should arrive well in advance of any invited guests to greet the presenters and the participants. The presenters should be introduced to the audience. The participants need to feel welcome and comfortable.

Program planning does not end when the event is over. Follow-up is very important. Return any equipment that was used promptly. Review the budget, to make certain that all the bills are paid. Clear away the publicity from bulletin boards or walls. A review of the participants' evaluations of the program must be completed. The planning committee should then evaluate the program's effectiveness. Send thank you notes to everyone who assisted with any of the arrangements, as well as to the resource people involved in the actual program. Recognizing the efforts of all the people responsible for arranging the program is a good way to gain support for future programs. Consideration should be given to any follow-up programs that might grow out of the original presentation.

Publicizing the Program

A well-planned program can turn into a disaster without good publicity. Remember, if no one knows, no one goes. . . . Display clearly on posters and other advertising materials the following basic information:

- who: name of the sponsoring group,
- what: name of the event using a catchy but descriptive title,
- when: day, date, and time, and
- where: location of the event.

All members of the sponsoring group need to be aware of the basic information concerning the event. Well informed group members often provide the best publicity.

A publicity campaign needs to be well planned. Start early by circulating "teasers" that will pique the curiosity of potential participants and stimulate discussions about the event. Getting students to talk about an event is an effective form of publicity in and of itself. The hall or floor should be saturated with a publicity "blitz" right before the event to underscore its importance. Advance publicity also lets students make plans to attend. Publicity that is haphazard and that does not gain the students' attention will result in poor attendance.

The information included in any publicity material needs to be clear and simple. Use creative, funny ideas that will catch students' attention. Catchy phrases, unusual logos, and graphics with splashes of color will have special appeal. Consider a variety of advertising vehicles, such as posters, flyers, table tents, and door hangers. Choose a combination that will be appropriate for the event. Where you display the advertising is also very important. Using table tents in the cafeteria can be very effective. Using posters on bulletin boards and in public areas can publicize the event not only to residents but to visitors as well. Door hangers can be useful to not only publicize the event but can promote an idea that reflects the goal of the event.

For broader publicity, use media such as radio and television. Announcements over a public address system can reach students quickly. Ads and personals in the campus newspaper can be effective throughout all phases of the publicity campaign. Personalizing publicity with individual invitations is an effective technique to gain support. Balloons and buttons that students enjoy collecting are effective promotional items. Publicity that looks exciting and upbeat will attract attention. Students are more likely to respond with interest. In effect, the publicity sets the tone for the event.

Evaluating the Program

An important step in developing and implementing a program is evaluation, especially for use in future planning. Participants as well as program planners need to evaluate each event. Each person attending a program should be given the opportunity to give feedback to the presentors and planners. A written evaluation form with a check list or short answer format is a useful tool to assess whether the program met the students' needs and whether the participants consider it a success. Asking for feedback is also a way to involve the participants and the audience members in future program planning.

When reviewing the program evaluations, consider the factors that contributed to the program's success or failure. Determine what worked well and what should be refined. This review will net valuable information for planning the next program. Assessing needs, successes, and failures is not the *final* step in the program planning process; it is the *first* step in planning the *next* successful program. One program often stimulates new and creative ideas for another. Evaluation is a needs assessment tool that can start the program planning process all over again.

Programming for Cultural Diversity

Programming plays an important role in fostering a sense of community and providing residents with learning opportunities. A community needs to be responsive to the individuality of all its members. Programming can be an important tool for creating a climate where residents learn to accept and respect individual differences among the members in their community.

Diversity surrounds a student on any campus, whether the institution is public, private, sectarian, non-sectarian, predominantly white or non-white. Through programming, you can expose students to new ideas and information about the diversity that exists in their environment. Each student is a reflection of his or her own heritage and therefore, represents some aspect of cultural diversity. Capitalizing on the resources and the talents inherent in students' diverse interests can encourage a meaningful exchange in a supportive environment. Learning more about that diversity can be the basis for some exciting program planning.

Three fundamental categories when programming for cultural diversity are race, religion, and ethnicity. Do not limit programming for cultural diversity to specific topics identified as minority issues. Instead, plan popular programming topics, such as personal grooming and male/female relationships, that appeal to the interests of both white and non-white audiences. For example, a workshop planned to explore male/female relationships should not only include the opportunity to explore the role of males and females in general, but also the role of the black, brown, Asian, and Hispanic male and female relationships in society. Figure 1 presents possible topics that can expose residents to the diversity all around them.

Effective program planning for cultural diversity considers both specific issues related to cultural diversity and popular topics of general interest seen from culturally diverse perspective. Residents can more readily learn mutual respect and understanding in a community where all members have a sense of belonging. This approach can enhance the sense of community.

Programs That Include Alcohol

Programs that include alcohol involve careful planning and the acceptance of responsibility and liability. You must be realistic about alcohol's use, acknowledging the consequences of misuse and having information and using it to promote a healthy environment in the residence hall and on the campus.

A successful party must include more elements than coming together to drink. A party should be a social program that offers the participants an enjoyable and rewarding social experience. Planning a party

---

Racial Diversity

Martin Luther King Day Celebration—I've Got A Dream
National Black History Month
Ebony/Ivory-Dance
Native American Awareness
Asian Awareness
Speak Out on Racism
Current events and their impact on racial relations
Music
Fashion

Religious Diversity

Ethics and Values Week
Awareness of World Religions
Important Celebrations and Holidays
Religions Within the Geographic Regions of the U.S.
Values Clarification
Theological Debate

Ethnic Diversity

International Awareness	Tracing Your Heritage—
International Dinners—Foods Around the World	Geneology
Customs, Celebrations	Literature
Hispanic Awareness	Linguistics/Language
Arts Festival	

Figure 1. Programs for cultural diversity.

where alcohol is served should follow the basic strategies for programming. Additional considerations involve compliance with the college/university policies and federal, state, and local laws governing the use of alcohol. Central to the planning process should be a basic understanding of what it means to be a good host or hostess.

Promoting the idea and value of responsible alcohol usage is essential, as identified by Keller (1985). The chart in Figure 2 provides helpful steps toward developing a plan for responsible use of alcohol. This process includes assessing the environment, identifying the situation, developing a plan of action, and finally evaluating the party's success or failure to prepare for the next program.

1. Plan a party around a central theme.
2. When alcohol is served, require identification and age verification.
3. When alcohol is served and the group includes underage students attending the event, use some method such as a hand stamp to identify the guests that may legally consume alcohol.
4. Provide only one source for dispensing alcohol; select a bartender who uses discretion in controlling the flow of alcohol.
5. Serve food.
6. Serve an alternate beverage that is a viable alternative such as mocktails and canned soda / pop (people sometimes switch from alcohol to non-alcoholic beverages before the party is over).
7. Serve beverages in reasonably sized containers.
8. Set a limit on the quantity of alcohol available to avoid overbuying and over-serving.
9. Stop serving alcohol about an hour before the party is scheduled to end.
10. Be aware if a guest has become intoxicated and take responsibility to see that this guest gets home safely. Do not let this person drive.
11. Advertise the party in good taste, emphasizing the theme, not the alcohol, as the publicity's focal point.
12. The party should be a social activity where alcohol is served as a refreshment rather than alcohol being the essential ingredient for the function's success.

Figure 2. Some programming guidelines or programs that include alcohol.

A Thematic Approach to Programming in a Residence Hall

In one thematic approach to programming, members of a staff decide at the beginning of the academic year to coordinate programming efforts that will challenge the residents, enhance their development, and provide a supportive environment at critical points throughout the school year. The target population living in the building is primarily freshmen and sophomores. The program concentrates on basic problems and issues related to learning about the university community and adjusting to a new environment. Goals for the program are based on intentional planning and development, as well as on the known concerns and needs of freshmen and sophomore residents. The theme they choose—"The Residence Hall Challenge . . . WE DARE YOU"—accurately reflects the goals and communicates a program message. The goals and theme set the stage for a year full of DARES!!! Their basic plan is set out in Figure 3.

Residents are challenged to get involved and to find their special place in the university setting. Attending hall activities as well as campus-wide activities is part of this challenge.

The first DARE that residents can accept takes place on the first weekend of the academic year (Labor Day Weekend). Many residents remain on campus. Publicity states "DARE to be there . . . Why not?"

The first football game of the season is an exciting way to promote school spirit and develop allegiance to the campus.

October: DARE TO BE FIT!

Residents are challenged to create a physically and mentally healthy lifestyle to offset the potentially busy and stressful year to come.

November & December: DARE TO BE AWARE!

During this season of giving, "DARE" promotes student awareness of both individual needs and the needs of others.

January & February: DARE NOT TO DESPAIR!

Because weather can be a depressing factor coupled with the long semester/quarter ahead, this theme stresses indoor "togetherness" and spirit-boosting activities. By this time in the year it is easy to begin to take things for granted, including friends, roommates, hall programs, and the importance of a positive attitude and outlook on life.

March: DARE TO BE A PAIR!

This theme provides students with opportunities to solidify and/or create relationships with members of the opposite sex, roommates, and friends. The importance of these relationships needs to be recognized and appreciated!

April & May: DARE TO BE PREPARED!

As the year comes to an end, the residents are challenged to prepare for the changes they are about to experience. Final exams present stresses and stretch tolerance levels. Leaving the close-knit floor community is stressful and residents anticipate detachment from new-found friends. Seeking summer employment and moving back home brings many more stresses.

Figure 3.

Summary

Programming in a residence hall is applied, intentional student development. The use of a theory or a concept supports and justifies the view that programming is an integral part of the educational process for students. Strategies for programming suggest a systematic process for the activities development and implementation. Programming plays a significant role in residence halls both as a tool that can bring about developmental change in students and as a means to shape the environment of the living unit.

Case Studies and Structured Group Experiences for Educational Programming

Case Study: Chris

Instructions: Read the case study which follows and answer the study questions which follow. After you have answered the study questions, share your answers in small groups with other RAs or in a class discussion. Draw from your own experience as an RA.

Chris is a resident advisor on a floor housing 50 freshmen. Four weeks have gone by since the residence hall opened. Chris begins to think about the freshmen living on the floor. Fall semester seems to be off to a positive start. Orientation is over, and the residents are settling into their own patterns of going to class, going home for the weekend, and hanging out with their friends. While no major problems seem to exist on the floor, the atmosphere is not really exciting. Something seems to be missing. Residents have started to establish their own routines. Some residents have even complained that "there doesn't seem to be anything to do around here." At the first floor meeting, Chris told the residents that any suggestions for activities were welcomed. To get the semester off to a good start, Chris had planned a Saturday night party for the residents two weeks after clases started but not everyone showed up.

A knock on the door interrupts this reflecting. Toni, Jamie, Bobbi, and Lou, four residents, ask if they can talk for a few minutes. Toni begins the discussion by stating, "We were talking at dinner about the floor. Other floors seem to have a lot more going on, a lot more things to do, more activities than our floor. So we decided that the resident advisor needed to do something to make the floor a more fun place to live."

Chris asks the four to explain what they mean. Jamie starts by saying "Over half the floor goes away on the weekends." Bobbi complains, "We don't seem to do anything as a group anymore. The people at the ends of the hall don't see each other. Nobody knows the two black students." Lou adds, "Everyone seems to just live here. Everyone seems to be going off in different directions. It feels so different than it did during orientation when we did things together and had fun. All that closeness at the beginning seems to be lost." Finally, Toni asks Chris, "As the RA, what are you going to do about this problem?"

Case Study Questions:

1. How can Toni's question be turned into a positive challenge for the RA and the residents? _____

_____

_____

_____

_____

_____

2. How can Toni involve others in the programming process? _____

_____

_____

_____

_____

_____

3. List at least twelve ways Toni can increase interaction among the residents on his/her floor.

    1. _____

    2. _____

    3. _____

    4. _____

    5. _____

    6. _____

    7. _____

    8. _____

    9. _____

  10. _____

  11. _____

  12. _____

Exercise: Educational Programming

Goals: The following exercise is designed to assist resident advisors apply student development theory or the wellness concept in planning and developing programs. The exercise takes the resident advisor through the process of developing an actual program plan that can be utilized in the residence hall.

Group Size: Small groups of about 4–6 students.

Time Required: Part A 45 minutes; Part B 45 minutes, Part C individual assignment

Materials: Newsprint; Magic markers and pencils; Student Development Approach to Programming Worksheet; Wellness Concept in Programming Worksheet; Program Planning Worksheet.

Physical Setting: Room with movable chairs and a chalkboard.

Process:

The exercise is divided into three parts. *Part A* is carried out in small groups with each group developing a year long program plan. *Part B* involves assembling the small groups into one large group with each small group making a presentation. *Part C* is carried out by each individual participant.

A: In a small group, develop a year-long program plan for a residence hall. For each month identify at least one program in each of the four program categories: social, educational/cultural, recreational, and community service.

1. Select one of the following as the basis for developing a year-long program plan, using as a guide one of the appropriate worksheets that accompanies this exercise:
   a. Student Development Theory
   b. Wellness Concept
2. Determine the target population for the program plan—upperclass/freshmen/all classes.
3. Decide the type of hall to use the program plan—single sexed/coed.
4. Develop a theme for the year.
5. Outline program topics for each month that will carry out this theme.
6. List the theme and the program suggestions for each month on newsprint.

B: After each group has completed Part A, the small groups will assemble into one large group.

1. Program plans completed by each group will be displayed.
2. Each group will be allotted time to briefly describe the program plan to everyone.

C: After each group has had the opportunity to present its program plan to everyone, each person will work individually to develop, in detail, a plan for one program using the Program Planning Worksheet.

Wellness Concept in Programming Worksheet

Dimension	Program Suggestions
Physiological	
Spiritual	
Intellectual	
Emotional Health	
Social	
Occupational	
Environmental	
Nutritional	

Student Development Approach to Programming

Vector	Program Suggestions
Achieving Competence	
Intellectual	
Physical	
Interpersonal	
Managing Emotions	
Developing Autonomy	
Establishing Identity	
Freeing Interpersonal Relationships	
Developing Purpose	
Developing Integrity	

Program Planning Checklist

A. *Before the program:*
  1. Formulate ideas; set goals
  2. Utilize the residents; appoint a committee
  3. Check campus and hall program calendars for possible conflict
  4. Identify a location and reserve the space
  5. Set the date and time
  6. Budget the cost of the program
  7. Contact resource people
  8. Plan program calendar
  9. Make arrangements for accommodating the needs of the guests/presentor/speaker (food, lodging, honorarium)
  10. Make arrangements for equipment (recreational or audio visual)
  11. Plan publicity schedule
  12. Confirm *all* arrangements one or two days prior to program

B. *During the Program:*
  1. Arrive early, set up, finalize details
  2. Make certain that the room is well lighted and ventilated
  3. Greet presentors, special guests
  4. Introduce presentors
  5. Make certain participants feel welcome and comfortable

C. *After the Program:*
  1. Return any equipment
  2. Pay bills
  3. Remove publicity from walls/bulletin boards
  4. Evaluate the program
  5. Send thank you notes to speaker/presentor as well as to all students who helped
  6. Consider follow-up programs
  7. Congratulate yourself on a job well done

Program Planning Worksheet

Program:

Objective:

Time:

Date:

Estimated Cost:

Arrangements	Type	Responsible Person	Completion Date
A. Speaker/Entertainment			
Food Arrangements			
Equipment			
Publicity			
Confirmation of Arrangements			

Arrangements	Type	Responsible Person	Completion Date
B. Program Set-Up			
C. Program Follow-Up			

CHAPTER 8

The Resident Assistant and Discipline

Dr. Alexandar Smith
Dennison University

The responsibility to enforce college rules and regulations and residence hall policies is a challenging and often difficult aspect of the resident assistant's responsibility. Enforcing policies, challenging or confronting residents about their behavior, interceding in problem situations, referring students, resolving interpersonal disputes, supporting positive behavior and discouraging antisocial behavior, and taking other actions designed to ensure that student rights are respected and a community of residents is supported are all tasks important to the RA's responsibility.

How you, as the resident assistant, carry out your responsibility for floor or building discipline can be directly linked to your effectiveness and success and to the degree of respect that others have for you. A discipline problem that is ignored, left unresolved, or one that is not responded to appropriately can frustrate your best intentions, cause morale problems on the floor, block the accomplishment of goals, disrupt an entire floor, and in other ways affect the quality of the experience for all floor members, including the residence hall staff. Further, a failure to set and enforce limits creates an environment that may be chaotic and certainly does not support the development and maturation of the residents on that floor or in that building.

This chapter reviews the institutional characteristics, traditions, and practices that can affect how you may be expected to handle discipline problems, explores reasons why discipline problems occur, and provides suggestions about how to respond to typical disciplinary problems. At the outset, you should understand that there is usually not one best approach or response to a discipline problem—in fact, there are often several. Understanding the institution's discipline system and the philosophy or educational principles behind that system will help you select the most appropriate response to a given problem. An optimal response is one that: 1) stops the problem behavior; 2) promotes constructive behavior change; 3) helps the individual involved in the incident to perceive or understand the consequences of his or her behavior; 4) protects the welfare of other residents; 5) promotes more mature behavior; and 6) is consistent with the objectives and practices of the college or university residence hall program. Although it may not be possible to meet all of these objectives when handling a disciplinary situation, your response and action should be directed toward meeting as many as possible.

Institutional Expectations and Traditions

Institutions differ in their expectations for resident assistants, in some of their policies and regulations, and in the structure of their discipline system. The type of residence hall and its traditions and reputation will also affect how you are expected to manage or respond to discipline problems. A male residence hall may have a different set of disciplinary issues or problems from a women's hall, for example. A building of upperclass students will differ in character and tone from a building that houses only freshmen, and as a result, the frequency and types of disciplinary problems may differ between them.

Institutions also differ in educational philosophy, mission, organization, and in how the discipline system is administered. These differences will be reflected in policies, social regulations, and in practice. Differences are also reflected by the range of residential environments available for students. These include buildings of different sizes and structure, interest houses or halls, program-oriented buildings, or a building with a unique history and tradition. Each environmental difference, whether at the institutional level or at the building level, will have an influence on your role as an RA and possibly on your disciplinary responsibility. Whether you are a new RA or a returning RA moving to a new building, you will have to determine what environmental influences and expectations influence how the discipline is to be handled. The later activity "Exercise: Institutional Characteristics and Disciplinary Expectations" will help you assess those institutional characteristics and expectations. Your appointment letter, a position description, staff manual, discussions with experienced or former RAs, and training workshops and classes—all these are important sources of information that can help answer these questions.

Your responsibility as an RA in disciplinary situations is determined by each institution's procedures and educational philosophy. In some settings, the RA may have only programming and advising responsibility and is expected only to report problems but has no other disciplinary responsibility. In another setting, the RA may have the authority to administer discipline sanctions such as fines or to impose restrictions, require restitution, or to take other action. Other typical RA disciplinary responsibilities can include investigation and preparation of incident reports for the university or college discipline or judicial office, for the building supervisor, or for the campus judicial board. An RA may be expected to advise or convene hall or building judicial councils, serve as a member of a judicial board, and help monitor judicial sanctions that have been imposed on residents. He or she may be asked to appear as a witness in judicial hearings and conduct informal judicial conferences. A clear understanding of your responsibility and authority for discipline is very important. Can you identify the key disciplinary responsibilities that you will have? Again, the exercise "Institutional Characteristics and Disciplinary Responsibility" will help you.

Disciplinary Problems—When and Why Do They Occur?

A discipline situation usually results whenever a student's or student group's behavior violates a rule, policy, or procedure; whenever a person's behavior disrupts or infringes on the rights of others; or whenever there is some loss or damage to personal or institutional property. Why do some individuals or particular living units seem to be involved in problem behavior or have a higher incidence of disciplinary problems than others? To fully and completely answer that question is beyond the scope of this chapter, but a general understanding of factors that influence the frequency or likelihood of a disciplinary problem can help you intervene or possibly prevent discipline situations from occurring.

One helpful model for understanding student behavior is to think of behavior as a function of the person and the environment. The interaction or transaction between environmental and individual characteristics determines the resulting behavior.

Environmental Factors

Institutional Policies: One important set of environmental variables is institutional or residence hall policies and regulations. What is considered a policy in one institutional setting may not be a policy in another institution. For example, the policies regarding the possession or use of alcohol in student rooms may differ from one institution to another. On one campus drinking a beer in the privacy of one's room may violate that institution's policy, but in another institution it may not. Generally speaking, the more numerous the institutional policies and regulations for student conduct, the more numerous the disciplinary violations.

Structure and Organization of the Residence Hall: Such factors as building size and design, proximity to other buildings, and number and type of residents are all environmental factors that contribute to discipline problems. Other factors such as gender, whether the building is an upperclass or freshman hall, or whether it is a special interest or general purpose hall may also influence the frequency of disciplinary problems you may encounter as the RA.

Group Norms: Sociologists who study groups believe that social or group norms influence individual behavior. Where the group norms in a particular living unit include some forms of antisocial behavior, for example, discipline problems may occur more frequently.

Institutional Characteristics: General institutional characteristics (such as whether the institution is public or private, coed or single sex; whether it has a religious affiliation; its geographical location; and mission) affect the character of the student body and the institutional values projected through its policies and practices. Those institutional characteristics shape the environment and influence disciplinary situations.

Other Characteristics: Other environmental conditions at your institution or in your living unit may have an important influence as well. Identifying and learning about them can help you in carrying out your disciplinary responsibilities (i.e., structure of campus social life and proximity to other social centers such as campus pub, college union, or fraternity houses; student attitudes toward administration; and frequency of campus programming).

Individual Differences

In addition to environmental characteristics, there are a wide range of individual differences and characteristics that determine behavior. Some are obvious, such as age, family background, socioeconomic background and experience, and gender. Other important individual characteristics include the following:

Levels or Stage of Maturation and Development: Psychologists (Astin, 1977; Chickering, 1971 and 1974; Erickson, 1968; and Perry, 1970) have documented the fact that there are different stages of socioemotional and cognitive development. Individuals progress through a sequence of stages at different rates. Chickering, for example, described seven vectors of development; one important vector was "managing emotions." A person who has not learned to manage his or her emotions effectively may have a greater potential to be involved in a discipline problem, such as verbal or physical harassment.

Level of Moral Judgment or Moral Maturity: Kohlberg, 1971 and 1975; Rest, 1974; Smith, 1978; and Turiel, 1974, have described different levels of moral judgment, moral reasoning, and moral maturity. Level of moral maturity is one important variable associated with moral behavior. Students who demonstrate more principled or a higher level of moral thinking are less likely to be involved in disciplinary problems (Smith, 1978).

Psychological and Personality Factors: Individual temperament or psychological and personality factors reflect important individual differences and behavior. A few students also suffer from major psychological disorders. A serious emotional disorder can contribute to behavior that causes the student to violate a policy or rule and require both a medical and/or counseling response and a disciplinary action.

Substance Abuse and Loss of Control: Surveys of factors contributing to disciplinary problems often note that the use of alcohol or other drugs is associated with discipline incidents such as vandalism, the destruction or defacing of property, and violence. Individuals are affected differently, and sometimes unpredictably, by alcohol or other drugs, but the impact of these substances on individual behavior cannot be denied.

These are just a few examples of individual factors that, when combined with environmental factors, directly determine student behavior. As an RA, you are not expected to be an authority in human behavior and motivation in order to handle disciplinary responsibilities. However, it is important to recognize that student behavior results from a complex set of individual and environmental factors. A discipline problem has both individual and environmental components.

Responding Appropriately to Disciplinary Problems

Response Style

Until they gain experience and confidence, most RAs find confronting or resolving a disciplinary problem to be an uncomfortable experience. You will not know for sure quite what to expect or how other students will respond to you as an RA. Some will challenge or test your authority. As RA, you may be uncertain at first about how to respond. The situation can seem intimidating. Experience will be the best teacher, but there are some basic attitudes and techniques to use that will make the disciplinary encounter less unsettling for you and more productive for all involved.

Stay under control. Because one important objective is to bring a behavior problem under control or to stop disruptive or offensive behavior, how one intervenes is important. If you lose your temper or get too emotionally involved, the problem can escalate. The immature, disruptive, or obnoxious behavior of some students can easily make many people angry, including you. Angry feelings are only natural in such situations, but it is important to keep those feelings under reasonable control. In most situations, a calm and reasoned approach and attitude will be a settling influence. An irritated or angry response will only add to or complicate the problem you hope to resolve.

Use common sense and good judgment. It is impossible to predict what types of disciplinary problems will occur. What is more, there is no textbook answer for every situation. Typically, RAs are selected in part for their maturity, responsibility, and good judgment. These traits and attributes are important guides to disciplinary situations, and there is no substitute for good common sense and judgment.

Avoid or minimize handling discipline in a public arena. One never knows how others will respond to discipline. Most people do not like to have their behavior questioned in public. In a group setting, you are outnumbered and can be put on the defensive or be distracted more easily. It is important to try to create one-on-one situations when imposing or following up on a discipline problem. Whenever possible, use a private setting, such as your room or the other student's room, or staff office, rather than the hallway, lounge, or a room full of students.

Know what is expected of you and from you. Residents will expect you to enforce policies, to know the rules, and to know what to do and how policies are to be enforced. Through training and contact with supervisors, it is very important to understand the limits of responsibility and to know how minor and major disciplinary problems are to be reported and acted upon.

Be flexible. Not every incident may be as it first appears. Discipline problems, as discussed earlier in this chapter, may be more complex than you first believe. Often there exists more than one interpretation or more than one option for a response. Sometimes a more informal rather than a formal approach is best. Sometimes the reverse is true. Be flexible so that you can respond effectively and appropriately to the situation at hand.

Be fair but firm. It is unrealistic to expect that everyone on the floor will like you and be your close friend, just as it is unrealistic to expect that individual students on the floor or in the living unit will like every other floor member. It is far more important that the residents perceive you, the RA, as fair. Fairness means responding to situations in a consistent and even-handed way and not jumping to conclusions or taking sides too quickly. Fairness also means that you will respond to a rule or policy violation by a friend or someone like a fraternity brother or sorority sister in the same way that you would for any other student.

Demonstrate sensitivity and concern for the rights and welfare of others. Both those who may be the victim and those who are about to be punished as a result of a disciplinary violation have rights, needs, and feelings. Expressing concern and sensitivity to individual rights and to the welfare and rights of community members is most important if a climate of respect and mutual consideration is to exist on the floor or in the living unit.

Be assertive, not aggressive. An assertive response is direct, positive, and clear communication about the behavior, problem or issue in question. Assertiveness in a disciplinary situation, as in other interpersonal situations, expresses a self-confidence and a respect for the rights and feelings of others. Assertiveness will help you maintain or gain control of the situation more quickly or easily.

Unlike aggressive responses (*"You jerk, why did you discharge that fire extinguisher?"*), an assertive response is not an attack on the person or persons who may be the source of the disciplinary problem. An assertive response describes or defines the behavior in question and its consequences for others. For example, you could respond to the unruly student who discharged the fire extinguisher by saying, "The fire extinguisher was emptied when it was sprayed down the hallway. Now only one fully charged extinguisher remains, and the safety of all of us on this floor and in this building is affected. The discharge of a fire extinguisher in a non-emergency situation is a major violation because the welfare of others is involved. I will have to report this. Tell me what happened."

Handling the intoxicated student. Many disciplinary problems are created by students who have had too much to drink. Your campus may have specific guidelines to follow for such situations. Attempting to have a rational conversation or to impose a discipline action on someone who has had too much to drink is ineffective. The situation at hand is simply a behavioral-management problem for the moment (or, in the extreme, a medical emergency), and the drunk student, who may be disruptive, needs to be guided to his or her room or escorted off the floor as quickly as possible (or request medical assistance). For this purpose, the student's friends and roommates should be asked to assist. You need to be firm and direct but not argumentative or threatening. The following day is the time to have that follow-up conversation with the student and to challenge or confront the abusive behavior.

The Response Sequence

When a problem situation occurs, there are four suggested steps to follow to address, respond to, and resolve the situation. Those steps involve response, assessment, decision, and action (RADA).

Step 1: Response Respond to the immediate problem behavior, complaint, or emergency. If the problem behavior is excessive noise or disruptive behavior, for example, the first step is to stop that behavior or at least bring it under control. The objective of the response in that situation is to stop the infringement on the rights of other residents. In a more serious situation, such as a fight, which might result in a personal injury, major destruction of property, or perhaps a fire alarm, respond to the immediate medical problem or crisis first.

Step 2: Assessment Once the crisis has been managed or the offensive behavior stopped, assess the situation to determine the cause of the problem. Collect information. Ask questions such as who, what, when, and why. If a possible policy violation or rule infraction occurred, or it is not clear exactly what happened and why, you may need to collect more information. This can involve identifying the names of possible witnesses, interviewing, or collecting witness statements.

Step 3: Decision After the preliminary assessment and information has been collected, it is time to decide whether some disciplinary action or further follow-up, such as a written report or further consultation, is required. Is some action needed, and if so, by whom?

Step 4: Action At this step, a specific action is taken. The action might be preparing a report, making a referral, imposing a fine, or issuing a warning. That action might involve calling Security if more investigation or assistance is needed or if a group of students should be dispersed. It might involve calling the building director or supervisor. It may require further response, assessment, decision, and action.

This four-step process outlined above may occur in either very rapid succession or almost simultaneously if the problem is minor, or it may stretch out over several days if the problem is more complex. It is a sequential process designed to lead to the optimal response objectives outlined at the beginning of this chapter and to help you handle disciplinary problems effectively.

Some Special Challenges

Occasionally, special issues or problems arise that may present a personal challenge or dilemma for you. Perhaps an issue places you in conflict with one of the expectations identified earlier in the chapter. Perhaps it results from job expectations that appear in conflict or difficult to resolve, such as handling both counseling and advising responsibilities and discipline responsibilities.

The RA as role model. Most institutions expect that you will serve as a positive role model for other students. That means that your personal behavior exemplifies high standards and is consistent with behavior expected of other students. You will face a personal dilemma if your behavior on occasion does violate rules and policies. Should such a situation arise, other students may believe that your efforts to enforce the same policy you violated to be hypocritical. If you elect not to enforce the policy, then your behavior will be at odds with the expectations of the hiring unit. As challenging as it may be to serve as a role model for others, it is an important expectation, and it is a responsibility that you should acknowledge and be sensitive to.

A related issue, one which also stems from the role model expectation, is how to handle and enforce policies with which you disagree. In accepting an RA position, it is important that you have a thorough understanding of policies that you are expected to enforce and the expectations that will be placed upon you. You should resolve potential conflicts at the time of hiring or before, but sometimes new policies or revised policies are approved and implemented during the year or after the hiring decision has been made. If that happens and the policy is one in which you strongly disagree or may be unwilling to enforce, then you have one or more decisions to make to resolve this ethical dilemma. One decision might be to accept the policy but work to change it within legitimate institutional decision-making structures. Another decision, after consulting with the staff supervisor, might have to involve resigning from the position. There are other possible decisions, but the important point to remember is the significance of your attitude and behavior for others while fulfilling the responsibilities and expectations of the resident assistant position.

The resident assistant as peer counselor/advisor and person responsible for discipline. Some RAs have a difficult time with the multiple responsibilities assigned to them, particularly when it involves both peer counseling and administering discipline. These two responsibilities in particular should not be perceived as incongruent or conflicting with one another. They are not, unless as you choose to handle or perceive them as such. Although you may have a preference for one of these responsibilities over the other, both counseling and discipline are responses to needs and to problems. Both the peer counseling response and the disciplinary intervention are designed to help influence, change, or modify behavior, and both are important RA intervention strategies and skills. They are intended to meet the needs of floor residents and to develop positive and supportive community norms and behavior on the floor or in the living unit. If, at the beginning of the year, you are clear in communicating to your floor residents that you have both responsibilities in counseling and discipline and are clear when you carry out these responsibilities, the potential for conflict is eliminated. The effective administration of discipline on your floor will create an environment that is supportive and will contribute to the education and development of individual residents.

Other special challenges may arise from your discipline responsibilities. It is often these challenges and related experiences that will be the most educational and maturing aspects of your position. They are challenges which your supervisor and other experienced RAs will be willing to discuss with you and assist you in resolving or meeting the challenge successfully.

Creating Positive Community Values/Norms

The previous sections of this chapter have introduced and illustrated the RA's various discipline responsibilities and have suggested strategies for approaching or resolving disciplinary situations as they occur. The ideal floor or living-unit environment would have very few, if any, disciplinary problems. Community norms and values would reflect and reinforce respect for others, and residents would exercise self-restraint and self-discipline. This is the ideal; this is the objective. It may not be the realistic setting. However, you will find that as an RA you have a significant influence on the development of community norms and expectations and on sustaining them. For this reason, your responsibility for discipline not only involves responding to problem situations but, perhaps more importantly, includes the responsibility for community-building. In this respect, there are several important tasks and activities that can be carried out.

Programming, which is covered in another chapter, is one of the most effective and important steps that you can take to inform and to educate floor residents. Programming related to community responsibility or to one of the causes or issues associated with discipline can be particularly useful and helpful.

Communicating clearly and thoroughly the expectations, important policies, and rules at floor meetings and through other approaches is also very important. Such communication should include not only what the policy is but why the policy exists. Policies and rules are created to address a concern or problem or to protect the rights and welfare of community residents. That communication should also include appropriate statements of expectations and limits, and also of consequences. It has already been pointed out that there may be a range in moral development and maturation level of the floor or living unit members. Communication, for that reason, needs to be framed with those developmental differences and objectives in mind. Communicate often, and communicate at different levels and by different means.

Finally, it is important to develop a sense of commitment and shared responsibility for the quality of community life on the floor or in the building. Everyone has a stake in building an environment that is nurturing rather than destructive, enhancing rather than demeaning, respectful rather than abusive. If all that responsibility rests only on your shoulders as the RA, and if you are the only one who enforces the policies or confronts inappropriate behavior, then the other residents are not accepting their community responsibilities. Once you are off the floor or away for the weekend, there is no standard and there may be frequent violations that occur in your absence. When most residents recognize and accept that they have a stake in maintaining the community atmosphere and are willing to act as their own agents, many more people will be involved in establishing norms and patterns of behavior that are supportive and positive. It is toward this end that you should work to help establish positive community values that will diminish or discourage incidents that could result in either minor or major disciplinary action.

Case Studies and Structured Group Experiences on Student Discipline

Case Studies: Substance Abuse

Instructions: This section consists of four case studies, each of which is followed by several questions. For each case assigned by your instructor, respond to each of the questions in the space provided, or use a separate sheet of paper for your responses to each question. You may then share your answers in small groups or as the basis for a class discussion.

1. A Case of Substance Abuse

Mary, a resident on your floor, appears to be someone who frequently smokes pot in her room, and it is alleged that she may also be using cocaine. Mary's roommate spoke to you earlier in the semester about a roommate change. Although the roommate would not specifically state that Mary's lifestyle and her use of drugs was the principal reason for her request, that was the implication in her discussion with you. You have had one conversation with Mary in which you confronted her with your supervisor, and she denied any use of illegal drugs.

Case Study Questions:

a. Should you confront Mary's roommate and ask her to provide you with a statement regarding Mary's alleged drug use? _____

_____

_____

_____

_____

_____

_____

b. What types of interventions are possible, and what recourses of action are available to you? _____

_____

_____

_____

_____

_____

_____

c. Do you have a right to require Mary to seek counseling and medical attention for her alleged drug-abuse problem? _____

_____

_____

_____

_____

_____

_____

d. What responsibility do you have to keep your professional staff supervisor informed? Should the problem be turned over to this staff person to handle? _____

_____

_____

_____

_____

_____

_____

2. A Case of Illegal Use of Fireworks

Fireworks and bottle rockets from room windows has been a semester-long problem for your building, but it has gotten significantly worse since spring break. On your return to the residence hall one evening, you spot a bottle rocket coming from a third floor window above the main entrance to the residence hall.

You run back to your hall and dash up to the third floor. Several doors to rooms in the general vicinity from which you observed the bottle rocket are open. You check each room. No one is in, but in one room the window is open and the screen is off. You see a bottle rocket on one of the student's desks. You hear laughter coming from a room at the end of the hall. You suspect that those involved in the incident are in there.

Case Study Questions:

a. Should you go immediately to the room from which you heard student voices and, if the residents of the room you suspect to be the location of illegal fireworks are present, confront them about their behavior? _____

_____

_____

_____

_____

_____

b. Since you did not actually see who discharged the fireworks and you can only determine that it was one of two possible rooms, what options are available to you if no one is willing to accept responsibility for the violation? _____

_____

_____

_____

_____

_____

_____

c. Is the presence of an unused bottle rocket in the room and the open window sufficient evidence on which to take disciplinary action if no one admits to discharging the bottle rocket and there are no witnesses? _____

_____

_____

_____

_____

_____

d. If the student you suspect does admit shooting several bottle rockets out of his window that evening, what penalties or discipline actions are appropriate for you to impose or initiate? _____

_____

_____

_____

_____

_____

3. A Case of a False Fire Alarm

Several evenings ago someone pulled the fire alarm on your floor at 2 A.M. The building was evacuated, and there were no suspects. The residents are very annoyed about what happened, and last night Annette, a resident from your coed floor, told you that she thought she knew who was responsible for setting off the false alarm. She says that she heard two residents of your floor talking about the fire alarm. One of them boasted that he had pulled the alarm on his way back to his room from a party on another floor. Annette tells you that she will tell you who she thinks is involved, but she wants to remain anonymous and does not want her name used.

Case Study Questions:

a. Identify several possible responses that the RA can make to Annette. What do you think is the best response to make to her? _____

_____

_____

_____

_____

_____

b. Should you confront the student suspected of the violation based on the information you have but without revealing its source? _____

_____

_____

_____

_____

_____

c. What is your next step if you confront the student suspected of pulling the false fire alarm and that student denies it? _____

_____

_____

_____

_____

_____

4. A Case of Disruptive Behavior

Joe, a resident on your floor, knocks on your door after midnight to complain about a party going on in the room next to his at the other end of the hall. Joe reports that he has knocked on their door twice already this evening and asked them to turn the music down and to hold the noise down. Nothing happened. When you follow Joe down the hall to the problem room, you discover a large party going on and 12 to 15 people (men and women) in that room. You recognize several people from your floor, but most of the people you have never seen before. The group has obviously been partying for a while and is getting very rowdy.

Case Study Questions:

a. Should you attempt to handle the situation yourself or should you call your building supervisor and/or Security? _____

_____

_____

_____

_____

_____

_____

b. If you decide to handle it yourself, what actions would you take to bring the problem of noise and disruptive behavior under control? _____

_____

_____

_____

_____

_____

c. If disciplinary action is appropriate, would you:
   (1) take that action that evening or wait until the next day? _____

_____

_____

_____

_____

   (2) discipline all the student guests who were present or just the regular roommate occupants who live there? (Explain your decision.) _____

_____

_____

_____

_____

_____

_____

_____

Exercise: Institutional Characteristics and Disciplinary Expectations

Goals
1. To help assess institutional characteristics and residence hall environments that influence disciplinary responsibilities.
2. To clarify RA disciplinary responsibilities.

Time Required: 20 to 90 minutes as in-class activity; one to three hours if assigned as out-of-class exercise that involves interviews and additional reading and research.

Group Size: Varied: individual exercise or as class exercise and discussion.

Physical Setting: Normal classroom or seminar setting.

Materials: 1. Copy of Institutional Characteristics and Disciplinary Expectations Worksheet; 2. Pencils for all participants; 3. Optional: position description, staff manual, college handbook, or other college publication that describes discipline system and/or RA responsibilities.

Process:
1. Instructor assigns as a reading the opening pages from Chapter Eight, sections from "The Resident Assistant and Discipline," to include the section "Institutional Expectations and Traditions" and other related reading material (5–10 minutes).
2. Distribute Institutional Characteristics and Disciplinary Expectations Exercise. Participants complete the exercise (15–20 minutes).
3. Instructor conducts a class discussion of institutional expectations and traditions that members believe influence discipline responsibilities (10–15 minutes).
4. Lecturette on RA's disciplinary responsibility. Outside resource persons might be invited to lead, such as campus judiciary officer. Question-and-answer session follows (20–40 minutes).
5. Optional. Various materials related to judicial and disciplinary responsibilities of the RA can be distributed and assigned as pre- or post-exercise reading. Part II of the exercise can be omitted.

Variations
1. Exercise could be used as a review or examination following a presentation and discussion of RA disciplinary responsibility.
2. Exercise could be structured to require all RAs or a smaller group of RAs to interview former staff members, building supervisor, college disciplinary officers, etc., to identify and clarify disciplinary responsibilities. Selected RAs or a smaller group of RAs could be asked to report on what they learned to entire class, to be followed by general class discussion.

Institutional Characteristics and Disciplinary Responsibility Exercise

Instructions: To help you assess and clarify the institutional characteristics and expectations that shape your disciplinary responsibilities, read and answer the following questions. (Your instructor may assign other material or interviews, which should be completed prior to completing this exercise.) Part I of this exercise should be completed in about 20 minutes, and Part II in 5 minutes.

Part I

1. What is the philosophy of residence life at my institution? (Is there one? How is it communicated? Can I articulate it to others?) _____

_____

_____

_____

_____

_____

2. What are my disciplinary responsibilities, and how am I expected to carry them out? _____
_____
_____
_____
_____
_____

3. What disciplinary authority do I have? _____
_____
_____
_____
_____
_____

4. What are the reporting lines (information channels) for disciplinary problems on my floor or in my building? _____
_____
_____
_____
_____
_____

5. How are institutional and residence hall policies communicated to students, and what is my responsibility in that communication process? _____
_____
_____
_____
_____
_____

6. Are there certain patterns or a history of disciplinary problems unique to the building I am assigned to? If so, how does that influence how discipline is to be handled? _____

_____

_____

_____

_____

_____

7. Note any other questions you have about your disciplinary responsibilities: _____

_____

_____

_____

_____

_____

Part II

When you have completed answering the questions above (or following class discussion if your instructor prefers), list the key disciplinary responsibilities that you have or will have as an RA (i.e., investigating, completing discipline reports, issuing fines):

a. _____

b. _____

c. _____

d. _____

e. _____

Do others in your class agree that these are the key responsibilities?
(circle) **Yes   No**

Exercise: Creating Role-Play Experiences

Goals
1. To create a pool of role-play experiences for use in RA workshops and other training experiences.
2. Have class (group) members identify typical disciplinary problems that occur on their campuses.
3. Through the use of individually developed role-play experiences, create in-class or out-of-class opportunities for class or group members to practice confronting discipline situations.

Group Size: Variable

Time Required: 45 to 60 minutes

Physical Setting: Moveable chairs

Materials: 1. Written instructions; 2. Pencil and paper or 4 × 6 note cards

Process:
1. Instructor assigns each individual or two small groups of 2 or 3 students the responsibility to develop one or two role-play situations as an out-of-class or as an in-class assignment.
2. Instructor indicates that each individual's (or group's) role play will be turned in to the instructor and that the instructor may use the role play as an in-class experience.
3. Instructions are given on how to construct a role-playing situation.
4. Instructor selects 3 to 5 of the role plays that represent typical but important discipline situations that the typical RA might be expected to handle.
5. Class (group) members volunteer or are called on to be role-play participants.
6. Role plays are done fishbowl style, with each role play presented in front of class (5–10 minutes for each role play).
7. Class members are asked to give feedback to participants after each role play and to offer other suggestions about how the RA might have handled the situation differently (5–10 minutes).
8. Instructor facilitates class discussion.
9. Another role play is selected and steps 5 through 8 are repeated.

Variations:
1. Instructor could prepare or utilize other role-playing experiences rather than asking class members to design role-play experiences.
2. After each role play has been critiqued, the role playing could be repeated with new participants.
3. Rather than fishbowl each experience in front of the entire class, divide the class into several smaller groups (6 to 8 each) with some members of the group participating while other group members observe. In second role playing, those who participated become observers and vice versa.
4. Rather than a general description and expectations to develop typical role play, the instructions could be modified to provide for role plays that illustrate only a certain type of problem (e.g., alcohol related, relationship violence, or a racial problem).

Instructions: Each class member or small group is expected to prepare two role-playing experiences. Each role play is to represent a fairly typical residence hall violation that an RA might be expected to confront.

Each role play should briefly describe the setting or context in general terms, without a large amount of detail. Role playing should identify between one and three persons plus the RA. Each character should have a brief role card that provides a brief description, orientation, and/or focus to suggest how that role might be carried out.

The description of role playing and each role card is to be legibly printed or typed on a 4 × 6 index card. The card is to be turned in to the instructor according to the instructor's directions.

Exercise: Residence Hall Infractions Worksheets: Examining RA Values and Attitudes Toward Residence Hall Violations

Goals:
1. To reflect and examine personal and group values and attitudes toward disciplinary violations;
2. To experience differences in individual attitudes and values toward disciplinary violations;
3. To explore effects of value judgments and differences in group decision-making;
4. To examine how differences in values and attitudes may give rise to inconsistent enforcement of disciplinary policies and create conflict among staff members.

Group Size: Between six and twelve participants; several groups may be directed simultaneously.

Time Required: 45 to 75 minutes.

Materials: 1. Copy of Residence Hall Infractions Worksheet; 2. Pencils for all participants.

Physical Setting: 1. A room large enough for groups to meet separately; 2. Blackboard and chalk or newsprint, easel, and marking pen.

Process:
1. Instructor distributes Residence Hall Infractions Worksheets to each participant. Participants are told that they have 15 minutes to complete this task.
2. Instructor forms groups of six to twelve persons and reads the instructions for group consensus from the Residence Hall Worksheet. Groups are told they have 20 minutes to complete the task.
3. Instructor monitors the group consensus process. If groups are finished early, the exercise can be stopped. If groups are unable to arrive at consensus, instructor can allot five more minutes to complete group ranking.
4. Optional, depending on time. Instructor assigns Part II of Ranking Experience (10–15 minutes).
5. Instructor asks each group to share its consensus ranking. Rankings are posted on the blackboard or on newsprint.
6. Instructor leads a class discussion on group differences in ranking. The discussion might include such topics as: the effect of personal values on ranking, how differences in ranking among individuals might affect consistency of discipline and policy enforcement within a building, and how value differences affect group decision-making.
7. Instructor asks groups to post or share the assumptions or principles identified in Part II.

Variations:
1. Individuals can be asked to complete Part II before groups are formed.
2. Rather than asking individuals to rank-order according to their individual preference, individual class members can be instructed to rank each item according to how some other person might rank them. For example, class members could be asked to rank these 12 items as they think their supervisor might rank them, or how a group of freshmen or a culturally different group might rank them.
3. Process observers can be assigned to each group to report on how the group handled conflict and group decision-making.

A Residence Hall Infractions Worksheet

PART I: Rank the following residence hall violations according to the importance or seriousness *you* attach to them. Place a (1) in front of the most serious violation, the number (2) before the second most important, etc., under the column marked Individual Ranking.

After members of your group have finished working individually, arrive at a consensus-ranking that each of you can agree to. The group has 20 minutes for this task. Do not choose a formal leader. Try to arrive at your group ranking by consensus rather than by voting or by averaging scores. The group ranking is entered in the column marked Group Ranking.

Individual Ranking	Group Ranking	
_____	_____	A. Breaking glass in the vending machine in the residence hall and stealing the candy.
_____	_____	B. Refusing to evacuate the building when the fire alarm sounds.
_____	_____	C. Opening an unlocked door and entering the room of a person of the opposite sex without authorization.
_____	_____	D. Pulling the fire alarm as a joke on the residents.
_____	_____	E. Getting into an argument and punching a roommate.
_____	_____	F. Blasting the stereo excessively during quiet hours.
_____	_____	G. Removing a chair from the residence hall lounge for personal use in a residence hall room.
_____	_____	H. Verbally harassing and intimidating another student who has reported a violation to the resident assistant.
_____	_____	I. Supplying drugs to other students.
_____	_____	J. Stealing a camera from another student.
_____	_____	K. Discharging bottle rockets from a residence hall window.
_____	_____	L. Furnishing a false ID to a staff member who is enforcing a building policy.

PART II:

When your group has finished its ranking, review the ranked list and identify those assumptions, principles, or criteria that the group used to determine the ranking of seriousness. In other words, why was letter _?_ ranked number 1; why was letter _?_ ranked number 12? (List 4–5 of those assumptions below). You have ten minutes for this task.

1. _____

2. _____

3. _____

4. _____

5. _____

CHAPTER 9

Mediation and Conflict Resolution

Dr. Barbara E. Engram
Hood College

According to an old saying, "If two people agree all the time, one of them is unnecessary." Differences of opinion are inevitable; without them, life would be boring. What is more, conflict can be productive. However, when two people who share a residence hall room have no effective means for resolving their differences, the results can be seriously disruptive for them and, occasionally, for those around them. Residence hall staff are often called to help resolve these snarled relationships.

Generally, students residing in residence halls are between the ages of eighteen and twenty-five, and for many this is their first experience in living away from home. For the first time, they are on their own to manage their affairs and their relationships without parents or other adults to intervene. Many may never have shared a room before. Others have shared a room, but when disputes arose, parents were available to restore peace. At one time, we even provided "parents" in residence halls, but today few colleges or universities employ housemothers. So students must learn to assume responsibility for their relationships and learn to resolve the conflicts that naturally and inevitably occur. Mediation services help students learn to resolve disputes effectively and productively. Such services also help students learn the skills needed to negotiate successfully on their own.

In this chapter, we will first look at definitions for various conflict or dispute resolution procedures, as well as the ways in which models of negotiation differ from each other. Then, a model for negotiations is presented with an example to show its use. The process of mediating, or facilitating, a negotiation is explained, and useful strategies for the mediator are presented. At the end of the chapter are exercises to help you develop your skills.

Conflict Resolution Procedures: Definitions

It is important to distinguish among negotiation, mediation, and arbitration, all of which are procedures used in resolving disputes or developing agreements where no dispute has arisen. In negotiation, two (or more) parties interact with each other to reach an agreement or resolve a dispute. In mediation (or mediated negotiation), an impartial outsider, the mediator, works with the negotiating parties to facilitate the negotiation process. The process itself remains essentially the same, with or without a mediator.

Arbitration is a third approach to dispute resolution in which an impartial outsider, after listening to all parties involved, decides how the dispute is to be resolved. In binding arbitration, the parties to the dispute have agreed to abide by the decision of the arbitrator(s). In working to help roommates find ways to resolve disputes and live together cooperatively, you will operate most often as a mediator. Your role will be that of an impartial outside party who helps the roommates use the negotiation process to resolve their differences.

Roommates may need the assistance of a mediator for a number of reasons. They may lack the skills necessary to negotiate an agreement. College students generally have had only limited experience in negotiating successfully. Or, a mediator may be needed to help roommates who are very emotional; people who are angry, frustrated, or otherwise upset are likely to have a hard time negotiating effectively. Negotiations can also be very difficult when students are dealing with sensitive subjects. In that situation, roommates may welcome the help of an impartial third party.

Conflict Resolution Models

Different models are used in conflict resolution. They draw from different fields and are used in different situations. Dispute resolution models are applied in international relations, labor-management contract negotiations, landlord-tenant disputes, divorce settlements and custody matters, and, most recently, in helping college roommates resolve disputes. Several features distinguish different models of negotiation. For example, whom do the negotiators represent? In international relations or labor-management negotiations, the negotiators represent large constituencies. In divorce mediation, wives and husbands are speaking directly for themselves. College roommates, too, are speaking directly in their own behalf.

Dispute resolution procedures can also vary in the extent to which they are adversarial/competitive or cooperative. Adversarial or competitive procedures operate on a "win-lose" basis; what one side wins is lost by the other side. This can produce agreements that are hard to enforce because they are not supported by the losing side. On the other hand, a cooperative situation more closely resembles teamwork; negotiators are joined in a problem-solving effort. They operate on a win-win basis; their goal is an agreement in which each party wins. A negotiation may switch from a competitive mode to a cooperative one, or vice versa. For example, a husband and wife may be adversarial in negotiating a property settlement but switch to a cooperative mode in arriving at an agreement on the custody of their children. In mediating disputes between college roommates, you may often be required to use all your skills to shift the disputants to a cooperative mode as they work toward an agreement.

Models used in dispute resolution may differ in the relative importance assigned to various goals or sub-goals. All dispute resolution procedures work toward producing an agreement, a settlement, a solution, or a contract. And, regardless of which model one uses, some learning takes place; participants know more when they finish than when they began. But the relative emphasis placed on learning skills varies. In some models, skills learning is incidental; in others, it assumes a more central role, becoming an important secondary goal. The latter is the case in the model presented here.

The Negotiation Process

As a mediator, your goal is to facilitate the process of negotiation between the roommates. Your skill as a mediator is grounded in your understanding of the negotiation process. One useful way to conceptualize negotiation is to see it as a three-stage process that is both cumulative and sequential. The process is cumulative in that each step builds upon previous ones; step two, for example, cannot be successfully completed unless step one was successfully completed. The process is sequential in that the steps must occur in a specific order. The three stages that comprise the negotiation process are outlined below.

Stage 1: Presenting Positions and Establishing Understanding

The goal of Stage 1 is to identify and understand the issue or problem. This may be relatively easy or very difficult. The event that brings people to negotiation may be straightforward. But it is also true that people often delay confronting a problem, so by the time negotiations begin they may be angry and impatient. One or both parties may have accumulated a list of offenses committed by the other, and what may have started out as a simple issue has grown complicated. Sometimes, people come to negotiation without a full and clear understanding of their own position and feelings. People who are particularly angry, frustrated, resentful, or upset may not be willing to listen to the other person's point of view.

In order to complete step one successfully, these problems must be resolved. Negotiators need to understand each other's position and feelings as well as their own. It is important to separate *understanding* the other person's point of view from *agreeing* with it; understanding is all that is needed at this point. A useful skill for accomplishing mutual understanding is active listening. (You may already be familiar with this skill, which is sometimes referred to as empathic listening; see Chapter 5.) Each person's position or point of view is presented in turn. The other person listens, and by accurately restating the position demonstrates his or her understanding of the speaker.

For example, one roommate might explain, "Look, when your friends come by to meet you to go to breakfast, they wake me up. It's really a pain when they come in the room talking when I want another half hour of sleep." The other roommate paraphrases, "My friends talking in the room when you're trying to sleep in the morning really annoys you." Notice that the paraphrase is short, and contains the important information in the speaker's statement.

Stage 2: Generating Solutions

When the issues have been presented and understood by the negotiating parties, they are ready to start the process of developing ideas that may be the basis for possible agreements. It is important to foster creativity here; the goal is to develop a number of possible solutions. At this point, attempting to find the one "best" solution is premature.

Remember, the overall goal is a mutually satisfying agreement. More energy and time may be needed to develop such an agreement, but there will be few problems in enforcing it. Solutions that are agreed to under duress, pressure, or to "keep the peace" seldom work. All too often the person who has given in to an agreement (or been pushed into it) begins to resent both the agreement and the other negotiator. This resentment may be expressed in covert or overt efforts to sabotage the agreement. For example, suppose a student agrees to late night parties and loud music in the room. The student was really opposed to these things but feared being considered unsociable. The student can vent resentment at the agreement by making a lot of noise in the morning when others are trying to sleep, by making negative comments about the roommate, or by being a "wet blanket" during the parties. Using imagination helps the parties find arrangements that appeal to both.

Stage 3: Developing the Specifics and Writing the Contract

At this stage, the negotiators work to finalize the specific details of the agreement. The goal is to produce a concise document, a written contract that both parties sign. Signing a contract serves to reinforce the commitment that comes from the development, in Stage Two, of a solution satisfying to all parties. A written contract also serves as a reminder of the details of the agreement. The contract contains a description of what each roommate agrees to do (or not to do). At times, other information, such as the date at which a trial agreement will be reviewed, may be included.

Suppose two students have reached the last stage of negotiation. The problem concerns one playing the stereo while the other is trying to study. The first might suggest, "Okay, I'll be more quiet while you're studying." That's certainly a friendly offer, but stated in that way it is too vague. Later, arguments could arise over whether this roommate is really being "quieter." Contrast that with the clear concise statement, "I agree to turn the volume on my stereo no higher than '4' on the dial while you are studying."

Sample Negotiation

Let's look at a negotiation between two roommates, Chris and Pat. A situation has come up and Chris, who is really angry, decides it's time to confront Pat.

Stage 1: Presenting Positions and Establishing Understanding

Chris, who is the "offended party," has initiated the negotiation and would probably speak first.

Chris: Pat, I get really irritated when you borrow my clothes without asking me. Last night when I was getting dressed to go out, I couldn't find my new blue sweater. It wasn't where I put it in my dresser. I looked all over and finally found it in your dirty laundry basket. So I had to change and was late. We missed the first part of the movie!

Pat: (demonstrates understanding of what Chris has said by paraphrasing) Umm . . . okay . . . so you got really mad when you couldn't find your sweater and then couldn't wear it because I had worn it already. My not telling you I was going to wear it really bothered you.

Chris: (adds a little more information) Yeah. Look, I don't want to be a grouch. It's just that in my family we never wore each other's clothes, and I'm just not used to it.

Pat: So this is a new situation to you, and you don't like it.

Chris: Yeah, that's about it. I'll listen now if you want to tell me your side of it.

Pat: Okay. Well, first off, I wouldn't have done it if I thought it was going to bother you. In my family we were always borrowing each other's stuff, and nobody cared about it as long as you cleaned what you used. That's why I had it in the laundry basket.

Chris: (in turn, demonstrating understanding) So from your point of view, you were just doing something which was usual in your family. You didn't think it would bother me.

Pat: Yeah. That's right.

COMMENTARY: Notice that each person shows understanding of the other by rephrasing what has been said. The person presenting a position is the one who decides whether the rephrasing is accurate. After the rephrasing, the speaker can add more information, correct errors, or, if satisfied, yield the floor to the other person. Neither is required to agree with the other's point of view.

Since both Chris and Pat have indicated that the paraphrases are accurate, they are ready to move on to Stage Two of the negotiation process, where they start generating ideas for possible agreements.

Stage 2: Generating Solutions

Pat: Well, I could just not ever borrow anything of yours.

Chris: Or, I think it might be okay, if you would let me know beforehand.

Pat: I'm willing to be responsible for cleaning anything I borrow.

Chris: Okay. You know, I've been thinking about it, and actually, there are only a few things I really don't feel comfortable lending. I'm not so much worried about the other stuff.

COMMENTARY: Chris and Pat have generated a number of different approaches that would solve the problem. They are ready to start developing the final agreement. They may choose one of the ideas or combine several. If either of them is uncomfortable with an idea, it is not used. Remember, to be workable, the final agreement must be supported by both parties.

Stage 3: Developing the Specifics and Writing the Contract

Chris: Suppose I tell you which things I don't want to lend. Then if you use the other things, it's okay with me.

Pat: That sounds fine. It seems fair to me that I agree to clean anything I use. I'm also willing to ask you, or let you know, before I use anything. I could let you know the day before.

Chris: Okay, that sounds fine to me.

COMMENTARY: At this point, the two roommates have a fairly specific contract, which details what each will do. Writing the agreement in contract form and signing it, formalizes their commitment to abide by it.

Any agreement represents the best plan the parties can make at that moment. Remember that in negotiating, people are essentially guessing about what will be the best course of action in the future, so all contracts are estimates, subject to change if conditions warrant. The first exercise, at the end of the chapter, will help you develop your skills in negotiating.

Mediating: Facilitating Negotiations

To mediate successfully you must perform a number of functions. You must establish and maintain an atmosphere that supports the negotiation process. You use your familiarity with the negotiation process to recognize when it is not functioning smoothly and use various skills and strategies to help bring it to a successful conclusion.

The Supportive Setting

People can and do negotiate when they are not experiencing a problem; indeed, it can be a very effective way to avoid problems. But most often you will be mediating a negotiation initiated to resolve a dispute. The students involved are likely to be upset, angry, or resentful. They may doubt that the negotiation process, even with the help of a mediator, will work.

Mediation should take place in a setting that insures privacy and freedom from disruptions and distractions. Participants should be as comfortable as possible. You may want to set up ground rules about such behaviors as smoking. Some mediators provide each participant with pen and paper for taking notes.

Set up a specific time and place for the session. Decide when the session will start and end. Some people prefer an open-ended session; they continue until an agreement is reached. Others prefer a specific session length, such as an hour or 90 minutes, and schedule additional sessions if negotiations have not been completed within that time. What probably matters most is that the negotiating parties know beforehand which approach is being used.

Impartiality

Maintaining an interpersonal atmosphere is also very important. The students involved in the negotiation need to know that they can trust you to be impartial. You may not feel neutral during the mediation sessions. One of the people involved may do or say things that you find offensive or that you believe to be selfish, childish, or objectionable for other reasons. Regardless of your personal feelings, what matters is that your behavior must be impartial at all times.

"Exercise: Behaving Impartially," at the end of this chapter, provides practice in presenting yourself as an impartial mediator.

Expertise

Students participating in negotiations that you mediate will look to you for expertise. Do not confuse this with being perfect! Competence requires that you have skills and work to use them effectively, that you be aware of your strengths and your limitations. When you are able to admit your mistakes or comfortably acknowledge that you do not have all the answers, others can quickly learn to trust your good sense. Until you have gained experience, make notes for yourself, or use an outline of the negotiation process.

Confidentiality

Your reputation for respecting confidentiality can make or break you as a negotiator. Few people are willing to discuss their problems with a person if they believe that what they say will be repeated to others. If your students believe that they can trust you, it will be easy for them to open up and discuss their feelings, experiences, and thoughts. Without an atmosphere conducive to openness, your efforts will be seriously, if not fatally, affected.

Setting Up the Sessions

The interactions you have with participants before the sessions even begin can have a strong effect on the success of your mediation efforts. Often, the process will start when Roommate A comes to you to request your help. At this initial meeting, you will hear that person's side of the story. If you and Roommate A agree that a mediated negotiation is an appropriate intervention, you must next decide how to involve Roommate B. Either you or Roommate A can invite Roommate B to participate in negotiations. If the situation has grown so tense that communications between the two are seriously disrupted, or if Roommate A is timid about inviting Roommate B to negotiate, it may be that you will offer the invitation. Whether you or Roomate A issues the invitation, it should be made clear that Roommate B is entitled to meet with you before negotiations actually begin. This arrangement establishes your impartiality. Roommate B may not even wish to meet beforehand, but the opportunity to do so establishes that you will listen to and be available to both parties.

Beginning the First Session

Your introduction of the first session sets the tone for the mediation, as well as providing information to the participants about what will be done and how. It establishes that this is to be a working session, with rules of operation and goals to be achieved. Explain the mediator's role in the proceedings. Assure participants that you will treat them impartially and that they are free to ask questions whenever they don't understand something.

The more emotional the participants are, the less likely they are to remember what is said, so a brief, general outline of the process is most useful at this point. You can explain additional details as the need arises.

When you are clear in your own mind about what you wish to say in the introduction, you can proceed smoothly and with confidence. The students who have come to you for help will be reassured that you know what you are doing. A rambling, unorganized introduction, on the other hand, creates an impression of incompetence that contributes nothing to the development of trust in the mediator. Use "Exercise: Introducing the Session," at the end of the chapter, to develop your skill in introducing the first session.

Strategies for Facilitating Negotiations

Remember that as a mediator you will be working with people who, because of emotions, lack of negotiating skills, interaction styles, or other factors, need your help to negotiate. Under the circumstances, do not expect things to proceed smoothly. This section presents strategies you can use to facilitate the negotiation process, to prevent problems, and to unsnarl some that do develop. You will not need to use them all in any given negotiation, but each will probably prove useful sooner or later.

Many of these strategies involve "correcting" people, getting them to stop what they are doing, or to do it differently. You must exercise skill and sensitivity to do this without causing the speaker to "lose face." A person who feels belittled, embarrassed, or humiliated by being corrected or who feels you have been judgmental or chastising will quickly lose any interest in cooperating in the negotiation process. One way to avoid this pitfall is to offer suggestions for a better way to do something without making comments about how it was done originally. Whenever you intervene to help negotiators change their approach, be sure to use your skills in expressing yourself in neutral language. "Exercise: Using Neutral Language" provides practice in using neutral language.

Prompt and Fade

This strategy helps people through a process new to them. For example, when explaining their position, many people have difficulty using neutral language. A prompt gives a specific structured approach that helps them to express themselves. To use a prompt, you might instruct the speaker to use the format, "When you . . . , I feel . . ." in order to express a complaint neutrally. If a roommate seems unable to use neutral expressions, even with a prompt, you can rephrase what was said and request the roommate to use that wording. Suppose one of the roommates, even with a prompt, says, "When you turn on your blow dryer in the morning, I feel you are being selfish and inconsiderate." You can say, "It sounds like that makes you angry. Try saying, 'When you turn on your blow dryer in the morning, I get really angry.' " As the roommates begin to use neutral language to express themselves, you "fade out"; gradually stop using the prompts until you can drop them altogether. To practice prompting, use the variation on the exercise on using neutral language.

Interrupting

All of our social training tells us not to interrupt others who are talking. We are taught to be polite and wait our turn. But what if the person who is talking is using non-neutral, inflammatory wording? The longer that person talks, the more upset the listener is likely to become. If your job is to help these people open up lines of communication, it might be best to stop the destructive statements and redirect them. Such an action minimizes the negative impact of non-neutral statements by one of the roommates.

As with other interventions, be sensitive to the speaker's feelings when you use this strategy. Use the interruption to guide the speaker toward more productive forms of expression; do not use this as an opportunity to admonish or chastise the speaker. Often, non-neutral expression occurs when the speaker is emotional. At such times, the speaker may not respond immediately to your gentle efforts to interrupt. Rather than raise your voice or become aggressive, try touching the speaker lightly on the arm. This will draw the speaker's attention and allow you to intervene.

Time-Outs

This technique is useful when you feel you should separate the participants. You may want to talk to one or both individually or feel that a period of time apart is necessary for the roommates to cool off when emotions are escalating. You simply announce that you are calling a time-out. (If you have explained what a time-out is during your introduction, participants will know what is happening; if not, briefly explain when you call it. Keep these points in mind when using time-out:

1. Never meet separately with only one party; have sessions with both. This avoids any misunderstanding about your impartiality.
2. While you are meeting with one of the roommates, give the other one a task. You could ask the roommate to think over the current issue being discussed, to consider points of possible agreement, etc. You do not want that person sitting there, wondering what you and the other person are talking about. Then, when you do meet with the person, be sure to ask about the results of the task you assigned.
3. You can use the private meeting with each person for any number of purposes. You may or may not discuss the same things with both people. It may be that you use the time to let one or the other (or both) ventilate emotions and calm down. You may wish to talk to one roommate about changing a course of action that threatens to sabotage the negotiation process altogether. The time-out allows you to do this privately.
4. Remember that the separate meetings are confidential. The mediator does not disclose anything that was discussed. The roommates may repeat things they said if they wish.

Writing Contracts

The critical issue in writing contracts is describing the agreed-upon behaviors in specific terms. A written contract should contain no vague or generalized language; there should be no judgment calls. Anyone who reads the contract and observes the roommates' behavior should be able to see clearly if the contract is being upheld. A contract that contains vague terms leads easily to the same dispute that made negotiation necessary in the first place.

Suppose, for example, one roommate agreed to "try to be quieter" in the evening. Arguments could easily erupt over whether the roommate was really trying, or whether the results were quieter or not. On the other hand, an agreement that when one roommate goes to bed or begins to study the other will use earphones to listen to the stereo describes the agreed-upon behavior exactly. "Exercise: Writing 'No-Loophole' Contracts" provides practice in mediating a negotiation between roommates from introducing the first session to writing the contract.

Conclusion

Negotiation and mediated negotiation are powerful techniques for problem-solving. They have the important advantage of empowering the disputants; rather than stepping in to control the actions of students in conflict, you can use these techniques to help students exercise control over their own behavior. Each successful negotiation, in addition to solving a specific problem, teaches students that cooperation, respect for others, and assuming responsibility for one's behavior are really worthwhile.

Case Studies and Structured Group Experiences for Mediation and Conflict Resolution

Case Study: Sandi and Julia

Instructions: Read the case study and respond to the questions which follow. First work alone. When you are finished, share your answers with other RAs in small group discussions or as the basis for a class-room discussion.

This dispute occurred about halfway through the fall semester. Both roommates are freshmen; they were assigned as roommates and had not met before arriving at college. They had had no major problems.

The Presenting Problem

Sandi came to the RA late one Sunday evening. She was upset, had clearly been crying, and was still near tears. She explained that when she returned to campus (she had spent the weekend visiting her boy-friend at his university's homecoming) her roommate, Julia, had confronted her angrily. She had accused Sandi of leaving the room "like a pigsty" and had stormed out, commenting that she was tired of cleaning up after Sandi. Sandi was hurt and insulted. As she talked, it became clear that she was also angry, though she denied those feelings.

Sandi wanted the RA to talk to Julia. She was not clear about her goals but essentially wanted the RA to fix the situation. When the RA first suggested that Sandi and Julia negotiate their differences, Sandi rejected the idea. She seemed afraid that Julia would "blow up" again and the situation would be even worse. The RA offered to serve as mediator, and Sandi reluctantly agreed. However, she didn't want to ask Julia to negotiate, so the RA offered to contact her.

The RA briefly explained her role as mediator. She pointed out that, in order to maintain impartiality, she would offer to meet privately with Julia since she was meeting privately with Sandi. She reassured Sandi that what she had said would be held in confidence. Sandi and the RA discussed what the RA would say to Julia in asking her to negotiate the dispute, and Sandi gave her permission for the RA to tell Julia that Sandi had come to see her and was upset about their confrontation on Sunday night. The RA got a list of times that Sandi would be available to meet.

When contacted by the RA, Julia was not surprised that her roommate had been upset but was a little suspicious and asked what Sandi had told the RA about her. The RA explained that what Sandi had said was confidential, as was anything Julia would say to her. She explained that she was available to meet privately with Julia, as she had with Sandi. She explained to Julia that the purpose of the negotiation would be to find a solution that both Sandi and Julia found acceptable. Julia agreed to the negotiation, and the RA scheduled a meeting for two days later. Julia felt she didn't need a separate meeting with the RA before negotiations began. The RA suggested that in the time before the negotiations, Julia think through her complaints and identify any major issues between her and her roommate. When the RA contacted Sandi to inform her of the meeting time, she suggested the same to her.

The Mediated Negotiation Session

When the roommates arrived for the session, the RA made them comfortable and briefly checked to see if any ground rules, such as no smoking, were needed. The roommates were seated in chairs facing each other rather than the mediator; this arrangement helped them talk to each other directly rather than through the mediator. The RA again briefly explained the goal of the negotiation process and her role as mediator. Because Sandi had initiated the process, she was asked to talk first.

Stage 1: Presenting Positions

At first, Sandi said very little. It was clear that she had no idea that her roommate had felt any dissatisfaction with her. She also felt that she did her share of cleaning up in the room. With some prompting from the RA, she did state that she had been upset when Julia yelled at her; she felt Julia could have just told her she was bothered about the room. Julia was more outspoken about her feelings. She listed a number of specific complaints. It seemed clear that Sandi was not a very good housekeeper. However, though Julia was outspoken, she had not been at all assertive in telling Sandi that she was bothered by her failure to help clean their room.

As the students talked to each other, a clearer picture of their relationship emerged. The primary issue focused on their differences around housekeeping. Sandi contributed very little, often left clothes lying around, her dresser drawers partially open, and her bed unmade. She occasionally made some efforts to clean up, but they were not effective. Julia, who had grown up with a working mother, was used to cleaning her own room. She had been upset about the room for some time but had said little about it apart from an occasional hint. Instead, she just cleaned up the room each week. It also became clear that they had different standards for what constituted a "clean" room and what must be done to accomplish that. Each had assumed that her standards were shared by the other.

A second issue had complicated matters. Julia expected her college roommate to be a "best friend" and felt rejected and hurt that Sandi went away every weekend. She ate her meals with Sandi and often invited Sandi to go with her to campus events. Sandi, who was shy and didn't know many people, depended on Julia for this companionship. Sandi, who admired Julia's ability to express herself, had been unaware of Julia's disappointment when she went away for weekends.

Stage 2: Generating Solutions

Julia spontaneously apologized for her "blow up" and acknowledged that she had contributed to the problem by not letting Sandi know when she was upset. At that, Sandi visibly relaxed and became much more talkative. The conversation then focused on ways to handle cleaning the room. Suggestions included dividing up tasks, taking turns cleaning the room, and working together. The standards for a "clean" room were also discussed.

Stage 3: The Contract

Julia suggested that they clean the room together. Sandi agreed and suggested Thursday after dinner for an hour. They made a list of what tasks would be accomplished. Julia also suggested that this time be used to discuss any problems between the roommates, and Sandi agreed. All these items were listed in the contract, which was signed and dated by both roommates. Copies of the contract were made for each roommate.

Case Study Questions:

1. List the techniques the RA used to help mediate the roommate conflict. _____

_____

_____

_____

_____

_____

_____

_____

_____

_____

_____

_____

_____

_____

_____

2. What should the RA do to follow-up? _____

_____

_____

_____

_____

_____

_____

_____

_____

_____

_____

_____

_____

_____

3. What should the RA do if one of the students does not fulfill the contract? _____

_____

_____

_____

_____

_____

_____

_____

_____

_____

_____

_____

4. What are the advantages of mediation over the RA resolving the dispute by taking sides or by arranging for a room change for one or both of the students? _____

_____

_____

_____

_____

_____

_____

_____

_____

_____

_____

_____

_____

5. From your experience as an RA, do you believe there are some situations which lend themselves to mediation better than others, if so what types. _____

_____

_____

_____

_____

_____

_____

_____

_____

_____

_____

_____

_____

_____

Exercise: Negotiation Skills

Goals:

1. To practice the three stages of negotiation
2. To practice observing negotiation, and identifying when the process is not being followed correctly.

Group Size: 4-member groups

Time Required: Approximately 40 minutes to 1 hour

Materials: None

Physical Setting: Table with chairs, or lounge chairs for participants

Process:

1. The facilitator explains the goals of the exercise to group members. The sections of the text that describe the three stages of the negotiation process and the example in the text are used to guide the role play.
2. In each 4-student group, two students will take the roles of the negotiators in Role Play #1 (below). The other two students will serve as observers. Each student negotiator selects and reads one of the role descriptions. (Take a few minutes to develop the character; think about the feelings, attitudes, and point of view that will emerge as you take the role.) The two observers review the stage descriptions in the text.
3. The students role play a negotiation, taking about 15 minutes. The observers interrupt only if the negotiators digress from the procedure described in the text. When the negotiation is complete, the two observers take the roles of negotiators and, using Role Play #2 (below), repeat the process described above.

Role Play #1

Roommate #1: You're a regular jogger and work to maintain your health through proper rest, nutrition, and fitness but you are not a health nut. You don't smoke and disapprove of smoking, but you also feel it's important to be accepting of others. You are willing to express your opinions, but don't want to sound "preachy."

Roommate #2: You smoke, and although you realize it has negative effects, it helps you relax. Your parents disapprove, and from time to time they tend to nag you about it. You had actually cut down quite a bit but you are working on a term paper which isn't going well at all, and you have smoked several cigarettes without even realizing it.

Situation: Roommate #1 walks into the room just as Roommate #2 lights up another cigarette. The window is closed, and the smoke in the room is really noticeable.

Role Play #2

Roommate #1: You are on a scholarship which requires that you maintain a high grade point average. You know you have to keep up with your schoolwork—if you get behind, you're in real trouble. Most of your friends are serious students, though you enjoy a good time as much as the next person.

Your roommate or, more accurately, your roommate's friends, are getting under your skin. They drop in at any time and seem unaware of your efforts to study. They talk freely and loudly, laugh, play the stereo, etc., even when you are pointedly trying to study.

Roommate #2: Though you would agree that an education is important, you don't see any reason to go overboard about it. You have a reputation as being a party person (and are proud of it). You like to have a lot of friends. You moved around a lot as a kid, and it's important to you that you can make friends easily and get along well with people. You think your roommate is being a bit stuffy, though by and large, except for this issue, you get along well together.

Situation: The friends of Roommate #2 have finally left the room. Roommate #1 feels really annoyed and has decided that it's time to talk this situation over and work out some way to prevent it happening again.

Exercise: Behaving Impartially

Goals:
1. To learn to identify behaviors which create the impression of partiality
2. To learn to replace these behaviors with ones showing impartiality

Group Size: Up to 30

Time Required: 20 minutes

Materials: Pencil and paper

Physical Setting: Classroom or lounge

Process:
1. Divide the class into small groups of 4 to 5.
2. Each group makes a list of specific behaviors that demonstrate partiality (for example, smiling at one of the students more often; sitting closer to one person than to the other).
3. Exchange lists between groups.
4. Still in small groups, go over the list you now have. For each description of a behavior indicating partiality, think of a way to change the behavior so that impartiality is demonstrated (for example, responding to each in turn; sitting at about the same distance from both roommates).
5. Reconvene, and share information in the lists with the whole class.

Exercise: Introducing the Session

Goals:
1. To learn to introduce the mediation session

Group Size: Up to 30

Time Required: 15 to 20 minutes

Materials: Pencil and paper

Physical Setting: Lounge or classroom

Process:
1. Working alone, make a list of things you want to include in your introduction to the mediation process. In your mind, practice how you might explain these things.
2. The class is divided into groups of three. One student takes the role of mediator, and the other two take the role of roommates who have come for mediated negotiations.
3. Role play the beginning of a session. As the roommates arrive, the mediator begins the session by seating them and taking a few moments to insure their comfort. The mediator then introduces the session, explaining the mediation process and the role of the mediator.
4. The roommates provide feedback to the mediator by responding to the questions below:
   a. was the presentation clear?
   b. did the mediator seem competent? confident?
   c. was the mediator impartial?
   d. did you feel free to ask questions?
5. Change roles, and repeat the exercise until everyone has practiced introducing the session.

Variations:
1. Learn to vary the introduction by instructing the roommates to take different roles and tailoring your introduction to them.
   For example:
   a. instruct one roommate to be skeptical about the chances for success.
   b. instruct one roommate to be concerned about the negotiator's impartiality (what did my roommate tell you about me when requesting this session?).
   c. instruct one roommate to take the role of a passive person who does not often speak up and frequently gives in to keep the peace. Try, in the introduction, to set the stage for this person to participate in the negotiations.
2. Practice with people who, unlike your classmates, know very little about negotiation. Ask friends to listen to your introduction and give you feedback using the questions above.

Exercise: Using Neutral Language

Goals:
1. To learn to reword statements using neutral language

Group Size: Up to 30

Time Required: 15 minutes

Materials: Paper and pen

Physical Setting: Classroom

Process:
1. Each person writes at least one inflammatory statement, using non-neutral language, such as those below.
   a. You never clean up your mess. I'm forever falling over your junk, and I'm sick of it!
   b. You're just too sensitive. You get all upset over nothing, and then you won't talk to me.
   c. You should go to bed at a more reasonable hour. It's dumb to stay up to all hours and then sleep late every morning.
   d. The real problem is that all you think about is having a good time. It never occurs to you that other people might want to study.
   e. It's just that stupid music. I mean, nobody listens to that stuff anymore. It's really boring!
2. Students take turns reading their statements to the group. Members of the group, at random or in a designated order, rephrase each statement in neutral language.

Variation:

To practice "Prompting," have a partner make inflammatory statements, using non-neutral language. Practice rewording the statements, using neutral language, and prompting your partner to use that wording. After a few minutes, stop and ask the partner for feedback; check to see if your prompts were offered in such a way that there was no "loss of face" for the partner. Change roles, and repeat the exercise.

Exercise: Writing "No-Loophole" Contracts

Goals:

1. To learn to write clear, concrete contracts

Group Size: Up to 30

Time Required: 1 hour

Materials: Paper and pen

Physical Setting: Classroom

Process:

1. The group breaks up into small groups of 3 or 4 members each. Each small group develops a situation statement. This briefly describes a dispute between two roommates and the position of each of them. For example:

   Roommate #1: You've always slept in a cold room, cozy under warm blankets and your favorite down comforter. When the window is closed, the room seems stuffy to you, you get too warm and don't sleep well.

   Roommate #2: Your roommate is freezing you out! Even under your blanket and bedspread, you end up shivering in the wee hours. You want that window closed!

2. Each small group passes its situation statement on to another small group. (If a group gets a statement similar to the one it wrote, exchange it with another group.) Using the second and third steps of the negotiation process, the small groups first develop lists of possible solutions and then select what they feel are the best for the contract. They write a contract for the two roommates, clearly specifying the behaviors each agrees to.

3. The large group reconvenes. Taking turns, each small group reads its situation statement and the contract it developed. The rest of the large group try to find loopholes in the contract. This can be treated as a game, or even a contest to see which group(s) can win by writing the most airtight contract.

Exercise: Mediating a Negotiation

Goal:
1. To practice mediating a full negotiation

Group Size: 6 to 10

Time Required: Approximately one hour (this may vary)

Materials: Pen and paper (for notes)

Physical Setting: Lounge or classroom setting

Process:
1. Two situations for mediated negotiation are given below. In each, the attitudes and behaviors of two students and an incident that brings them to mediated negotiation are outlined. The personalities of the roommates, their attitudes, and their reactions can be developed more fully as the role play unfolds. Before the role play begins, decide on the sex of the roommates and give them names.
2. Each of the role plays calls for two roommates and one mediator. Periodically, rotate new people into the various roles.
3. The role play can be stopped (for example, after the mediator has finished the introduction to the first session) so that the class can discuss the mediation and give feedback on the role play. New people can be rotated into the roles and either proceed to the next phase of the negotiation or try a different approach to the phase just completed.
4. Remember that one advantage to role play is that it allows you to experiment. If you approach the role play situation determined to play it safe, you may miss out on a good opportunity to learn.

Role Play Situation #1

Student A: You are Hispanic and have just come to this country to attend college. Many of your Hispanic friends grew up here. You like it in America but plan to return home after you complete graduate work. You don't say so often, but you really feel dedicated to helping the people in your country. You come from an upper middle class family; your father is a professional and your mother is a traditional homemaker. You enjoy people and have always been outgoing. Your friends frequently stop by your room to visit or listen to music, which you love. Without even realizing it, you tend to slip into speaking Spanish when you are all together. It seems so much easier and more comfortable, and you seem to express yourselves better, though you are fluent in English.

Student B: You come from a white, middle class family. Neither of your parents is college educated, though both are intelligent and hard working. Your father started his own business, and your mother worked along with him, keeping the books. The business prospered, and you grew up in a nice home. Your high school was predominantly white and you have had only very limited contact with people from different cultures and races. Your father has occasionally hired Hispanic workers, but it never seemed to work out, and you have heard him comment about their lack of ambition. It really bothers you when your roommate's friends speak Spanish. Sometimes they don't switch to English when you come in. As they talk and laugh, it seems they are talking about you. You feel they are rude. You also don't like their music. You have requested this negotiation because you feel the music is too loud and disruptive to you when you want to study or relax.

Role Play Situation #2

Student A: You are really angry about an incident that occurred this past weekend. You were tired, so instead of going to the mixer you just went back to your room and fell into bed. You were awakened several hours later when your roommate and date, both obviously drunk, came sneaking into the room. There was a lot of giggling and other noises, and you strongly suspect they were having sexual intercourse. You didn't say anything at the time—you were so shocked that you frankly didn't know what to do. You're not a prude, but you think your roommate's behavior was outrageous. When you tried to bring the subject up, it was not taken seriously, so you have requested a negotiation.

Student B: You feel your roommate is making a big deal about the whole thing. It's not like you do this sort of thing regularly. This weekend, you admit, you got a little tipsy, and behaved a bit impulsively, but you think that's no reason to react as if you had no morals at all. Besides, your roommate, being awake, certainly had the opportunity to make a noise, or say something instead of just lying there like some sort of voyeur! The more you think about it, the more annoyed you get. Up until now, you thought you two were getting along okay, but you certainly don't like this prudish streak!!

Insuring the Well-Being of Your Residents

4

CHAPTER 10

Wellness Promotion and Residence Life

Dr. Kent D. Beeler,
Eastern Illinois University

The concept of wellness is based on the principle of connectedness among the mind, body, and spirit, and can be traced to the ancient Greeks, who pursued this harmony. The term *wellness* and the related movement, however, are of recent origin. Halbert L. Dunn, a retired public health physician, stressed the holistic nature of wellness and described high-level wellness as significantly more than the absence of sickness and disease. His series of 29 lectures (1961) in the late 1950s to a Unitarian Church in Washington, D.C., marked the beginning of the wellness movement in this country (Ardell, 1984).

Synonyms for wellness include positive lifestyle, personal well-being, holistic health, self-care, health promotion, life directions, lifestyle improvement, and choice living. Wellness definitions are equally diverse. John Travis (1977), another wellness pioneer, stated that high-level wellness means giving care to the physical self, using the mind constructively, channelling stress energies positively, expressing emotions effectively, becoming creatively involved with others, and staying in touch with the environment. Kenneth Pelletier (1979) viewed wellness as ". . . an approach to health care which encourages individuals to seek lifestyles which enable them to achieve their highest potential for well-being" (p. 13).

Wellness is composed of a broad spectrum of daily choices, each involving some degree of health risk or benefit, that collectively represent a lifestyle. Patterns of personal habits, behaviors, and attitudes reflect individual priorities. Wellness promotion, itself, is a conscious and deliberate approach to establish and maintain positive life directions and is concerned with all aspects of one's well-being.

Clearly, wellness is more than jogging and eating carrot sticks, with a little stress management thrown in. Nor is wellness telling others how they should live healthful lives. It is important to understand that wellness does not occur overnight; it is a life-long process. Acceptance of personal responsibility is at the heart of any successful self-care formula.

The notion of specific programs to enhance personal well-being has now reached higher education, following earlier applications in business-industry and health-care settings. Importantly, wellness programs are highly compatible with curricular and co-curricular missions of postsecondary education. "Helping people to understand themselves, think clearly and rationally, recognize the interconnections of their total functioning, and assume increasing degrees of self-directedness is the goal of both universities and the wellness approach" (Elsenrath, 1984, p. 96).

The University of Wisconsin-Stevens Point (UW–SP) implemented the first campus wellness format in the early 1970s. About 100 similar projects were identified in 1984 (McDonald, 1983). Now, about 20 percent of colleges and universities have health promotion plans (McMillan, 1986).

Wellness programs in residence life are also rapidly gaining favor. An Association of College and University Housing Officers-International (ACUHO-I) survey showed that 30 percent of residence hall programs had incorporated wellness as a model or philosophy for programming and student development, and 30 percent were in the process of developing one (Johnson, 1984).

The next section examines the quality of life in America today. The need for balancing wellness components is then discussed, followed by a description of major lifestyle dimensions and sample indicators. The status of wellness in college student affairs and residence life is reviewed, with needs and benefits of choice-living education identified. The final section deals with implementing wellness promotion with residents. The involvement of resident assistants in personal well-being is highlighted, and important precepts are listed for designing healthy lifestyle programs on campus. The second section of this chapter includes a case study and four exercises to further your understanding of self-care aspects. Six positive lifestyle projects are included. You are encouraged to refer to all these activities; they will help enhance your knowledge of how wellness can be meaningfully applied in residence life.

Quality of Life in Contemporary Society

In 1900, the primary cause of death in the United States was infectious disease. Medical practitioners responded by launching the first revolution in American public health care. Through research and education, disease after disease—influenza, tuberculosis, polio, and smallpox—has virtually been stamped out. In the mid-1980s, citizens' lives are again being threatened. This time, however, traditional medicine is not fully equipped to do battle (Seffrin & Torabi, 1984). Richard Palmer, a past president of the American Medical Association, reported that only ten percent of all factors that cause illness are factors physicians are trained to treat.

John Travis (1981), first physician to formally offer wellness education and services to the public and health professionals, has characterized today's medical practice as revealing severe signs of limitations. Labeled the treatment model, contemporary medicine is built upon diagnosing disease, repairing injury, and eliminating symptoms. The aspect usually missing is prevention; methods implicit in the treatment model do little to encourage patients to behave responsibly.

The second major advance in health care, then, deals with what individuals are willing to do for themselves. Being accountable for living more wisely is at the forefront of the attack on diseases of lifestyle. A major obstacle to this significant shift is society's conditioning to rely on others to ensure its good health. The cultural resistance to accommodating wellness practices is considerable. Present norms do not promote active, informed participation in personal health care. Major changes in societal behaviors, attitudes, and values will be required to change cultural expectations.

The U.S. Center for Disease Control (*Ten Leading Causes*, 1975) reported on the influence of four factors on premature death—lifestyle, environment, medicine, and heredity. The National Wellness Institute (UW–SP) (1984) created a quality of life circle based on this information, as shown in Figure 1.

Remarkably, individuals can do things for themselves that actually determine over one-half (53 percent) of their lifestyle. With assistance of doctors, hospitals, and others in the health-care system, 10 percent more can be self-managed and added to the 21 percent represented by environmentally-controlled influences. Only 16 percent of our quality of life and health is determined by factors—genes and body makeup—beyond personal decisions. The message is clear: Get into control of all lifestyle components.

Wellness leaders Donald Ardell and Mark Tager (1982) designed a simple form that provides a quick check on your level of well-being. The first exercise in this chapter—"Wellness/Worseness Continuum"—allows you to assign a letter grade to your current lifestyle performance.

Wellness as Balance

The word *wellness* is sometimes used to describe superficial approaches, which does not do full justice to concepts associated with the term (Travis, 1981). In particular, the physical wellness component often receives disproportionate attention; many even equate physical fitness to wellness. A major reason for the overplay given the physical aspect is its prominence as a functional entry point into lifestyle improvement. Additionally, physical changes are simple to observe and monitor. At the same time, physical well-being dramatically influences all other wellness dimensions.

THE QUALITY OF LIFE DIAGRAM

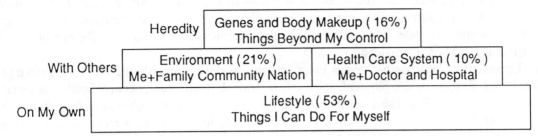

Figure 1. Quality of life diagram. National Wellness Institute (1984). Adapted from *Life-style assessment questionnaire* (4th ed.). Stevens Point, WI: University of Wisconsin at Stevens Point.

U.S. Senator William Proxmire (1973), well-known fitness enthusiast, puts the case for regular exercise this way:

> If you exercise enough you will be leaner, stronger, more energetic. You'll love life, enjoy the smell of flowers, the taste of your food, the cold, and the bracing freshness of a morning breeze. You can literally exercise your way out of boredom, listlessness, anxiety . . . And you'll look so much better. The heavy jowls, the sagging stomach, the yellowish or pallid complexion will diminish and then vanish with exercise. Exercise won't grow hair on your head, alas. And it won't give you the nose you want, won't make you taller, won't change your bone structure. But it will do just about everything else and everything else is plenty. It will put a warm, pink color in your cheeks. It will eliminate the bulges and sags and fat. It will put firmness in your muscles, put a brightness in your eye (p. 31).

What do college students do to stay physically active? The Gallop Organization interviewed over 500 full-time undergraduates at 100 institutions to find out. The results showed that three of every four students (78 percent) participated in physical fitness activities, aside from walking to classes and similar necessities. Running was the most popular activity (34 percent), followed by weight training (22 percent), walking (19 percent), and swimming (18 percent). Aerobics, calisthenics/exercise, racket sports, basketball/baseball/football, and bicycling were clustered next ("Phys. ed. shapes up," 1985, March).

All of us should be encouraged to engage in physical activity of all types. But an integrated lifestyle is the key to profitable well-being. The wellness theme holds that individuals take a comprehensive self-care approach. The development and interdependence of all self-care aspects is at the heart of becoming a whole person. Kenneth Cooper (1982), aerobics proponent, stated, "The human body is just another part of the universe that is meant to be in perfect balance" (p. 11).

Famed cardiologist Paul Dudley White remarked that the body, mind, and soul are inextricably woven together, and whatever helps or hurts one of these three sides of the whole person helps or hurts the other two. To further understand the need for lifestyle equilibrium, read the later case study about Ed Excess. You will identify with this campus escapade and see exaggerated examples of the poor quality wellness that college students exhibit.

Wellness Dimensions and Indicators

Travis (1981) declared, "I think it is imperative that our first step as individuals, when moving into the field of wellness, be to examine our own lives" (p. 2). An early step in subscribing to high-level wellness is to get comprehensive information about how we are now functioning. There are numerous health hazard appraisal programs available, including computerized processed and self- or hand-scored questionnaires (Leafgren & Elsenrath, 1986). The Health 80's System (Medical Datamation, Belleville, OH) has been adopted at over 200 institutions as a replacement for the traditional pre-enrollment physical examination of students.

Other prominent assessment instruments used with campus populations include Lifestyle Assessment Questionnaire and Test Well from the National Wellness Institute, UW–SP. William Hettler, director of health services at that institution, has put together an abbreviated health style inventory ("Taking stock," 1986). To get an informal index of your current status, complete the inventory at the end of this chapter. A brief self-interpretation is provided.

The University of Wisconsin–Stevens Point wellness model is probably the most recognized in higher education; its six dimensions are physical, spiritual, emotional, intellectual, occupational, and social. Other institutions use some or all of these components or may combine them with cultural-aesthetics, environmental, or similar aspects. Campus wellness programs sometimes deal with more specific foci, such as sexuality, career planning, drug-alcohol-tobacco abuse, nutrition-diet, human awareness, and stress-time management. There is no common agreement about which wellness promotional thrusts should be emphasized. What is agreed, however, is that wellness is multidimensional.

Aid Association for Lutherans, a fraternal benefit society, has designed self-care materials for member use. The wellness dimensions and indicators (Figure 2) are partly based on *Well Now!* (undated) You can find relative indication of your present well-being in six dimensions by reading this compilation.

Social (Intentionally building and maintaining close and rewarding relationships with others)
- going out of the way to greet and meet others
- making a special effort to support those who have experienced a setback
- complimenting family members, friends, and associates on their accomplishments

Physical (Having a strong healthy body)
- maintaining ideal body weight and following recommended nutritional guidelines and dietary habits
- conducting continuous physical activity (minimum of 20–30 minutes at least three times a week)
- using leisure time to participate in individual or group activities that increase general fitness level

Emotional (Having the ability to feel and deal constructively with feelings)
- sharing feelings freely with others
- considering what can be done to remove personal obstacles and barriers
- telling others how much their friendship or companionship is appreciated

Spiritual (Working toward inner peace and harmony)
- finding something in every situation for which to give thanks
- pursuing opportunities for spiritual growth and development
- putting religious beliefs into daily practice

Intellectual (Being in the process of learning throughout life)
- finding out how something works so it can be repaired
- discussing the same reading, movie, play, etc. with others
- investigating new topics of personal interest

Environmental (Using and managing resources responsibly)
- making changes to conserve energy
- using public transportation or car pools and walking or bicycling when possible
- recycling clothing, glass, aluminum, etc.

Figure 2. Wellness dimensions and indicators. Adapted from *Well Now!* (undated) Appleton, WI: Aid Association for Lutherans.

Wellness in College Student Affairs and Residence Life

Within the past decade, a family of college student development theories (cognitive development, psychosocial, person-environment interaction, and humanistic-existential) and process models (COSPA I and II, T.H.E., and ecosystems) have emerged in the professional literature. The wellness model is comprehensive enough, yet generic enough, to align with and complement any of these orientations (Warner, 1985; Krivoski & Warner, 1986).

From inception, the student personnel profession has adopted the important orientation of responding to the whole student, attending to individual differences, and working with them at their developmental level (Knefelkamp, Widick, & Parker, 1978). The ultimate goal of college student development is to facilitate optimum human functioning. This is certainly harmonious with the wellness philosophy (Leafgren, 1984; Leafgren & Elsenrath, 1986).

In reality, student affairs divisions have been doing wellness promotion all along. This is not always apparent, since these efforts have seldom been formalized. Upon closer scrutiny it can be seen that wellness improvement has been encouraged by services, activities, and programs provided largely by these professionals. Figure 3 shows an alignment of college student personnel functions with wellness dimensions (Beeler, 1985).

This fractionalized approach does offer some health-enhancement benefits for students. But it lacks cohesion and does not communicate the idea that wellness is wholeness and is an integration of all self-care dimensions.

Intentional wellness promotion for students in higher education and residence life is still essentially a new phenomenon. This situation is starting to change, as colleges and universities hire wellness coordinators and directors to design and implement campus healthy lifestyle formats. Some central housing units have budgeted positions for activities directors to work exclusively with hall programming. In a few cases, these specialists use the wellness theme as the centerpiece.

Housing operations are almost always self-supporting, so generating income to meet revenue bond commitments usually requires a high rate of student occupancy. Shifting demographics of the college-attending population prompt residence life policymakers to look for new ways to attract and keep occupants and to meet their special needs. There is a clear trend to create special-interest halls, wings, and floors, including ones featuring wellness. Institutions with healthy lifestyle housing units include Miami University (OH), James Madison University (VA), Michigan State University, Western Illinois University, Western Michigan University, University of North Carolina-Charlotte, and Illinois State University.

Residence hall professionals and paraprofessionals, particularly RAs, are increasingly involved with student development. They are attempting to design programs that focus on the mini-life cycle of the campus years. A student development approach that can transcend the diversity of both staff and residents is wellness promotion. Historically, hall occupants have been overloaded with social and physical-recreational activities, often to the exclusion of other important lifestyle dimensions. The wellness model is a vehicle RAs and residence life educators can use for proactive, intentional, and balanced programming in the halls (Warner, 1985).

Functions	Dimensions
1. Counseling Center	1. Emotional
2. Recreation-Intramurals	2. Physical
3. Career Planning and Placement	3. Occupational/Vocational
4. Student Activities and Residence Life	4. Social
5. Campus Ministries	5. Spiritual/Religious
6. Student Union, Museums, and Theatre	6. Cultural/Aesthetics
7. Academic Courses and Curricular Activities	7. Intellectual

Figure 3. College student personnel functions and wellness dimensions. Beeler, K. D. (1985a); Wellness promotion in higher education and college student affairs. *College Student Affairs Journal*, 3, 10–22.

Needs and Benefits of Campus Wellness Promotion

The transition from high school to college is characterized by many changes, often described as adaptive stress. For instance, home-sickness, new freedoms, fitness activity modifications, nutritional choices, and social and value challenges may contribute to an actual decline in a student's health. Successful wellness promotion accelerates students' adjustment to college life, offers them a positive direction, and makes them feel like the institution cares.

What are some representative areas in which undergraduates show poor quality self-care considerations? *Newsweek on Campus* polls have reported college student opinions about eating habits and alcohol-drug usage. Data were collected by the Gallup Organization from 516 face-to-face interviews held at 100 institutions. Here are selected findings:

- twenty-nine percent considered themselves overweight
- nearly two-thirds said undergraduates eat more junk food than other Americans
- thirty-six percent of females and nineteen percent of males usually ate snacks instead of regular meals
- over one in three admitted they binged-and-purged or knew someone who did ("Newsweek on Campus," 1987).
- fifty-three percent indicated alcohol abuse on campus was a serious or a somewhat serious problem
- fifty-four percent had tried marijuana and twenty-three percent cocaine
- marijuana was reported by seventy-four percent as the most used drug ("On Campus Poll," 1987).

Such student behavioral patterns certainly reflect a need for healthy lifestyle educational programming on campus and within residence halls.

Health destinies can be significantly shaped during the collegiate experience. The landmark publication, *Healthy People* (1979), points out that the young adult years are relatively healthy times. Levin (1979), however, suggested that a major gap in self-care education programs exists for the college population. Students certainly establish a lifestyle within the daily routine of campus life. Wellness involves making intelligent decisions from when we wake in the morning until we go to bed at night; it involves choices in eating, drinking, exercising, driving, shopping, cleaning, working, studying, socializing, relaxing, and loving.

A study of college students' attitudes toward health acknowledged the validity of the wellness model used at University of Wisconsin–Stevens Point. Survey respondents concurred that all six dimensions (physical, emotional, social, spiritual, occupational, and intellectual) were important in wellness. The results seemed to indicate that undergraduates are becoming more aware of the complex interactions among health, behaviors, and emotions (Archer, Probert, & Gage, 1985). It is also fortunate that the college years represent a time of openness to changing damaging personal regimens.

An ACUHO-I survey (Johnson, 1984) of member institutions with wellness programming reported the following benefits for hall residents:

- increase in physical activity (36 percent)
- more awareness of good nutrition and diet (28 percent)
- better able to handle stress (25 percent)
- fewer smokers (17 percent)
- generally healthier and happier (13 percent)
- less alcohol consumption (8 percent)

The study also asked respondents to record residence staff benefits observed since implementing the wellness concept in the halls. Listed were these positive changes:

- increase in physical activity (27 percent)
- better ability to handle stress (24 percent)
- increased awareness of good nutrition and diet (24 percent)
- improved attitude and staff/resident interaction (15 percent)
- generally healthier and happier (13 percent)
- fewer smokers (13 percent)

Cohen (1980) suggested that most student health services would be better named student illness services because their primary function is to alleviate symptoms and cure illnesses. Generally, all students pay for medical services through student activity or user fees. They pay the assessment, whether or not they use the services. In effect, healthy students are subsidizing the cost of sick ones. The presence of wellness activities for the entire campus population would equalize the unfairness of health center financing.

Research is emerging that documents the dividends from investment in healthy lifestyle promotion. Several studies have provided key arguments for institutions to implement wellness programs for students. One important reason is the increased probability of better enrollee recruitment and retention ratios (Hettler, 1980; Monaghan, 1984). A correlation has also been found between poor handling of undesirable life events and lowered grade point averages (Knapp & Magee, 1979). It follows that wellness promotion can assist individuals to better negotiate pressures that develop during college years.

There is evidence that undergraduates who exhibit positive self-care will have a competitive edge in employment, given comparable academic credentials (Hettler, 1980). The point is that wellness-oriented graduates are frequently hired before non-healthy candidates with accompanying medical risks. Companies are interested in doing what is possible to reduce health and life insurance premiums for their employees.

RAs and Wellness Promotion

As an RA, you will be viewed as an important example of personal wellness. Residents quickly see a discrepancy when staff members advocate but do not follow wellness tenets. Any gap prompts potential healthy lifestyle converts to question the worth of related wellness programming. The participation of all residence life personnel in positive lifestyle promotional activities is crucial. RAs, in particular, must be proactive in spreading the important message of quality self-care and modeling its outcomes. There is little doubt that credibility is a by-product of participation and a powerful base for convincing others (Opatz, 1985).

It is important to recognize that students do not follow a uniform pattern of development during their collegiate experience. Each year is different for each resident, a fact that underlines the value of considerable breadth in wellness programming. Another reminder is that initial response to related promotional activities usually comes from those already exhibiting a positive lifestyle. Getting additional participant involvement becomes more difficult; you must select strategies carefully to attract students not yet sold on the value of personal wellness.

An effective way to determine the global interest of residents regarding various wellness dimensions is to examine their current status. You can use the Hall Residents Wellness Inventory at the end of this chapter, patterned after one used at Michigan State University, to assess the wellness priorities of any campus living unit. A profile of hall occupants' survey results will reveal wellness aspects deserving attention or enhancement. RAs can then design and implement programs to meet these needs. Sample topics for wellness promotion appear in Figure 4. Keep your residents in mind as you review this list and add other subjects that come to mind.

Environmental	Intellectual
pollution	study skills
water safety	mini-computers
conservation	word processors
accident prevention	test anxiety
recycling resources	time management
population growth	decision-making
nuclear issues	goal setting
	problem solving
	public speaking
	personal finances
Spiritual	**Social-Emotional**
birth control	assertiveness training
yoga-meditation	human relation skill
non-Western religions	conflict resolution
sexual harrassment	adjustment to college life
death and dying	dating skills
religious cults	overcoming phobias
civil rights	expressing personal feelings
human sexuality	motivation
humanitarianism	dealing with parent/family
alternative sexual lifestyles	handicapped awareness
Physical	**Occupational-Vocational**
nutrition and diet	career exploration
self-protection	job search skills
progressive relaxation	life/career planning
fitness assessment	selecting academic majors
first aid—CPR	scholarships, grants, and loans
smoking cessation	placement center services
weight control	on- and off-campus employment
aerobics	life after college
drug/alcohol/tobacco abuse	identifying job skills
eating disorders	academic assistance services
exercise programs	
arts and crafts	
stress management	

Figure 4. Wellness programming topics.

Precepts for Healthy Lifestyle Promotion in Residence Life

Ardell and Tager (1982) suggested that RAs follow the classic planning process when creating a wellness format and wellness-oriented programs and activities. The basic steps are these: 1) identify the problem or need; 2) brainstorm ideal solutions and desired states; 3) think about available resources; 4) make a choice; 5) create a plan; 6) carry out the plan and develop support for maintaining it; and 7) evaluate and adjust as necessary.

Any blueprint for self-care needs to be premised on sound precepts. Beeler (in press) has recommended these for review:

1. The wellness enterprise involves the interrelationship of the mind, body, and spirit. All dimensions of personal well-being should be developed, monitored, and balanced.
2. Lifestyles are unique and personal. There is no single model for wellness. Self-care should be tailored to meet idiosyncratic needs, preferences, and values. But all components of choice living emphasize one thing: finding positive ways to increase prospects for a well life.
3. Daily habits, attitudes, and behaviors represent decisions and routines that are cumulatively health-depleting or health-enhancing. They yield patterns of life-long consequences.
4. Individuals are superior experts on themselves; they serve as their own best consultants and resources. Yet, wellness can not be done totally alone, nor can it be done for others.
5. High-level wellness depends on understanding and accepting the first principle of ecology: everything affects everything else. Thus, the need for an integrated lifestyle that acknowledges all positive life-style aspects.
6. Benefits accrue when any wellness dimension is developed. But when all components are put together, the combined effect is even greater than the sum of all the parts.
7. Individuals must take charge and be responsible for their own life directions. Personal commitment is at the heart of any successful self-care strategy; it is life insurance in the truest sense of the term.
8. A healthy lifestyle is a process rather than a goal. It is a journey, with each day offering unique paths. As long as individuals are engaged in improving personal wellness, they are moving in the right direction. The final documentation of success is the body, which, in effect, is one's autobiography.

Helpful print resources for starting a personal lifestyle enhancement program include *Planning for Wellness* (Ardell & Tager, 1982), *Improving Your Odds* (Tager & Harris, undated), *Wellness Workbook for Helping Professionals* (Travis, 1981), *Fitness: The Facts* (undated), and *Well on Your Way* (Palmetto Health Systems, 1985). Handbook series dealing with wellness promotion and stress management are also available (Tubesing & Tubesing, 1988a; 1988b).

Conclusion

The importance of personal wellness for you and the residents you serve is effectively recited in this wellness parable from Santayana's *The Super Script:*

> One night, in ancient times, three horsemen were riding across a desert. As they crossed the dry bed of a river, out of the darkness a voice called "Halt."
> They obeyed. The voice then told them to dismount, pick up a handful of pebbles, put the pebbles in their pockets and remount.
> The voice then said, "You have done as I commanded. Tomorrow at sunup you will be both glad and sorry." Mystified, the horsemen rode on.
> When the sun rose, they reached into their pockets and found that a miracle had happened. The pebbles had been transformed into diamonds, rubies, and other precious stones. They remembered the warning. They were both glad and sorry—glad they had taken some, and sorry they had not taken more.

And this is the real story of wellness!

Case Studies and Structured Group Experiences for Wellness Promotion in Residence Life

Case Study: Ed Excess

Instructions: Read the case study and answer the questions that follow. First answer the questions alone, then share your answers in small groups or in class discussion with RAs.

ED EXCESS, 22, COLLEGE SENIOR, SUDDENLY HOSPITALIZED IN SERIOUS CONDITION

Special to the *Daily Campus News*

On a Friday during the middle of the spring semester of his freshman year, Ed Excess, 18, awoke to a tremendous clap of thunder and flash of lightning. With a ringing headache and upset stomach, he moved to the residence hall window and looked out through bleary eyes. Written in fiery letters across the early morning sky was a startling message:

"SOMEONE IS TRYING TO KILL YOU, ED EXCESS, BEWARE!"

With shaking hands and a trembling body, Excess quickly opened his first cigarette package of the day. But his mind quickly returned to the prophetic statement. He didn't question its meaning; you don't challenge one like that. Ed's only inquiry was, "Who"? Excess picked up his shower tote, made sure the aspirin and Alka-Seltzer were there, and left for the bathroom. Shortly later, after changing into some slightly snug clothes, he took the elevator from the first floor to the dining service.

Passing up the pancakes and syrup, he settled for fried eggs, which he freely salted, and sausage, which he liberally dosed with catsup. His double order of white toast was covered with butter and jelly. Still feeling anxious from the frightening proclamation, Excess turned to Ivan Eaton and told him, "Someone's out to kill me!" "Who?," asked his shocked roommate. Ed slowly stirred cream and sugar into his third cup of coffee and shook his head. "I just don't know."

Concerned though he was of the danger, Excess could hardly go to the campus police with such a tale. He decided his only course of action was to go about his daily routine and hope to outsmart his would-be murderer.

On his way to class, Excess tried to think of an ingenuous way to deceive this potential killer. Wondering if the all-night cramming and No Doz would pay off, he slumped into his chair for the 9:00 A.M. economics test. The final bell rang with Ed still stuck in the middle of the exam. Feeling exhausted, he blew off his other classes for the morning.

What he really needed was some relaxation at the movie theatre or downtown games room. Getting his car from the parking lot, he noticed the fuel gauge was on empty. Excess pulled into the gas station

Case Study. Ed Excess. Adapted from Tubesing, N. L., & Tubesing, D. A. (1983). Grabwell Grommet. *Structured exercises in wellness promotion* (vol. 1). Duluth, MN: Whole Person Press.

cursing the 7 m.p.g. and rolled down the windows to free the smoke coming in from the rusted-out exhaust system. He charged the fill-up on his credit card and shrugged at the 21 percent interest owed on the balance, which was at the maximum.

Then he suddenly remembered the upcoming 1:00 P.M. appointment with the hall director; something about the 12 write-ups from the RA staff. On his return to campus, his attention turned again to finding a clever way to outwit his deadly pursuer. But the frustration of making up time by beating traffic lights and switching lanes occupied him wholly. Excess didn't hear the siren of the emergency vehicle until it was directly behind him; he vowed to keep the car stereo turned down in the future.

At the hall cafeteria his favorites—beef strogonoff and cherry pie ala mode—were featured, but Ed knew he didn't have time to stand in line. Instead, he stopped at a fast food outlet for a quick lunch— double burger, large fry, and giant soft drink. He later determined it was the large soft serve that required him to use a whole roll of Tums, although it could be argued that the box of brownies was the real culprit.

Following the stressful session with the hall director, Excess returned to this room for a few winks before starting research on a term paper. It was his roommates's jam box that woke him about 4:00 P.M.; Ed was also slightly irritated because he missed the afternoon soaps on television. However, there was enough time to get to the Friday Club meeting at a local bar. There, Excess was in a good mood as he feasted on hors d'oeuvres of fried chicken wings and slammed down his third pitcher of beer. The smoke-filled room made his eyes water, but that was a small price to pay for winning a free T-shirt by placing third in the drink-a-thon.

While Excess couldn't escape the ominous death threat, he took salvation in the fact he hadn't panicked. "I simply must live my life as usual," he quietly reminded himself. As the weeks passed, Excess manfully stuck to his regular habits and began to take a perverse pleasure in his ability to survive. "Whoever is trying to get me," he said proudly to his roommate, "hasn't been successful." "I'd still be on guard," cautioned Ivan Eaton as they shared a sack of potato chips and a can of cashews with a six-pack of Jolt.

Ed's pride grew as he followed his regular routine over the next seven semesters. It was just before spring break in his senior year when, complaining of dizzyness and nausea, he was rushed to the emergency room of the local hospital.

Following a thorough physical examination, the doctor reported to Excess that the outlook for an immediate and complete recovery was not encouraging without significant lifestyle changes. It seems Ed suffered from early cases of emphysema, arteriosclerosis, duodenal ulcers, and cirrhosis of the liver. He also checked in with high blood pressure and a high cholesterol count, too much body fat, and circulatory insufficiency.

As he shared the box of chocolate-covered cherries during visiting hours, Excess took pride in reporting to his roommate that "whoever is after me hasn't gotten me yet; I'm just too smart for him"!

Case Study Questions:

1. What negative health behaviors did Ed Excess exhibit?_____

_____

_____

_____

_____

_____

_____

_____

_____

_____

2. List five ways Ed Excess could improve his lifestyle.

1. _____
   _____

2. _____
   _____

3. _____
   _____

4. _____
   _____

5. _____
   _____

3. As Ed Excess's RA how could you help?

_____
_____
_____
_____
_____
_____
_____
_____
_____
_____
_____
_____

4. What program could you develop to help Ed Excess and other residents develop a healthier lifestyle—List ten—be creative.

1. _____
2. _____
3. _____
4. _____
5. _____
6. _____
7. _____
8. _____
9. _____
10. _____

Exercise: Wellness/Worseness Continuum

Goals:

1. To help participants get an informal index of their wellness status;
2. To encourage participants to improve the quality of their current lifestyle.

Group Size: Unlimited

Time Required: 20 to 30 minutes for group of 15 to 25

Materials: 1. Copies of Wellness/Worseness Continuum worksheet for each participant; 2. Pencil or pen for each participant.

Physical Setting: Classroom or meeting room; preferably with deskchairs.

Process

1. The facilitator introduces the exercise to participants and indicates that completing it will provide a letter grade that represents the quality of their current lifestyle.
2. Facilitator distributes copies of Wellness/Worseness Continuum worksheet to participants.
3. After participants complete the worksheet, they are asked to share what grade they assigned themselves and reasons for it. Participants in A-B wellness range are requested to describe what they do to maintain their letter grades. Participants in D-F worseness range are asked to describe what they can do to improve their letter grades. Participants in the C normal health range can outline what they can do to earn a higher letter grade.
4. Facilitator can ask participants to record their earned letter grade on a slip of paper; a breakdown of letter grades can then be compiled and shared with the group.

Wellness/Worseness Continuum
First, carefully examine the characteristics listed under wellness, normal health, and worseness.

Wellness A+	Normal Health C	Worseness F−
positive self-concept	absence of illness	low self-esteem
monitor wellness signs	no pain	monitor illness signs
focus on vitality	not sick	focus on disease
aliveness		boredom
energy		fatigue
calm and accountable		hostility and blame
interdependence		dependence
health-enhancing		health-risk habits
at cause		at effect
joy		no fun

Now circle the letter grade that honestly represents the quality of your current lifestyle.

Wellness	Normal Health	Worseness
A+ A A− B+ B B−	C+ C C−	D+ D D− F+ F F−

Wellness/Worseness Continuum. Adapted from Ardell, D. B., & Tager, M. J. (1982). *Planning for wellness: A guidebook for achieving optimal health* (2nd. ed.). Dubuque, IA: Kendall/Hunt.

Exercise: Health Style Inventory

Goals:

1. To acquaint participants with representative aspects of a healthy lifestyle and to have them gauge their personal level;
2. To encourage participants to make adjustments that lead to an improved lifestyle.

Group Size: Unlimited

Time Required: 20 to 30 minutes for group of 15 to 25.

Materials: 1. Copies of Health Style Inventory for each participant; 2. Pencil or pen for each participant.

Physical Setting: Classroom or meeting room, preferably with deskchairs

Process

1. The facilitator comments about the value of inventorying one's health style.
2. Facilitator distributes copies of Health Style Inventory worksheets to participants.
3. After participants complete worksheets, they are to total their "Yes" answers and review the interpretation of scores.
4. Facilitator asks participants what they discovered about themselves as a result of taking the Inventory.
5. Facilitator can ask participants to record their "Yes" total on a slip of paper; an interpretive breakdown can be shared with the group.

Health Style Inventory William Hettler, M.D.

Directions: Write yes or no on the line to the left of each question.

_____ 1. Do you like your job (being a full-time college student)?

_____ 2. Do you awaken rested and refreshed every morning?

_____ 3. Do you wear a seat belt?

_____ 4. Do you weigh within 5 pounds of your ideal body weight?

_____ 5. Do you know how to measure your resting heart rate?

_____ 6. Is your heart rate less than 60 beats per minute?

_____ 7. Do you know how to measure your blood pressure?

_____ 8. Do you refrain from tobacco products—cigarettes, cigars, and smokeless varieties?

_____ 9. Do you know three ways to reduce stress or anxiety without the use of drugs?

_____ 10. Do you have fewer than three alcoholic drinks a week, on the average?

Interpretation

9–10 yes answers: Be proud of yourself—you are doing well!
6–8 yes answers: Room for improvement in your self-care!
5 or fewer yes answers: Your health style is at risk!

Exercise 3. Health Style Inventory. Adapted from Taking stock of your health: A self-scoring questionnaire (*Chronicle of Higher Education,* February 19, 1986, p. 22).

Exercise: Hall Resident Wellness Inventory

Goals:

1. To provide participants with an informal profile of their current lifestyle status;
2. To show participants which of their wellness dimensions needs to be upgraded or enhanced.

Group Size: Unlimited

Time Required: 20 to 30 minutes for group of 15 to 25

Materials: 1. Copies of Hall Resident Wellness Inventory for each participant; 2. Pencil or pen for each participant.

Physical Setting: Classroom or meeting room, preferably with deskchairs

Process:

1. The facilitator introduces the exercise to participants and requests their cooperation in completing a copy of the Hall Resident Wellness Inventory.
2. Before distributing copies of the Inventory, the facilitator informs participants that the results will be used to plan hall programs and activities promoting a positive lifestyle.
3. After participants have completed the Inventory, the facilitator tallies group responses in each of the six sections within the instrument. These results provide a quick overview of hall residents' expected behaviors in terms of various wellness dimensions.

Hall Resident Wellness Inventory

Dear Resident:

This inventory will give you an informal profile of your current wellness status (positive lifestyle) in each of six dimensions. Your responses will also help the residence hall staff get an overall idea of the wellness level of fellow residents.

The staff can then plan programs and activities to enhance what you are already doing well. As importantly, we can provide opportunities for you to develop wellness aspects needing attention.

Please Complete the Following Information

Male _____   Female _____   Academic Semester/Year _____   Freshman _____
Sophomore _____   Junior _____   Senior _____   Transfer _____

New to campus residence halls? yes _____   no _____

Number of previous semesters in campus residence halls _____

Directions: Please circle the number that best represents your response to each Wellness Inventory item.

Use this Scale:

1 = Mostly True   4 = Somewhat Untrue
2 = Somewhat True   5 = Mostly Untrue
3 = Undecided

Emotional

1. I am able to deal with the pressures of college life.	1 2 3 4 5
2. I can resolve issues with my parents and family members.	1 2 3 4 5
3. I can establish friendships easily.	1 2 3 4 5
4. I am comfortable expressing my feelings with others.	1 2 3 4 5
5. I am considerate of other floor residents' feelings.	1 2 3 4 5
6. I take responsibility for my own behavior.	1 2 3 4 5
7. I expect that floor residents will successfully share their feelings and emotions.	1 2 3 4 5

Intellectual

1. I believe my study habits are adequate.	1 2 3 4 5
2. I can handle my personal finances satisfactorily.	1 2 3 4 5
3. I am able to effectively schedule my time.	1 2 3 4 5
4. I feel capable of making important decisions.	1 2 3 4 5
5. I know how to set and reach goals and objectives.	1 2 3 4 5
6. I understand the value of mini-computers and word processors.	1 2 3 4 5
7. I expect that floor residents will take their academic studies seriously.	1 2 3 4 5

Social

1. I anticipate working out any problems with my roommate(s) or suitemates.	1 2 3 4 5
2. I like to have some private time on occasion.	1 2 3 4 5
3. I feel skillful in human relations.	1 2 3 4 5
4. I am able to assert myself when necessary.	1 2 3 4 5
5. I feel secure going places where I might not know anyone.	1 2 3 4 5
6. I believe it is important for floor residents to do things together.	1 2 3 4 5
7. I expect that floor residents will work out satisfactory compromises on community issues (noise, study time, visitation hours, etc.).	1 2 3 4 5

Physical

1. I am within 5–10 pounds of my ideal body weight.	1 2 3 4 5
2. I understand the seriousness of eating disorders (bulimia, anorexia nervosa, etc.)	1 2 3 4 5
3. I intend to exercise regularly (20 to 30 minutes of continuous activity at least three times a week).	1 2 3 4 5

Hall Residents Wellness Inventory. Adapted from Well-Come to Wellness (undated). East Lansing, MI: University Housing Office, Michigan State University.

4. I know and use ways to handle stress.   1   2   3   4   5

5. I am knowledgeable about birth control methods and post-pregnancy options.   1   2   3   4   5

6. I know how to protect myself from sexual assault (including date rape).   1   2   3   4   5

7. I expect that floor residents will not have a problem with getting drunk or high.   1   2   3   4   5

Spiritual

1. I am comfortable with others who have a different sexual orientation than mine (gay, straight, bisexual).   1   2   3   4   5

2. I take time out for spiritual growth and development.   1   2   3   4   5

3. I anticipate my values and beliefs will be challenged by floor residents.   1   2   3   4   5

4. I intend to expand my awareness of different ethnic, racial, and religious groups.   1   2   3   4   5

5. I am tolerant of others' views about life's issues.   1   2   3   4   5

6. I am able to set personal limits in an intimate relationship.   1   2   3   4   5

7. I expect that floor residents will satisfactorily handle harrassment about their sexual, religious, or racial orientation.   1   2   3   4   5

Occupational

1. I have decided upon my academic areas of study (major and minors).   1   2   3   4   5

2. I have identified my career interests, skills, and abilities.   1   2   3   4   5

3. I understand job search skills (resume preparation, interviewing, follow-up, etc.)   1   2   3   4   5

4. I know about available campus resources (academic assistance center, career and placement office, etc.).   1   2   3   4   5

5. I have decided my career plans following college.   1   2   3   4   5

6. I have a good idea how marriage, family, and career fit together.   1   2   3   4   5

7. I expect that floor residents will have well-defined career and life plans.   1   2   3   4   5

Check the wellness areas you generally need to further develop:

Emotional _____   Social _____   Spiritual _____

Intellectual _____   Physical _____   Occupational _____

Please return the Wellness Inventory to your Resident Assistant (RA) whose name is _____

(Print)

THANK YOU!

CHAPTER 11

Managing Stress

Dr. Gary Gintner,
Louisiana State University

Recently a university department head asked me to help him identify the cause of his program's 50 percent drop-out rate. Interviews with staff and students and a review of academic records revealed an interesting pattern. Indexes of academic achievement (e.g., grade point average, SAT scores) were not associated with whether or not students remained in the program. Some students even maintained a grade point average of 3.5 (scale of 4 = A) and higher before leaving the program. Instead, the interviews revealed that the stress generated by academic, personal, and family demands was the most common reason given for leaving.

Research shows that stress may not only cut university aspirations short but also may undermine professional careers as the result of stress-related disorders (e.g., alcoholism, depression, and heart disease). Stress costs business over four billion dollars per year in the form of hospitalization expenses, retraining costs, and decreased productivity (Pelletier, 1982). From this perspective, learning to manage stress may not only be an essential university "survival" skill, but also a long-term career necessity.

This chapter will present an approach to stress management based on the principle that certain types of coping strategies work best for certain types of stress. Like picking warm clothing for a cold day, effective stress management matches the coping plan to the anticipated challenge.

Basic Principles of Stress Management

Stress can be defined as the perception of a demand that exceeds or taxes one's coping ability (Lazarus & Folkman, 1984). As long as coping abilities match or exceed the weight of stress demands, the individual feels free of excessive tension. However, as demands outweigh coping resources, a state of imbalance develops, with the body being burdened with a weight beyond its carrying capacity. Just as you might be able to carry a heavy load for a short distance, the body can tolerate temporary imbalance and bounce back. However, if the situation persists, signs of excessive stress appear, followed by exhaustion or the development of stress-related illnesses. The next section will examine how you can recognize signs of stress imbalance in order to take preventive action.

Stress Signs

A pilot uses his or her flight instrument panel to indicate course direction and potential engine trouble. Adjusting actions in relations to these indicators insures that he or she will reach the destination and avoid mechanical problems. In the same way, the body is equipped with its own indicators of stress. These signs are mainly the result of a mobilization response as the body gets ready for a demand called the "fight-flight" response (Selye, 1975). Muscles brace, pupils dilate, breathing quickens, and heart rate and blood

Table 1 *Signs of Excessive Stress*

Physiological	Psychological	Behavioral
• Sore muscles	• Worrying	• Overindulgence in substance (e.g., drinking, drugs, food)
• Upset stomach	• Difficulty concentrating	• Difficulty sleeping
• Headaches	• Being forgetful	• Annoyed easily
• Racing heart	• Feeling nervous	• Difficulty sitting still
• Diarrhea	• Feeling out of control	• Difficulty relaxing
• Sweaty hands	• Feeling sad	• Staying to yourself
• Dry mouth	• Down on yourself	
• Restlessness	• Feeling time pressure	

pressure increase. A number of stress chemicals are released to free up energy reserves in case they are needed. Like pressing the accelerator pedal down in a car, the human engine races. Our stress signs are like a car's temperature indicator signaling impending "overheating" if something is not done.

Stress signs can appear in three pathways: physiological (e.g., body symptoms), psychological (e.g., alterations in thinking and feeling), or behavioral. Table 1 lists some characteristic signs for each of these three pathways. While some of us may respond solely with physiological indicators (e.g., "tension headaches"), most people have signs in at least two pathways. The important thing is to be aware of your characteristic signs. The exercise entitled "What are your Stress Signs?" at the end of the chapter presents these stress signs in a questionnaire format so that you can identify your key stress indicators. Recognizing stress signs may not only alert you to impending stress imbalance; it may also suggest to you the potential cause of the imbalance.

Sources of Stress

Stress can originate in either the environment or the person. While external circumstances and demands may stress us beyond our capacity, our behavior and reactions may also create stress and set up future stressful episodes. For example, the individual who keeps his roommate awake each night with loud music is in a sense shaping a stressful future environment for himself in the form of hostile reactions. So it is important to be cognizant of those stresses that are due to external demands and those that we bring on ourselves.

Environmental Sources of Stress

Stressful life events There are two sources of environmental stress: major stressful life events and daily hassles. The former consists of life situations that demand significant change or adjustment, such as starting college, changing majors, moving, or the death or serious illness of a family member. As major life situations start to pile up, you might think of yourself as accumulating stress risk points (Rahe & Arthur, 1978). The *College Schedule of Recent Events* is a commonly used questionnaire that provides a list of stressful life events, with stress point values given for each event. The scale includes events such as a broken steady relationship (70 points), starting college (50 points), changing field of study (41 points), and working while attending school (38 points). Marx, Garrity, and Bowers (1975) found that the number of points a college student earned in the year just past predicted the frequency and duration of illness episodes (e.g., colds, flu, etc.) during the following six months. There is growing evidence that disruptive events such as these have the physiological consequence of lowering our immune response, thereby making us more vulnerable to illness (Borysenko, 1984).

Hassles Ordinary daily hassles are also a source of stress. These include roommate difficulties, losing things, concerns about school, work overload, and financial worry. As these become more frequent, students are liable to feel more stressed and annoyed, and, consequently, are at greater risk of becoming sick. In fact, research has shown that hassles are a better predictor of subsequent illness than major stressful life events (Lazarus & Folkman, 1984). So it is important to be cognizant of your "hassle index" because it may be a more subtle and potentially detrimental source of day in and day out stress.

Person Sources

Cognitive Why is it that one individual who experiences a major stressful event or a hassle reacts with alarm, while another shows disappointment and goes on? The answer lies in the definition of stress, which, as you may recall, stated that the perception of a demand is the critical event. In other words, the way we perceive what is at stake in a particular situation will either reduce or heighten the magnitude of our stress reactions (Lazarus & Folkman, 1984).

When we tell ourselves that either our actions or the world "must" or "should" be a certain way, we inadvertently raise the stakes of situations that may counter these beliefs (Ellis & Grieger, 1977). For example, the student who believes he *must* be "right" about every decision is liable to become quite upset or overly defensive when he is wrong. Similarly, the resident assistant (RA) who believes he "should" be in control of the situation 100 percent of the time may become quite annoyed by a student who questions the rules on the RA's floor. In both cases the particular "belief" colors the perception of the situation so it is seen as personally threatening.

Three beliefs that may be particularly stress-inducing are:

1. "I have to have everybody like me all the time or I am a bad person."
2. "I have to be perfectly competent all the time with no mistakes."
3. "The world has to be fair!"

Notice that all three are unrealistic and reflect "all or none" thinking. For example, belief #1 assumes that one's personal worth is based on others' approval and that one exception undermines total worth. As a result of this position, these individuals have particular difficulty being assertive or saying "no," for fear of disapproval. Those who hold belief #2 cannot allow themselves to make mistakes or to be fallible. Situations that threaten complete mastery, such as a difficult course are especially stressful. Belief #3 is exemplified in individuals who are constantly wary of getting what they feel they deserve and who become agitated when things are not equitable. You can notice your own unrealistic beliefs when you hear yourself saying the words "must," "ought," "should," and "have to" when you talk about yourself.

The way we talk to ourselves as we approach, deal with, and recover from stress also affects how stressed we feel (Meichenbaum, 1977). As a demanding situation approaches, worrying about the worst possible outcome tends to exacerbate a person's stress response. For example, imagine the body's reaction to "I know I'm not going to do well on this test—it's so hard!" Notice that this negative thinking never indicates how to cope with the situation. Rather, it is liable to increase the individual's anxiety and prompt avoidance of studying or just giving up. Worrying can be self-defeating and stress-generating if it does not result in a plan of action for dealing with the problem. The coping section will discuss how to change these stress-inducing beliefs and negative self-talk.

Behavioral Personal sources of stress also include self-defeating habits and life skill deficits. Self-defeating habits include such things as excessive alcohol consumption, "partying" too much, or waiting until the last minute to start studying for an exam. Notice that while partying and procrastination may be rewarding in the short-run, the long-term consequences may be quite disruptive (e.g., "all nighters," DWIs, or flunking out).

A second set of behavioral sources of stress are life skill deficits in areas such as social interaction skills, assertion, decision-making, and time management. These behaviors are learned and are not a matter of will power. For example, the student who does not manage time wisely may not know how to prioritize and consequently feels like he never has enough time to get things done. Although specialized training in these skills is beyond the scope of this chapter, other chapters in this book are excellent resources.

By now you probably have an idea of some of your stress sources. At the end of the chapter, the third exercise contains the *Sources of Stress Inventory,* which may help you pinpoint your key stress areas more clearly. Stress management works most effectively when you tailor coping plans to the specific stress sources you have targeted.

Coping With Stress

In this section we will examine ways of both pinpointing your stress and designing coping plans to address these situations.

Pinpointing

An important stress management skill is the ability to specify what triggers your stress so that your coping efforts are focused on the appropriate target. A useful technique is to monitor your identified stress source each day, noting the following:

| Time | Place | What's happening? | What do you do? | Stress Rating 1 (low)–10 (high) |

You might place these headings on an index card that you carry in a pocket or purse. Whenever a stressful episode occurs, make an entry. At the end of the week, note your stress ratings to identify situations, places, or coping responses that make your stress worse or better. Are there certain people who are "stress carriers"? Are there things you do in reaction to situations that result in a higher stress rating? Are there places or activities that are consistently associated with higher ratings? These data will be useful in tailoring your coping strategies. For example, one student who rated the academic area as a high source of stress monitored her study time. She found that the presence of a particular person consistently undermined her attention to her work. Her focused stress management plan was directed at minimizing this person's disruptive influence, which resulted in better grades on her tests.

Coping Strategies

By self-monitoring or simply listing stressful episodes over a two week period, you can identify a set of "high risk situations" for future stress episodes (Marlatt & Gordon, 1985). You will probably notice that some of the situations are changeable (e.g., negative thinking, inadequate studying, or agreeing to take on a demanding project), while others are outside of your control and just need to be accepted or tolerated (e.g., worries about a sick parent, waiting for exam results). Table 2 lists cognitive and behavioral coping strategies that work best with either controllable or uncontrollable sources of stress. The strategies that are designed to meet controllable or modifiable stress sources demand problem-focused coping, which entails interacting and approaching the problem source in an effort to reduce it. Uncontrollable situations, however, demand emotion-focused coping, which reduces our internal emotional and physiological responses to help us better tolerate the situation.

Part of your stress problem may be that you are using the wrong type of coping strategy for the situation that confronts you. For example, some students cope with the pressure of a major term paper (i.e., a controllable source of stress) by distracting themselves until the last possible moment. In this situation an emotion-focused strategy (i.e., distraction to reduce internal anxiety) is applied to a situation that would have a better outcome had problem-focused coping (e.g., planning and writing) been employed. Likewise, some situations that must be accepted (e.g., end of a romantic relationship) are sometimes handled by problem-focused coping strategies such as incessantly calling the partner and trying to mend the relationship. These efforts all interfere with accepting and resolving the loss and produce greater long-term stress. The rest of this section will give examples of problem-focused and emotion-focused coping to illustrate how coping is matched to the demands of the stressor.

Table 2 *Cognitive and Behavioral Coping Strategies for Controllable and Uncontrollable Stress*

Type of Coping

	Behavioral	**Cognitive**
Controllable	• Planning or prearranging activities • Seeking information to solve problems • Talking with resource individuals • Confronting the stress carrier • Avoiding situations that trigger stress • Arrange situation to encourage coping • Self-contract desired behavior	• Coping Self-Statements • Mental rehearsal • Disputing unrealistic beliefs
Uncontrollable	• Avoid reminders • Physical Exercise • Relaxation • Leisure Activities • Social support	• Narrowing down worrying time • Reappraisal: look for silver lining • Thought stopping • Positive comparison

Problem-Focused Coping

Changeable sources of stress can include novel situations (e.g., starting college, a new apartment or roommate), coping with workload, hassles in our relationships with others, and our self-defeating thinking and behavior. The two upper boxes in Table 2 list some behavioral and cognitive problem-focused coping strategies that may help reduce these modifiable stress sources.

The impact of numerous demands (e.g., academic workload) can be minimized by planning your work time, rewarding yourself for schedule adherence, avoiding time wasters, and arranging the environment to encourage your desired activity. For example, the tension of midterm week can be markedly reduced by arranging a study schedule far in advance of a test. Since smaller amounts of study time are needed at each sitting, studying becomes markedly less aversive than the "all nighter." In order to stick to the schedule, avoid situations that guarantee distraction (e.g., studying in the lobby or union). Rather, you might find a special time of day or a place that would encourage and "cue" studying. One student, who had spent most of her library time socializing, changed her study area to an empty room in her dorm.

If you do come up with a good activity schedule, it might be useful to make a contract with yourself that establishes a reward for sticking to the plan each week (e.g., special night out, special activity). Contracting is especially important if you targeted self-defeating behaviors like excessive partying as a stress source. Finally, picking a specific time to do your weekly planning (e.g., 10-minutes on Sunday night) will ensure continuity and maintenance of your study and work planning.

If the source of stress is an interpersonal situation (e.g., an annoying floor-mate), then the best course may be to confront and deal with the "stress carrier." This may entail expressing your feelings, making a request, or simply being able to say "no" when you want. It may also include avoiding the "stress carrier" under certain situations (e.g., when the individual is intoxicated, broke, or angry). For example, RAs are frequently confronted with complaints about noisy or disruptive individuals on their floor. How can the RA deal with this situation? First, think of what you want to say ahead of time. A helpful device is to put your assertion in the format, "I feel . . . ," "When you . . . ," "I would appreciate it if you would . . ." This lets the other person know what is bothering you and how to rectify it. Notice there is no name calling or character assassination. While you may feel good saying it, putting down the other person is not likely to cultivate a cooperative response.

Next, with the help of someone who is not involved in the problem, rehearse what you want to say as if you were talking to the disruptive individual. It is important to maintain eye contact and use a firm tone of voice. Lastly, set a time when you will talk with the individual, making sure to avoid times when a favorable response is less likely (e.g., at 2:00 A.M. when they are drunk). If someone else must do the confronting, the RA can coach the individual through the above steps. It is useful to rehearse or role-play the situation several times to help make the response more proficient.

If you anticipate confronting a novel situation (e.g., starting college, starting a new program or major), it is especially useful to get as much information as possible about the situation or program ahead of time. Talking to resource individuals who are familiar with the area can also provide useful information. These strategies work because they reduce the anxiety generated by the situation's uncertainty, making the situation appear more familiar and manageable. For example, I knew an RA who made it a regular practice to check with the new students on her floor about how they were acclimating to campus life. She found it particularly helpful to put them in contact with key resource people such as academic advisors and heads of social groups.

The upper right-hand box of Table 2 lists a number of cognitive coping strategies that either help prepare us for effective coping or modify thinking that may be the stress source itself. Coping self-statements are designed to change negative thinking (e.g., "I'm going to fail!") to problem-focused thinking, which is more positive and task-oriented. The next time you catch yourself thinking negatively you might say the following to yourself:

> "Stop! That's not going to help now. What is it that I have to do right now to change this situation? If I just . . . things will probably work out. The important thing is to stick to my plan."

Although this appears simple, you will have to practice interrupting automatic negative thinking. Take a minute to think of an upcoming situation about which you have been worried, and see if you can think of some good coping self-statements. For example, an RA who anticipates a heated floor meeting can think ahead of time what he or she would like to say and what to do if he or she begins to feel threatened.

Mental rehearsal is similar to coping self-talk except you imagine yourself coping with the situation as you would like. For example, if you are fearful of how you will present yourself in a confrontation with someone, you might do the following:

> Find a quiet place, and get yourself comfortable. Take a few minutes just to relax and clear your mind. Then, almost as if you were watching a movie, picture yourself approaching the situation (e.g., the stress carrier). You notice that you become a bit nervous. You calm yourself by coping self-talk (e.g., Don't worry. Take a deep breath and remember what you'd like to say.") You confront the situation and your words and manner flow as you would like. Then imagine yourself feeling good about how you presented yourself.

By using mental rehearsal several times prior to an anticipated stressful event, you will also desensitize yourself to the situation. Exposing yourself to the situation in imagery allows you to coordinate your thinking, words, and action. Not surprisingly, professional athletes use mental rehearsal prior to a big match to maximize their performance and minimize the interference of anxiety. You might consider it the next time you anticipate confronting challenges such as a major exam, an important date, or a verbal presentation.

Sometimes the negative self-talk, however, is only part of a major underlying unrealistic belief. Woolfolk and Richardson (1978) suggest a four-step process in changing stress generating beliefs:

1. Write the unrealistic "must," "should," or "have to" belief in one or two sentences. Example: "I have to have everyone like me. I feel awful if I've disappointed someone!"
2. Identify the negative statements you tell yourself when you do not meet this expectation. Example: "I feel awful because disappointing others means I'm selfish, incompetent, and an unlovable person."

3. Now dispute the reality of the belief by thinking of reasons why the belief is unrealistic or irrational. Example: "Just because I displease someone does not mean I'm bad. It just means a difference of opinion. It would be impossible to please everybody—you would always do things their way and never assert your own needs or interests."
4. Put yourself in a situation that challenges the unrealistic belief and see how it turns out. For example, say "no" to a friend when you want to, and see what happens. Does your friend stop calling because you expressed your opinion?

The four steps listed above have been found to be a useful way of changing unrealistic beliefs, but you need to practice the disputing regularly. Take 10 minutes a day to think of situations and reasons that counter the unrealistic ideas. Try to develop a more realistic belief that you repeat to yourself, like "It would be nice to have people like me, but sometimes others may not like what I do."

Remember that problem-focused techniques demand interacting with the source of your stress, be it a situation, a person, or your own thoughts and behavior. Although problem-focused coping may appear more stressful in the short-run, the long-term consequences may actually eliminate the source of your tension. Reminding yourself of the long-term payoff is one way you can maintain your motivation to tackle the problem.

Emotion-Focused Coping

Emotion-focused coping reduces our internal response to stress without actually changing the stress source itself. In a negative sense, drinking when stressed may be considered an emotion-focused strategy, since alcohol deadens internal physiological stress reactions. But there is a whole set of adaptive ways of using emotion-focused strategies, especially when we have to tolerate an uncomfortable situation (e.g., seeing your ex-boyfriend with a new mate). The lower two boxes of Table 2 list some ways that action and thinking-oriented strategies can reduce our internal discomfort.

Behavioral strategies can help reduce our physiological and emotional response to stress in three major ways. First, avoiding reminders of the stressful event limit the cues in our environment that can trigger our internal discomfort. For example, if you are thinking too much about a former romance, you might temporarily avoid places where you regularly went together. You might also remove any pictures or momentos in your room. In this way, you begin to increase the distance between you and the past relationship, thereby easing the process of acceptance.

The second way that behavioral strategies can help us tolerate stress is through the tension-releasing benefits of certain activities. Research has shown that physical exercise results in decreased muscle tension and anxiety, as well as speedier physiological recovery from stress (Sime, 1984). Planning as little as three 20-minute exercise sessions per week can be sufficient to reap these benefits. Cooper (1977) provides guidelines for starting and maintaining a sound exercise program.

Relaxation training is another tension-reducing activity. Two familiar forms are meditation and rhythmic breathing. Research has shown that the muscular relaxation, mental calmness, and lower resting blood pressure can be attained through regular relaxation (Benson, 1977). The "Let Yourself Relax" exercise at the end of this chapter describes one type of relaxation exercise you might consider. In developing your facility to relax, consider these recommendations:

1. When you are just beginning, find a quiet place where you will be undisturbed for 20 minutes. Try to practice at a regular time each day, when you are not too tense. Turning the lights down and taking the phone off the hook reduces potential distractions.
2. Once you can relax easily during low stress times, shift your relaxation period to a time when you feel tense or uptight (e.g., after studying in the afternoon each day).
3. As your relaxation skills improve, you can use your calming technique prior to or during high stress episodes such as an exam or before a confrontation. During these times, just use the portion of your exercise in which you typically feel quite relaxed. By repeating this portion, you can cue your relaxation response more rapidly.

As you can tell, relaxation may not only help reduce daily tension, but it may also moderate the stress we feel as we actively confront situations.

A third way that an activity can help us tolerate stress is through the enjoyment and social support it provides. For example, leisure activities such as hobbies and artistic endeavors are more than just releases of tension. Like depositing money in a bank account, pleasant and rewarding activities enrich our quality of life and counteract the stream of "withdrawals" our stressful obligations make. If you need to add some quality-enhancing activities to your lifestyle, experiment until you find something that you like. You might also think of a pleasant activity that you used to do (e.g., playing the guitar). Because RAs spend much of their time with floor and school obligations, it is especially important for them to schedule pleasant events into their weekly routine.

While certain activities are one hedge against our stress level, the way we appraise a situation can also enhance tolerance and acceptance. For example, if you are spending too much time thinking about an ex-boyfriend, you can use a narrowing strategy: Avoid thinking about him by narrowing down your "worry time" to a specific 15-minute time period during the day. If thoughts occur at other times, you might use a thought-stopping technique:

1. As soon as you have a thought about him, yell "Stop!" to yourself.

2. Imagine a large red stop sign as clearly as you can.

3. Then, engage in an engrossing activity, or just use coping self-statements.

These procedures break the automatic chain of worry thoughts and block cognition with an alternative input. Some situations may not be pleasant to accept, but limiting unproductive worrying is one way to reduce strain on your system.

A second way we can modify our thoughts about an unpleasant event is by focusing on some positive consequence of the situation. Did the experience provide something of value that will help you cope in the future? For example, a dissolved romantic relationship may provide key information about what type of partner is good for you and what type guarantees turmoil. Likewise, failure in one academic area may suggest another academic area more suited to your particular talents.

Another way you can think more positively is through focusing on aspects of the situation that are either favorable or not as bad as they could be. The disappointed straight A student who gets his first B might reassure himself by saying, "It could be a lot worse—at least my first non-A is a B." The injured athlete might console himself by thinking, "At least the broken leg will heal—some injuries mean the end of an athletic career." If there is some disappointment you have to accept, try to focus on something you have learned by the experience. Frequently this type of thinking generates an idea for an alternative avenue for gratification.

Conclusion

In summary, try to remember these stress management principles as you cope with daily stress:

1. Stress occurs when we perceive that demands exceed our coping resources.
2. As this occurs, a state of internal imbalance develops, signaled by stress signs.
3. These signs can alert us to take corrective action as well as indicate the potential source of stress.
4. While some stress sources are external situations (e.g., major life events or hassles), others are the result of our self-defeating habits, negative self-talk, and unrealistic beliefs.
5. Once you have recognized a potential stress source, try to self-monitor it to specify the problem more clearly.
6. If the targeted stress source is within your control to change, choose a coping strategy that helps you reduce the source (i.e., problem-focused coping).

7. However, if the stress source is beyond your power to change, choose a strategy that helps you reduce your internal stress response (i.e., emotion-focused coping) in order to tolerate the situation more easily.
8. Problem-focused and emotion-focused strategies frequently can be used to facilitate each other (e.g., relaxing before a confrontation).

The next section presents three case examples that will help you to practice applying these principles. The last section contains practical exercises to help you build your stress management skills.

Case Studies and Structured Group Exercises for Managing Stress

Each of these cases are variations on an actual problem a student has presented at a stress seminar. After a brief description of the problem, there is a series of questions to help you think through the case. You might ask yourself these questions when you are thinking of your own stress management plan.

Instructions: Read the case studies and respond to the questions which follow. First work alone. When you are finished, share your answers with other RAs in small group discussions or as the basis for a classroom discussion.

Case Study: Kallen

Kallen transferred this semester from a small community college to a large state university. At the community college she was able to maintain a straight A average "without studying much." However, the courses at the large university are not only more difficult; they also demand considerably more reading. She reports that she is behind in all her classes, with two major tests scheduled in one week. She also has a major sorority activity coming up this weekend, which she feels obligated to attend since she's a new pledge.

She reports that the demands of school and her social activities have her running "like crazy." She admits that she is having trouble falling asleep at night because she worries so much about her first round of tests at the "big university." When she sits down to study, she starts to feel nervous and finds it difficult to concentrate. She admits that she has done a lot of "nervous eating," resulting in a 5-pound weight gain over the past five weeks. She feels like the walls are closing in on her and is sure that she will fail.

Questions for Kallen's Case Study

1. What are some of Kallen's stress signs? Try to include each pathway. _____

_____

_____

_____

_____

_____

_____

_____

_____

2. List some of her stress sources. _____
_____
_____
_____
_____
_____
_____
_____

3. Which are controllable? _____
_____
_____
_____
_____
_____
_____
_____

4. Looking at Table 2, what strategies might help her? _____
_____
_____
_____
_____
_____
_____

5. What could she do to reduce her nervousness while studying? _____
_____
_____
_____
_____
_____
_____

Case Study: Wade

Wade attended a stress seminar because of the stress involved in his senior year student teaching practicum. He's been placed at a "rough" high school, where it is not uncommon for students to bring knives to class and "mouth off." He reports feeling like a failure because he is unable to get all of his students to listen to him and hand in their assignments. When he is asked for more specific information, however, he reports that only three of the students are actually uncooperative (which for this school is doing quite well).

Wade reports coming home at the end of the day and worrying about how he mishandled a situation or how he made several "stupid mistakes." He notices that his stomach "really churns" during these times. He admits he wishes he could run away from the situation. Each morning he comes to the school feeling nervous, thinking to himself, "Boy, I wonder if this is going to be another horrible day? I wonder what stupid thing I'll do today?"

Questions for Wade's Case Study

1. What are some of Wade's stress signs? _____

_____

_____

_____

_____

_____

_____

_____

2. Which parts of his stress does he bring on himself, and which are inherent in the school system?

_____

_____

_____

_____

_____

_____

_____

3. How might he self-monitor a relevant source of stress? _____

_____

_____

_____

_____

_____

_____

4. How might he use his self-monitoring to design a stress-management plan? What would you include?

_____

_____

_____

_____

_____

_____

_____

_____

Case Study: Adam

Adam almost flunked out last semester. During finals week he pulled three "all nighters" resulting in a series of severe headaches and two D grades. As a result, he made up his mind that this semester would be different. He realized that he had partied too much early in the semester, leaving his studies to the last minute. He decided to make a plan where he would study two hours each day starting the first week of the semester. He monitored his study time during the first week to see what situations kept him on his plan and what situations sidetracked him. He got a list of some of these "high risk situations" and tried to develop a plan of action for them. For example, one was a friend who tempted Adam to go to the bar with the line, "You can study when you get back." As you might expect, studying never occurred on his return. He developed a response to the friend, saying that he would meet him at the bar, when he was done. Another part of his plan was to build in some fun activities each week as a "reward" for the effort he was putting into studying. Not surprisingly, at the end of the semester, he got eight hours of sleep each night during finals week.

Questions for Adam's Case Study

1. List some of Adam's stress management strategies. _____

_____

_____

_____

_____

_____

_____

_____

_____

_____

_____

_____

2. Which were problem-focused and which were more emotion-focused? _____

_____

_____

_____

_____

_____

_____

_____

_____

_____

Exercises: What Presses Your Stress Button?

Goal:

1. To break the ice and have group members get to know each other.
2. To illustrate environmental and personal sources of stress.

Group Size: 5 to 30

Time Required: Approximately 30 minutes

Materials: Blackboard or large easel

Physical Setting: Have group members arrange their chairs in a large circle.

Process:

1. The facilitator asks each member to introduce themselves and complete the sentence, "One thing that presses my stress button is. . . ."
2. Each example is written on the board or on a sheet of paper as it is given.
3. After each member has taken a turn, the group members are asked to indicate which of the responses are caused by external sources and which are self-generated. Are there any situations in which both are important?

Variation

An individual can do the exercise on his or her own by taking a sheet of paper and drawing a line down the middle. On the right-hand side of the page, list external stress sources. Use the left-hand column for self-generated sources.

Exercise: What Are Your Stress Signs?

Goals:

1. To help participants identify their characteristic signs of stress.
2. To help participants become aware of how stress manifests itself in thoughts, feelings, bodily responses and behavior.
3. To help participants identify an early sign of stress.

Group Size: Unlimited

Time Required: 30 minutes

Materials: Pencil or pen; Stress Signs Questionnaire

Physical Setting: No special requirements

Process

1. Ask the group to complete the *Stress Signs Questionnaire.*
2. After completing the questionnaire, ask participants to share what they learned about their stress indicators. Are there any signs that are early indicators of stress build-up?

Stress Signs Questionnaire

Instructions: For each item below circle the number which best describes how often you have experienced each of the following in the *past month*.

Physiological	Never	Seldom	Often	Very often
1. Sore muscles	1	2	3	4
2. Upset stomach	1	2	3	4
3. Headaches	1	2	3	4
4. Racing heart	1	2	3	4
5. Diarrhea	1	2	3	4
6. Sweaty hands	1	2	3	4
7. Dry mouth	1	2	3	4
8. Restlessness	1	2	3	4

Psychological

	Never	Seldom	Often	Very often
1. Worrying	1	2	3	4
2. Difficulty concentrating	1	2	3	4
3. Being forgetful	1	2	3	4
4. Feeling nervous	1	2	3	4
5. Feeling out of control	1	2	3	4
6. Feeling sad	1	2	3	4
7. Feeling down on yourself	1	2	3	4
8. Feeling time pressure	1	2	3	4

Behavioral

	Never	Seldom	Often	Very often
1. Overindulgence in a substance (e.g., drinking, drugs, food)	1	2	3	4
2. Difficulty sleeping	1	2	3	4
3. Annoyed easily	1	2	3	4
4. Difficulty sitting still	1	2	3	4
5. Staying to yourself	1	2	3	4
6. Difficulty relaxing	1	2	3	4
7. Rushing around	1	2	3	4
8. Accident prone	1	2	3	4

Exercise: Identifying Stress Sources

Goals:

1. To help participants identify key stress areas.
2. To illustrate how some stress sources are changeable, while others demand tolerance or acceptance.

Group Size: 5 to 50

Time Required: Approximately 30 minutes

Materials: Pencil or pen; the Sources of Stress Inventory.

Process:

1. Ask participants to complete the Sources of Stress Inventory on the following page.
2. Ask participants to discuss what they became aware of in doing the exercise. Which stress sources are changeable and probably demand problem-focused coping efforts? Which entail learning to control internal responses (i.e., emotion-focused coping)? Which may use both?
3. To evaluate how much stress these stress sources are generating (i.e., the sum of all their ratings), participants can be given these values:

High Stress	= Greater than 99
Moderate	= 85–99
Average	= 54–84
Moderately low	= 39–53
Very low stress	= Less than 39

SOURCES OF STRESS INVENTORY

Instructions: Below you will find some common sources of stress for college students. For each item, rate how stressful it was for *you* during the past semester. Using the following scale, circle the number to rate your stress:

Not at all Stressful	A little bit	Moderate	Quite a Bit	Very Stressful
1	2	3	4	5

Academic

1. Getting the grades I'd like to get   1 2 3 4 5
2. Studying as much as I should   1 2 3 4 5
3. Writing papers for class   1 2 3 4 5
4. Studying for an exam   1 2 3 4 5
5. Indecisions about a career or major   1 2 3 4 5

Total Items 1–5 _____

Interpersonal

6. Not having enough friends   1 2 3 4 5
7. Problems with roommates   1 2 3 4 5
8. Not getting along with others   1 2 3 4 5
9. Feeling disappointed by friends   1 2 3 4 5
10. Difficulty speaking up for myself to others   1 2 3 4 5

Total Items 6–10 _____

Dating

11. Not mixing well with the opposite sex   1 2 3 4 5
12. Not enough dates   1 2 3 4 5
13. Disappointing love affair   1 2 3 4 5
14. Not sure what I want in a relationship   1 2 3 4 5
15. Feeling nervous on a date   1 2 3 4 5

Total Items 11–15 _____

Family

16. Misunderstood by family members   1 2 3 4 5
17. Interference of family members into my personal life   1 2 3 4 5
18. Unhappy family life   1 2 3 4 5
19. Being away from home   1 2 3 4 5
20. Not being treated like an adult   1 2 3 4 5

Total Items 16–20 _____

Financial

21. Difficulty managing my money   1 2 3 4 5
22. Making ends meet   1 2 3 4 5
23. Not enough money for education   1 2 3 4 5
24. Being wasteful with my money   1 2 3 4 5
25. Having an uncertain source of income   1 2 3 4 5

Total Items 21–25 _____

Intrapersonal

26.	Wanting to be more popular	1	2	3	4	5
27.	Tend to be too self-critical	1	2	3	4	5
28.	Having to please everybody	1	2	3	4	5
29.	Unsure of my values	1	2	3	4	5
30.	Not knowing what I really want	1	2	3	4	5

Total Items 26–30 _____

Exercise: Let Yourself Relax

Goals:

1. To get acquainted with a relaxation exercise.
2. To become aware of how the body feels when relaxed.
3. To identify parts of the body which are difficult and easy to relax.
4. To suggest how a portion of the relaxation exercise can be used in stressful episodes.

Group Size: Up to 50

Time Required: 45 minutes

Materials: None

Physical Setting: Find a room free of interruptions or intrusive noise. A comfortable setting in which you can dim the lights enhances the exercise's impact.

Process:

1. Describe to the group that a relaxation exercise is a way of calming your mind or body. Point out that relaxation is a skill, and that like any skill some people get the knack right away, while others require somewhat more practice. Tell them that the exercise will take about 15 minutes.
2. The facilitator asks everyone to get in a comfortable position in their chairs with both feet on the floor and arms uncrossed.
3. Dim the lights in the room.
4. Begin the exercise by saying, "I am going to give you some things to focus on and some things to think about. As much as you'd like, allow yourself to follow my instructions. First, just slowly close your eyes."
5. Read this script in a slow monotone tone of voice:

> For a few minutes I'd like you to focus your attention on your breathing. Try to get your breathing nice and even and regular (3-second pause) so that the same amount of time is taken breathing in (pause) as breathing out (pause). Nice even, regular, rhythmic breathing (pause). If your mind wanders (pause), just gently and easily (pause) bring your attention back (pause) to your breathing (pause) noticing how even, regular and rhythmic (pause) your breathing is becoming (pause). Nice balanced, even, breathing (pause).

> As you are relaxing (pause) notice that sensation (pause) at the tip of your nose (pause) where the air feels slightly cooler when you breath in (pause) and slightly warmer as you breath out (pause). Allow your attention to focus on that sensation (pause) of coolness as you breathe in and warmth as you breathe out (pause for 10 seconds). If your mind wanders (pause) just bring your attention back to coolness as you breathe in and warmth as you breathe out (pause 10 seconds).

> You're feeling more and more relaxed and calm (pause). There's a comfortable warm feeling on the top of your head (pause). The warm feeling is spreading downward (pause) across all sides of your head (pause). Warmth spreads down the back of your head (pause), the sides of your head (pause), and across your forehead (pause). You can feel the warmth spread across your eyebrows and eyelids (pause). Your forehead and eyelids are growing warm, relaxed, and heavy (pause). The warmth spreads across your cheeks, your mouth, and into your chin (pause). Your whole face is growing pleasantly warmer and relaxed (pause).

> The warmth spreads into your neck and your shoulders (pause). Your neck and shoulders are growing heavy, relaxed, and warm. The warmth spreads down (pause), into your upper arms (pause), into your forearms (pause), and into your hands (pause). Your arms and hands are growing heavy, relaxed and warm (pause).

> The warmth spreads down (pause) down across your back (pause) and into the small of your back (pause). Your whole back area (pause) is growing pleasantly heavier and warm (pause).

The warmth spreads down (pause) across your chest (pause). Your breathing is easy (pause), comfortable (pause), and relaxed (pause). Nice, balanced, even, breathing (pause).

The warmth spreads down (pause) across your stomach area (pause) and into your legs (pause). Your thighs (pause), your knees (pause), and your calves (pause) are growing heavy (pause), relaxed (pause), and warm (pause). You can even feel the warmth (pause) spreading into your toes (pause). Your whole body (pause) heavy (pause), relaxed (pause), and warm (pause). The calmness even reaches into your mind (pause). Your mind is at peace (calm) and your body is calm (pause). Your mind is at peace (calm) and your body is calm (15 second pause).

As you're relaxing, let yourself think of a pleasant and relaxing scene like a waterfall (10 second pause), a country lake (10 second pause), or a beautiful flower (10 second pause). Pick a scene (pause) and allow your mind (pause) to think about it for the next few minutes (10 second pause). What colors do you notice? (10 second pause). Are there any sounds? (10 second pause). Are there other sensations you notice? (10 second pause) Just let yourself stay with the scene (15 second pause).

As you're relaxing (pause) notice how your muscles feel (pause). Notice the comfortable sensations (pause) in your body of heaviness and warmth (pause). Some of you (pause) may even feel (pause) comfortable tingling (10 second pause).

As you practice this exercise (pause), you might notice it (pause) getting easier and easier (pause). I'm going to count backwards (pause) from five to one (pause). When I get to one (pause) allow your eyes to open (pause). Five, feeling calm, and relaxed (pause). Four, at peace with yourself (pause). Three, coming up (pause). Two, noticing sounds around you (pause). One, open your eyes.

6. Processing of exercise

   Ask participants the following questions:
   1. What did they notice about relaxing?
   2. Which parts of their body were easy to relax, and which parts were particularly difficult?
   3. How might you use an exercise like this for stress management?
   4. Ask participants about the part of the exercise during which they felt the most relaxed. This portion can be used prior to or during a stressful episode as a way of moderating tension quickly.

Variation:

The exercise can be done individually by having the script read into a tape recorder. The tape can then be used for daily practice.

Exercise: Stress Management Planning

Goals:

1. To show participants how to specify a stress source.
2. To teach participants how to develop a stress management plan for a specific situation.

Group Size: Up to 30

Time Required: Approximately 45 minutes

Materials: 1. Sheet of 8½″ × 11″ paper; 2. Pencil or pen

Physical Setting: It may be necessary to have tables to write on, although a tablet of paper is sufficient.

Process:

1. The facilitator tells the group members that the purpose of this exercise is to develop a stress-management plan for *one* of their sources of stress.
2. Each of the questions in section 3 are read out loud or completed in the space provided. After each question, the facilitator asks if there is any questions. In the event a participant has difficulty with any portion, the facilitator asks the group to help answer the question or help problem-solve.
3. Stress Management Planning Guide

    a. Pick a stress source from the *Sources of Stress Questionnaire* that you would like to work on:

    _____ .

    b. Try to write the problem as specifically as you can: _____

    _____ .

    c. What makes the problem worse? _____

    _____ .

    d. What makes the stress source less problematic? _____

    _____ .

    e. Now turn your problem into a goal by stating it as something you want to increase, decrease, or a skill you want to learn: My goal is to _____

    _____ .

    f. Look at Table 3 and pick a coping strategy that will help you meet your goal: I will _____

    _____ .

    (If you are going to use coping self-statements, write down two statements you might use). _____

    g. Are there situations, people, or times which might undermine your plan (i.e., high risk situations)? What could you do for each of the situations you listed under #3?

High risk situation	*Plan*
1. _____	1. _____
2. _____	2. _____
3. _____	3. _____

h. Do you need to add pleasant or rewarding events into your lifestyle as a stress buffer? If yes, write down one activity and write down when you could do it in the following week:

Activity: _____

When: _____

i. Try to summarize your stress plan:

My stress plan is to: _____

_____

_____

4. Ask participants what they became aware of in constructing their stress plans. What did they realize about their stress source as they planned to modify it? _____

_____

_____

CHAPTER 12

Substance Abuse: Food, Alcohol, and Drugs

Dr. Nancy I. Mathews,
Louisiana State University

This chapter contains a discussion of three categories of self-abuse prevalent among college students. All three are indicated by a preoccupation with a particular substance: eating disorders, alcohol abuse, and drug abuse. All three are by nature compulsive diseases, requiring professional medical and psychological assistance to alleviate the problem. This chapter discusses each category separately in a section that includes the definition of the problem in the college population, the physical and psychological symptoms, and the treatment of the disorder. At the conclusion of this chapter, resident assistants should be able to identify and differentiate symptoms of each type of abuse and be able to counsel students exhibiting these symptoms in order to facilitate their treatment by medical and psychological professionals.

Eating Disorders

Problem Definition

An eating disorder is a disturbed eating behavior which some individuals begin as a means of controlling weight but which gradually takes control of their lives by becoming a compulsive method of reducing anxiety. People with eating disorders may try to manage their weight by severely restricting their food consumption, engaging in uncontrollable binge eating, or a combination of the two. Furthermore, they may vomit after eating, take diuretics (water pills), diet pills or laxatives, or engage in excessive exercise.

Some people with eating disorders are emaciated in appearance, others are overweight or obese, yet others are of average weight. While it may not be easy to identify these people by appearance alone, it is important to be able to recognize the symptoms associated with these disorders because they are life-threatening.

There are several sociocultural factors that contribute to the increased incidence of eating disorders among today's young adult population. Western culture places great emphasis on the meaning of food; it is used symbolically as a gift of love, a reward for good behavior, or as a punishment for wrongdoing. People eat food to manage stress, avoid failure, fight depression or loneliness, and avoid sexual feelings (ACHA, 1984).

American society also emphasizes that the ideal person is fashionably slim. Fifty-six percent of all women diet today for cosmetic reasons, not for health reasons. Similarly, our culture displays a revulsion for obesity and excessive eating, which may lead overeaters to develop feelings of self-hatred, anxiety, and self-doubt (Schwartz, Thompson, and Johnson, 1982).

The issue is compounded by a college environment that challenges students with conflicting values, encouraging eating and drinking as part of all social occasions, but discouraging the results of these behaviors. It is in this paradoxical environment that students are facing a stressful transition into an adult world that requires separation from their families and high school friends, the selection of a career, and the ability to deal with complex social relationships. Some students may try to soothe the resulting stress by reverting to eating behaviors learned earlier in life, such as binging followed by guilt-induced fasting. Most of these individuals appear to have vulnerable personalities that encourage them to engage in repetitive, habitual behaviors.

To compound the issue, there is considerable research indicating that many people with eating disorders come from overprotective families in which rigid rules discourage them from becoming independent and learning how to resolve their interpersonal conflicts. Therefore, they try to take control over some part of their lives by structuring their eating behaviors. In addition to familial influences, it is known that abnormal eating behaviors are learned from peers. One study found that many bulimics had another vomiter as their closest friend (Schwartz et al., 1982).

Thus, the specific causes of eating disorders are multiple and complex. It appears that a combination of psychological, environmental, and physiological factors may cause eating disorders to surface: societal norms, maladaptive family relationships, learned behaviors, personality disorders, and perhaps even a biological predisposition toward developing the illness (NICHHD, no date).

Two common types of eating disorders, anorexia nervosa and bulimia, will be discussed in the following sections. It is important to note that while each disorder can operate as a separate entity, combinations of the two also are common. Some researchers have attempted to solve that problem by renaming these combination disorders as "bulimia nervosa," "bulimarexia," "dysrexia," or "anorexia bulimia nervosa" (Holmgren et al., 1983). In order to simplify the understanding of these disorders, anorexia nervosa and bulimia will be described first as separate disorders. Then the combined disorders will be discussed.

Anorexia Nervosa

Anorexia nervosa is a misleading term that means loss of appetite due to nervousness. Actually, a person with anorexia nervosa has no loss of appetite at all, but instead uses extreme self-control to suppress the appetite because of an irrational fear of becoming obese (APA, 1980).

Most anorexics (90–94 percent) are adolescent or young adult females who begin to exhibit symptoms between the ages of 12 to 18 years; the other 6 to 10 percent are adolescent males (NICHHD, no date). Anorexia nervosa, not as common as bulimia, encompasses only .5 to 1 percent of the population. Although most of these cases come from white, middle- to upper-middle income families, it is not unusual to find them among all racial and economic groups today. The disorder can be halted if it is identified in time, but, unfortunately, 15 to 21 percent of these patients die because they literally starve themselves before help is received (APA, 1980).

Anorexia nervosa begins when a young woman initiates a rigid diet that leads to a significant weight loss (15 percent to 25 percent of her original body weight). Her goal thus reinforced, she still refuses to eat and to maintain a normal weight for her age and height. She becomes preoccupied with her body size, based on an inaccurate belief that she is fat, even though she has developed an emaciated appearance. The anorexic may use laxatives, diuretics, or excessive exercise as an additional means of controlling her weight. Some anorexics demonstrate a preoccupation with food by reading recipes, frequently talking about food, hoarding, or tearing food into small pieces. She also may have an elaborate system of labeling particular types of food as "good" or "bad" (APA, 1980).

As the disorder progresses, the anorexic's endocrine function becomes impaired, leading to delayed sexual development and the cessation of menstruation (amenorrhea). Malnutrition develops, causing dry skin, loss of head hair, disruption in sleep patterns, fatigue, and the inability to think clearly. She also may display a growth of fine body hair on the arms and legs (lanugo), which may be the body's way of compensating for the typical low blood pressure and an inability to maintain a normal body temperature. Most of these patients are dehydrated, which causes difficulties with constipation and urination. If medical and psychological help is not sought, the heart, brain, and kidneys will shrink and eventually fail to function.

The most prevalent psychological symptom is denial of the problem; the anorexic refuses to seek help because she does not believe she is too thin. She is obsessed with her appearance and believes that her behavior will make her more desirable and attractive to others. Sometimes other compulsive habits accompany the problem, such as frequent weighings and hand washing.

The anorexic tends to be a perfectionistic, high achieving model daughter. She does not exhibit rebellion outwardly but approaches high parental expectations and family conflicts by being compliant and obedient, then attempts to gain control over her life by disciplining her eating behavior. She has low self-esteem, lacks the confidence to act independently, and is socially withdrawn and depressed.

Bulimia

Bulimia is a misleading term that means "ox hunger." Although the bulimic person rapidly consumes a large amount of food, binge eating is a means of easing psychological pain, not the result of excessive appetite or physical hunger (Mitchell & Pyle, 1982).

As a group, bulimics tend to be slightly older than anorexics; they begin their eating patterns between the ages of 15 to 18 and typically do not seek treatment until their twenties or later. As in anorexia nervosa, this disorder predominantly affects females (4 to 19 percent of the population). Less than 5 percent of this group is male (Kreipe & Carafos, 1985; Mitchell & Pyle, 1982). Some reports indicate that this incidence rate is low since all bulimics will not seek help for their disorder, and families and friends may not identify the problem readily.

Bulimia is the uncontrolled consumption of a large quantity of food within a discrete period of time, typically about two hours. The eating usually is terminated by abdominal pain, sleep, social interruption, or self-induced vomiting. The vomiting decreases the pain of abdominal distention and, at the same time, reduces the anxiety associated with overeating (APA, 1980). This binge-purge cycle may occur several times a week or as frequently as every day (Mitchell & Pyle, 1982). It occurs episodically, alternating with periods of restrictive dieting and normal eating. The bulimic frequently chooses highly caloric food that has a soft texture, is digested easily, and can be eaten quickly with little or no chewing. The bulimic usually is a secretive eater; for example, some only binge at night.

The bulimic shows great concern about her body image and appearance and repeatedly attempts to lose the weight gained from binge eating. In addition to methods typically used by the anorexic (fasting and using laxatives or diuretics), the bulimic may use ipecac to induce vomiting. As a result of the combination of binging and purging, she displays frequent weight fluctuations of greater than ten pounds. Yet most of these young women are either of normal weight or only slightly overweight, unlike the anorexic who is extremely thin (APA, 1980).

Other physical symptoms associated with overeating and forceful vomiting include dehydration and electrolyte imbalance, swelling and infection of the salivary glands, dental decay and gum disease, and muscle weakness and cramps. If the condition continues, internal bleeding, perforation of the esophagus and stomach, and heart irregularities may cause heart failure and death (ACHA, 1984; Mitchell & Pyle, 1982; APA, 1980).

Although the anorexic denies that she has a problem, the bulimic is aware that her eating pattern is abnormal. She knows that eating dominates her life, and that she is unable to control both the binging and the vomiting. She feels a great deal of shame and guilt for her impulsive behaviors and exhibits symptoms of chronic depression. The disorder becomes a vicious cycle of eating to reduce anxiety and then vomiting to reduce anxiety about overeating. Other compulsive problems sometimes are associated with bulimia, such as alcohol and drug abuse, or shoplifting—often food (APA, 1980; Mitchell & Pyle, 1982).

Combined Disorders

As mentioned earlier, combinations of these two disorders are likely to occur, and some confusion exists among researchers about whether anorexia nervosa and bulimia are in actuality extremes of the same disorder. Some, but not all, individuals exhibiting one eating disorder exhibited a different eating disorder earlier in life (Holmgren et al., 1983). Therefore, attempts have been made to compare the anorexic, who restricts her food intake, with the bulimic, who either just binges or binges, restricts food intake, and also purges (Halmi, 1983; Norman & Herzog, 1983; Holmgren et al., 1983). Those who have exhibited symptoms of both extremes have certain personality characteristics that distinguish them from those who have exhibited symptoms of only one disorder. Nevertheless, it is more useful to find the similarities among the disorders, with the understanding that all eating disorders are life-threatening and therapy should be sought immediately.

All eating disorders are habitual and compulsive in nature, which means that they occur repeatedly and result from some psychological pressure that makes little logical sense and results in negative emotional consequences. These disorders are also addictive, in the sense that individuals believe they can never satisfy their cravings (Gormally, 1984). The anorexic fears losing control of her desire to lose weight and ultimately becoming obese; similarly, the bulimic fears she will be unable to control her craving for food and will become obese. Both disorders are centered around a preoccupation with food and eating (Holmgren et al., 1983).

Treatment

The resident assistant should place educational literature about anorexia and bulimia in high traffic areas so that students who suspect they have a problem will be able to educate themselves about the disorder. Frequently, roommates and other friends will notice the problem and will seek advice before the afflicted person does. If you suspect the problem, it is important to talk with the student about it. She will need knowledge about the symptoms and characteristics of the disorder and information about where she can seek help on campus. The RA should stress the fact that eating disorders are life-threatening but that they are curable. The individual may feel more comfortable if the RA or a close friend accompanies her on the first visit to the health service. It is essential that she receives professional treatment.

Treatment consists of appropriate medical care for the physical symptoms, including drug therapy and hospitalization when necessary. Psychological care may include behavioral modification, nutritional education, individual psychotherapy, group counseling, and/or family counseling (NICHHD, no date). The patient learns to gain control over her impulses, to express her emotions appropriately, and to be more assertive and independent in interpersonal relationships.

Alcohol Abuse

Problem Definition

The consumption of alcohol is an integral part of the college experience. No other population in the United States has a larger proportion of drinkers. It is estimated that 90 to 94 percent of students begin to drink before they reach college, and both men and women drink more as they progress from freshman to senior year (Mills, Neal, & Peed-Neal, 1983).

The problems associated with alcohol consumption are widespread on college campuses. A recent national survey of 202 colleges found that 61 percent of residence hall damage, 60 percent of violent behavior, 34 percent of emotional difficulties, and 29 percent of academic problems are all alcohol related (Gadaleto & Anderson, 1986). Other problems typically associated with college drinking include missing classes due to hangovers and injuries or deaths from falls, fights, or driving an automobile (Mills et al., 1983). Additionally, many deaths or near deaths are reported every year caused by drinking alone—not in combination with some other variable such as driving while drinking (Blimling & Miltenberger, 1981). Despite the fact that most problems associated with college drinking diminish after college (Mills et al., 1983), there is strong evidence that alcohol abuse develops within the first five years after regular drinking is established, and heavy drinking in adolescence is likely to be associated with later alcohol dependence (APA, 1980).

Although research has determined that genetics greatly affect alcohol use (50 percent of all alcoholics have an alcoholic parent), inheritance is not the only factor. In some population subgroups (religious, ethnic, geographic, or socioeconomic), alcohol consumption is considered part of sex-role orientation or transition to adult status. Thus, young males may drink to symbolize their virility, their independence, or their manhood (Leigh, 1985). Other influential cultural factors include drinking alcohol as part of religious ceremonies, meals, or social rituals, and the institution of alcohol policies and other social regulations. For example, many campuses have established policies regulating the use of alcohol dictating that parties can be held only under certain circumstances, restricting the time, place, and amount of alcohol allowed, and setting out other requirements such as serving food and nonalcoholic beverages.

Environmental factors also influence drinking patterns. Most students learn to drink from the groups with whom they closely identify and socialize: their families and peer groups. The family role relationships and drinking history determine what drinking behaviors students perceive as expected or normal and later may choose to emulate (Leigh, 1985). Many social customs reinforce the belief that experimentation with alcohol is part of the process of growing up. Furthermore, student peers reinforce excessive drinking behaviors by laughing at drunken actions, joking about a particular person's performance on a given occasion, and labeling excessive drinkers with pet nicknames (Blimling & Miltenberger, 1984). Similarly, different types of college environments will encourage or discourage alcohol use. For example, on some campuses intoxication is routinely associated with fraternity pledging, football games, or special traditions, yet may not be socially accepted at basketball games, formal dances, or theatre events.

There have been many attempts to isolate personality factors that might determine alcohol abuse. There is a slight indication that problem drinkers in the college environment feel inadequate, have a negative self-concept, and lack self-acceptance (Dennison, Prevet, & Affleck, 1980; Solomon & Keeley, 1982). Other researchers report that drug abuse (including alcohol) among college students may be related to dissatisfaction with life, such as boredom and feelings of being unappreciated, unrecognized, or unhealthy (Wright & Moore, 1982). It should be noted that attempts to define an alcoholic or pre-alcoholic personality among the general adult population have been contradictory at best (NIAAA, 1980). Research indicates that most drinking problems among college students are likely to occur as acute events that are situationally defined, not chronic conditions (Mills et al., 1981). Nevertheless, the RA should never ignore the problem drinker by assuming he or she is just passing through a stage. Alcohol abuse and dependence are the result of recurring actions over a long period, all signaling the need for professional help.

Symptoms of Problem Drinking

Alcohol is the shortened term for ethyl alcohol, a depressant drug that slows the activity of the central nervous system and the brain. The substance has the power to alter moods and induce sedation, intoxication, or unconsciousness. The beverage alcohol is absorbed into the bloodstream directly from the walls of the stomach and the small intestine and is carried to every other part of the body.

The effects of alcohol are influenced by each person's body weight, speed of drinking, choice of beverage, accompanying food consumption, mood, and previous drinking experience. In general, one drink can be burned by the average-weight person within one and one-half hours. The definition of one drink is based on the percent of alcohol in the particular beverage and its typical serving size. Thus, a 12-ounce beer, a 5-ounce glass of wine, a 3-ounce glass of fortified sherry or port, a 1.5-ounce shot of hard liquor such as whiskey or vodka, and one mixed cocktail all produce identical effects on the body. If alcohol consumption increases beyond the recommended one drink every hour and a half, changes in mood and behavior progress from 1) a relaxed, sociable state, to 2) impaired motor activity, to 3) mental disorientation, to 4) a barely conscious stupor, and then to 5) coma and death (NIAAA, 1980).

There are three behavioral risk factors commonly associated with problem drinking among college students: consuming more than five drinks on each drinking occasion, an increase in the frequency of drinking occasions, and an increase in the frequency of intoxication (Mills et al., 1983). Additionally, there are three main patterns of chronic alcohol abuse among all populations: 1) the regular daily intake of large amounts, 2) regular heavy drinking limited to weekends, or 3) long periods of sobriety interspersed with binges of daily heavy drinking that last for weeks or months (APA, 1980). These factors are strong indications that social drinking has become problem drinking.

Alcoholism is a progressive disease that develops over a period of time. The individual drinks in order to function or to cope with life events and gradually develops a psychological and physical dependence upon alcohol. Alcoholics cannot control the amount of alcohol they consume and repeatedly drink more than they intend until intoxicated. Alcoholics also have developed a tolerance for alcohol and need to consume greater amounts to produce the same effect a lesser dose once generated. Alcoholics cannot stop drinking altogether without experiencing withdrawal symptoms that include extreme nervousness, anxiety, perspiration, nausea, trembling, confusion, panic, hallucinations, and potentially fatal convulsions. The disease has negative social and occupational consequences and eventually destroys the health of the affected person (ACA, no date).

The American Council on Alcoholism has produced a list of symptoms that, in addition to the above main description, indicate an individual has a drinking problem:

1. drinks increasing amounts of alcohol and is intoxicated often;

2. preoccupied with drinking to the exclusion of other activities;

3. makes promises to quit but breaks them;

4. exhibits behavioral and personality changes (tense, irritable, mood fluctuations);

5. conceals drinking or drinks alone;

6. experiences "blackouts," during which he or she was able to function but cannot now remember any of the events that occurred during that period of intoxication;

7. drinks before stressful events or to relieve anxiety, loneliness, or depression (before a party, school, or work);

8. denies or makes excuses for drinking, and becomes angry or defensive if someone mentions it;

9. loses interest in appearance and hygiene;

10. develops poor health (loss of appetite, respiratory infections, depression, or nervousness);

11. experiences problems with family, friends, counselors, professors, employers, and the legal establishment (absenteeism, poor academic work, social isolation, divorce, accidents, or arrests for intoxication) (ACA, no date, p. 2).

The many health risks associated with alcohol abuse include the following: 1) damage to the central nervous system and brain, resulting in changes in sensation, perception, motor control, and emotional control; 2) damage to the heart, lungs, and liver; 3) cancer of the esophagus, mouth, throat, larynx, and liver, the risk of which greatly increases if the drinker also smokes; 4) several muscular diseases; 5) gastritis, ulcers, and pancreatitis; 6) pneumonia and respiratory infections; 7) malnutrition and anemia; and 8) mental disorders (NIAAA, 1982). Of course, these health risks only are associated with alcoholism, not the responsible intake of limited amounts of alcohol.

Treatment

Because most students have already experimented with alcohol before arriving on campus, the resident assistant should encourage the responsible use of alcohol instead of preaching abstinence. Responsible drinking entails obeying state and university regulations regarding drinking and driving, not drinking beyond the individual tolerance level, recognizing another person's right not to drink, providing food and nonalcoholic beverages at all social events where alcohol will be served, and discouraging inappropriate or irresponsible drinking behavior. With the recent changes in laws affecting the drinking age, however, this issue has become more complicated. While it is reasonable to expect a responsible person to obey state laws and university regulations on drinking, it also is reasonable to expect the college student to conform to group norms. The student culture probably will reinforce the importance of obeying regulations in situations in which there is a high risk of getting caught but probably will condone unauthorized drinking when that same risk is low.

The resident assistant must know and be able to identify problem drinking behaviors; must intervene when inappropriate behavior is damaging the building, other residents, or the drinker; and must see that the problem drinker receives appropriate medical and counseling assistance. Approach any intoxicated person with care. Realize that the brain has been anesthetized by alcohol and thinking will be impaired so that atypical behavior, such as violence or mood changes, may surface. The RA should seek assistance from another staff member or responsible student to help the intoxicated person into bed. Use a calm, rational approach. Although disciplinary action for violent behavior is essential (such as separation from other people or removal from the building by police), delay any discussion about drinking behavior until the student is sober and can talk sensibly.

There is no quick way to sober up an intoxicated person; a cold shower, coffee, oxygen, or exercise will not improve the situation. Bed rest, taking analgesics such as aspirin or acetaminophen for pain, and ingesting food when the stomach can tolerate it are the best means of helping the body recover from alcohol poisoning. The general rule is that it takes one and one-half hours for each drink to become metabolized, but hangover symptoms can persist for some time thereafter. When students "pass out," turn them on their sides, so that they do not accidentally inhale vomitus, and monitor their breathing. Seek medical care immediately if the skin tone is purplish, breathing is irregular, or if the person appears to be in a coma and does not respond to gentle shaking.

The RA should be able to distinguish between alcoholic behavior and the occasional irresponsible use of alcohol by a student who does not display the symptoms of problem drinking. Alcoholics are suffering from a disease that requires help from medical and psychological professionals, although the individuals are usually the last to realize it because of their denial patterns. Do not hesitate to discuss the issue with a problem drinker, delineating the particular behaviors that indicate he or she needs assistance. Sometimes a group confrontation involving roommates, classmates, and other staff members helps the drinker face the reality of his or her behavior. During the confrontation all the people involved should thoroughly explore the behaviors they have observed and the feelings they have experienced. Offer hope to the person by indicating that alcoholism is a treatable disease. Refer the drinker to the campus health services, inform your hall director, and also provide a list of community agencies that can provide assistance.

It is important for the RA to seek the assistance and support of his or her supervisor when dealing with alcohol abuse problems. There are no simple remedies or counseling strategies that will work in each situation. In extreme cases involving repeated damage to the residence hall and its inhabitants, it may be necessary, after providing fair warning, for the hall director or other housing official to confront the individual with the option of either accepting treatment or losing the privilege of remaining in the residence hall or at the college. It is not uncommon for the alcoholic to lose all support systems before he or she realizes the need for treatment.

Professional treatment consists of three stages. The first is the immediate management of acute intoxication and withdrawal symptoms. This may not require in-patient hospitalization in all cases, but usually involves the administration of anticonvulsive medications, vitamin and nutritional therapy, and sleep. The second stage involves treating the related health problems brought on by drinking so the body can begin to heal itself.

The last stage involves long-term behavior change so that the destructive drinking patterns do not continue. This phase may include participation in counseling or psychotherapy (individual, group, and/or family) to learn to cope with life problems, social self-help groups such as Alcoholics Anonymous, and possibly academic and career counseling. In some cases, the drug disulfiram (Antabase) is taken daily to discourage the return of the disease. When combined with alcohol, disulfiram causes headache and nausea. The only "cure" for alcoholism is total sobriety and maintenance of daily control over the urge to drink alcohol in order to cope with personal and social problems.

Drug Abuse

Problem Definition

Drug abuse is indicated by a pattern of repeated intake of a chemical substance* for the purpose of altering mood and behavior, eventually causing social, school, or employment problems. These problems typically include a failure to meet obligations to others; absenteeism; the inappropriate expression of emotions; erratic behavior; arrest for possession, purchase, or sale of a drug; accidents; and a general deterioration in appearance and health. The affected person usually remains intoxicated by the drug and continues to use it, despite the related social, physical, and emotional problems (APA, 1980).

Progressive use generally leads to a tolerance for the substance and a physical or psychological dependence upon it. An individual is considered to have developed a tolerance when his or her body has become so adapted to the drug that increasing amounts are needed to achieve the desired effect. The individual is psychologically or physically dependent when specific withdrawal symptoms follow ceasing or reducing the intake of the substance; the dependent person has reached a stage of needing the drug in order to adequately function on a daily basis (DSM III, 1980). These unpleasant, painful, and sometimes life-threatening symptoms differ according to the specific drug and may include anxiety, nervousness, trembling, nausea, chills or sweating, hallucinations, and life-threatening convulsions.

As with alcohol use, a majority of students appear to have experimented with drugs before coming to the college campus. The National Institute on Drug Abuse (1983) reported that 57 percent of high school seniors have tried marijuana, 16 percent have tried cocaine, and 9 percent have used other opiates. Another study (ADAMHA, 1986) found that 28 percent of 18- to 25-year-olds (the traditional college population) have tried cocaine. Furthermore, it has been demonstrated that drug abuse is the second most common psychiatric disorder, after alcohol abuse, among this age group. The incidence for the 18- to 25-year-old population exhibiting the clinical symptoms of the problem is approximately 11 to 17 percent with more males (6–11 percent) than females (3–6 percent) (Myers et al., 1984; Robins et al., 1984).

As with alcohol abuse, there have been many attempts to explain drug use by adolescents and young adults. Although drugs are accessible and knowledge about them is readily available, the mere presence of drugs is not sufficient to explain why some students choose to use them experimentally, others become heavy users, and others never try them at all. There is some indication that conditions of early life may place a young person at risk for developing multiple problem behaviors. Engaging in a variety of deviant activities eventually may become part of that person's identity. Students who lack self-confidence, are socially isolated, and are experiencing negative emotions are more likely to fall into this category than those who are self-satisfied and have a set of strong values and beliefs shared by family and friends (Oetting & Beauvais, 1986).

Despite the indication that familial and personality factors may be of some consequence, 95 percent of drug use among the adolescent population can be accounted for by the influence of peers alone (Oetting & Beauvais, 1986). It is in the peer cluster, a small group of best friends or a couple, that drugs are first provided and experimentation begins. Since the peer cluster shares beliefs, values, and rationales about drug use, their common behavior gives the members a group identity. Group membership supports the continued use of drugs and isolates the student from people who might be of some influence in stopping it.

Students say they use drugs because they like the feeling the specific drug causes, it is an expected party behavior among friends, and the drugs relieve feelings of boredom, anxiety, or unhappiness (Oetting & Beauvais, 1986). Among adolescents, drugs generally are used sporadically in socially confined situations. It is only when the individual has become chemically dependent or has a serious psychological or physical problem that drug use is likely to occur outside the group.

---

*Note: Although alcohol is classified as a drug, it typically is discussed separately because its use is legal in our society, unlike most of the other drugs discussed in this section.

It is important for the resident assistant to be able to identify the symptoms of abuse discussed in this section because all drugs, including alcohol, can produce serious side effects. At the least, drug use may limit the normal process of experiencing the breadth of college life. Because drugs impair the mind, they increase the likelihood of accidents and violent behavior. Drug abuse can reduce the body's resistance to infections and bring about malnutrition, organic damage, and mental illness. An overdose can cause psychosis, convulsions, coma, and death.

The effects of different drugs will vary, depending on what substance is used, how much is taken, previous drug experience, and the health, personality, and surroundings of the user. Combining one drug with another in order to heighten or to counteract the effects of a substance and to avoid withdrawal symptoms, multiplies the health risks (NIDA, 1984). In essence, one drug added to another drug does not equal two doses, but instead may have the effect of four or more doses. This chemical reaction, known as synergism, is particularly important, because frequent drug abusers are likely to combine drugs. Information about the symptoms, methods of intake, side effects, and health risks associated with the six classes of drugs will be defined in the next section.

Marijuana

Marijuana and hashish (called grass, pot, weed, and hash) are products of the cannabis plant. Cannabis may be smoked in a pipe or cigarette (called a joint or reefer) or eaten. The drug's effects can be felt immediately and persist for about three hours. Because cannabis is stored in the fat tissues of the body, its presence can be detected in urine tests up to a week after taken. When burned, it characteristically produces a sweet odor, which may be noticed on the skin or clothing of persons who have been in a smoke-filled room for some time. Cannabis intoxication results in altered mood and perception. The user feels euphoric (varying from elation to relaxed indifference) and experiences a slowed sense of time. Cannabis increases the heart rate, stimulates the appetite, causes the eyes to become bloodshot and the mouth to feel dry, and provokes laughter. Its use commonly impairs judgment and physical coordination and, in some people, may cause a panic attack or a loss of reality awareness. The health risks associated with cannabis use are much greater than those of tobacco smoking. They include lung damage, chronic emphysema, and cancer. Research also has shown that marijuana affects the sex hormones, causing reduced fertility and premature babies (APA, 1980; NIDA, 1984).

Stimulants

Stimulants, as the name implies, speed up the action of the central nervous system and the brain. This category of drugs contains amphetamines (called speed, uppers, bennies, dexies, and pep or diet pills), cocaine (called coke, crack, snow, flake, and rock), and caffeine (normally found in coffee, tea, colas, cocoa, chocolate, and tablets for pain, colds, or to keep users awake). Amphetamines are usually taken as a tablet or capsule or are injected intravenously. Cocaine may be sniffed into the nose through a small straw, smoked in a pipe or cigarette, or modified into a liquid form and injected intravenously. The cocaine user experiences an immediate "rush" and the effects usually disappear within 6 to 24 hours. Amphetamines usually produce a slower, more lasting effect.

People intoxicated by stimulants typically are elated, restless, overactive, anxious, and talkative. Physical symptoms include accelerated heart and breathing rates, dilated pupils, decreased appetite, elevated blood pressure, tremors, sweating or chills, and possibly nausea and vomiting. Because of the method of administration, cocaine sniffers also will exhibit a runny or congested nose and nosebleeds. It is not uncommon for stimulant users to display violent or aggressive behavior, suspiciousness or paranoia, and hallucinations about bugs crawling under the skin. After the immediate effects have subsided, users feel fatigued due to disturbed sleep patterns, depressed, and even suicidal. Health risks associated with stimulant use include malnutrition, mental illness, seizures, stroke, heart failure, and death.

Although caffeine is not a controlled substance, overuse of this drug can cause effects similar to those mentioned above. Additional negative effects include increased urination, headaches, stomach complaints and ulcers, irregular heart rates, and heart disease (APA, 1980; NIDA, 1984).

Depressants

The drugs in this category include barbiturates (called barbs, downers, blues, or goof balls), sedatives or tranquilizers (such as valium or librium), hypnotics such as methaqualone (called ludes or sopors), and alcohol. As with alcohol use, depressants slow down the activity of the central nervous system and the brain, producing effects such as slurred speech, drowsiness, loss of coordination, slowed reflexes, confusion, and faulty judgment. Furthermore, the user's mood may be unstable, causing irritability and aggressive behavior.

The use of depressants is particularly dangerous when combined with alcohol. Since both drugs are in the same classification, the mixture can cause an overdose, which in turn can cause a loss of memory, coma, and death. A person experiencing withdrawal from depressants will demonstrate tremors, nausea and vomiting, sweating, elevated heart rate and blood pressure, anxiety, and depression (APA, 1980; NIDA, 1984).

Hallucinogens

Hallucinogens distort perception, sensations, emotions, and thinking so that consciousness is clouded. The person may see or hear things that are not present in reality. Drugs included in this classification are usually known by initials rather than their longer chemical names: LSD (called acid), mescaline, DMT, MDA, MDMA (called ecstacy), and PCP (called angel dust).

Most of the hallucinogens, with the exception of PCP, are taken orally and bring about perceptual changes while the person is fully alert. Users may "see" geometric shapes, objects, or people that are not present, may confuse one sense (such as vision) with another sense (hearing), may feel they are outside their bodies, or may perceive that they are smaller or larger than they really are. Their judgment is impaired, and they may become anxious, depressed, or afraid they are becoming insane. Physical symptoms include dilated pupils, increased heart rate, sweating, tremors, and uncoordinated movements. The drug's effects are noticed within one hour and may last from six hours to as long as three days. Sometimes the user will experience a "flashback" of the hallucination after the drug is no longer in the body. Health risks associated with hallucinogens include injuring the self or others, convulsions, brain damage, coma, and death.

PCP sometimes is placed in a separate category because it rarely causes a pure hallucinosis (APA, 1980); that is, although there is a noticeably disturbed state of awareness, the person usually does not see or hear things that are not present. PCP can be smoked or inhaled, and the effects may be felt almost immediately and persist for three to six hours. An intoxicated person's eyes will move rapidly vertically or horizontally. The user will exhibit an increased heart rate and blood pressure, inarticulate speech, and impaired muscular coordination. PCP causes euphoria, agitation, anxiety, unstable emotions, a feeling of slowed time, and a loss of pain sensation. The intoxicated person's behavior may be unpredictable, impulsive, and violent. Health risks of PCP use include harm to the self and others, depression, convulsions, brain damage, suicide, and death (APA, 1980; NIDA, 1984).

Opiates (Narcotics)

Opiates are used to decrease the perception of pain and to increase feelings of relaxation. As such, the results may appear similar to those of alcohol or barbiturate intoxication, except that opiates cause the pupils to become constricted (unless the person has taken an overdose, in which case, the pupils will be dilated). The drugs in this classification include heroin (called smack, junk, or scag), morphine (called dreamer), opium, and codeine. They are taken orally, injected intravenously, sniffed into the nose, or injected just under the skin. The effects usually are noticed immediately and can last approximately four to six hours. Symptoms of opiate intoxication include lethargy, apathy, and loss of judgment. The individual may alternate between alertness and drowsiness, exhibit slurred speech, and have impaired attention and memory. Symptoms of withdrawal are nausea, vomiting, diarrhea, chills or sweating, runny nose and eyes, and sleeplessness. Health risks associated with opiate use include skin abscesses, pneumonia and hepatitis, malnutrition, heart disease, diabetes, coma, and death.

Methadone is a synthetic drug that has been used to help addicts withdraw safely from opiates. Although its use produces milder effects, it can also be abused, just like the opiates, if taken in large quantities in an uncontrolled, non-medical setting (APA, 1980, NIDA, 1984).

Inhalants

Inhalants are chemical vapors that are breathed into the lungs, causing a slowing of the central nervous system and brain. Most of the substances in this classification are not intended to be used as drugs. Their normal, daily applications are misused in order to alter the functions of the mind and body. These substances include aerosol sprays (such as cookware sprays or hair sprays), solvents (such as nail polish remover, cleaning fluids, or furniture refinishing products), paints, glue, liquid paper, and gasoline. This category does contain some drugs developed for medical use: nitrous oxide (called laughing gas), amyl nitrite (called poppers or snappers), and butyl nitrite (called locker room or rush). These substances are taken in a variety of manners, such as sniffing directly from the container, breathing the vapors from a paper bag, or leaving the container open in a small enclosure where there is poor ventilation. The effects are noticed immediately but usually last only a few minutes unless the user continues taking the substance within a given period of time.

Abuse of inhalants results in decreased heart and breathing rates; a flushed face and neck; dizziness and headache; nausea and vomiting; sneezing, coughing, and nosebleeds; loss of coordination and appetite; and confusion and decreased judgment. In higher doses, violent behavior, unconsciousness, or immediate death can occur because oxygen in the lungs is displaced, leading to suffocation or respiratory depression. Long-term use results in fatigue, weight loss, permanent damage to the nervous system, and organic failure (NIDA, 1984). An accidental inhalation reaction resulting from the normal use of these substances is common among people who use the products without adequate ventilation.

Designer Drugs

The so-called "designer drugs" are synthetic chemical facsimiles of illicit drugs found in several of the above categories (stimulants, hallucinogens, and narcotics). Thousands of types of drugs are manufactured relatively easily in small laboratories throughout America as a low-cost high-profit substitute for drugs that are listed as illegal and are difficult to import.

The greatest hazard associated with these ever-changing drugs is the lack of quality control over potency, dilution, and formula. The results of these chemical experiments have produced disastrous physical consequences, such as psychosis, instant paralysis and brain damage, and immediate death. In addition, people develop a tolerance to these chemicals relatively quickly, leading to the possibility of overdose. Students should be made aware of the fact that the next seemingly innocuous dose of "ecstasy" (a hallucinogenic amphetamine also known as MDM) can be unpredictable.

AIDS and Drug Use

Although it is well-publicized that the AIDS (Acquired Immune Deficiency Syndrome) virus is easily transmitted by blood, most intravenous drug users are so dependent on their drug that they will not abstain in order to locate a sterile needle if one is not handy. Thus, AIDS is epidemic among IV drug users who share needles.

Many college students experiment with drug use as they are exploring their sexual identity. They discover that alcohol reduces inhibitions and learn from their peers that various drugs supposedly increase sexual pleasure. Unfortunately, they frequently are unaware that drug use can affect their judgment regarding the avoidance of risky sexual behaviors. Also, there is increasing evidence that drug use suppresses the immune system, so the body is less able to fight the AIDS virus. Residential hall programming about alcohol and drugs always should include a discussion of AIDS, and vice versa.

Co-Dependency

Co-dependency is a term used to describe some family members of various types of abusers including alcohol, drug, violent, or sexual abusers. The family members are labeled co-dependents because they are not abusers themselves, but they are extremely dependent on the abuser, highly tolerant of the abusive behavior, and unable to separate themselves from the abusive situation.

College students who reveal the pain associated with co-dependence need professional counseling. The resident assistant can help by showing concern and encouraging the student to seek help from a mental health counselor or from community self-help groups such as AL-ANON or Adult Children of Alcoholics (ACA).

Caution

It is important for the resident assistant to be aware of the fact that many physical and mental conditions mimic the symptoms of drug withdrawal. For example, a diabetic experiencing an insulin reaction may lose motor control, collapse, perspire profusely, and exhibit mental confusion or irritability. Similarly, a schizophrenic may exhibit behaviors indicating a clouded state of consciousness, such as confused speech and hallucinations. Therefore, it is necessary to question the afflicted person to determine what he or she believes is causing the discomfort and to seek medical help immediately, even if that person denies a problem exists or says that the symptoms will pass, given some time. Ask the person specific questions regarding previous occurrence of the symptoms, what drugs or conditions might be causing the reaction, and what has helped in the past to relieve them. Realize that these symptoms, whatever the cause, are serious and can be life-threatening.

Treatment

Resident assistants should counsel students who indicate by their behaviors that they have been repeatedly taking one or more drugs and that their drug use is causing social, academic, or family difficulties. Students need to be told what specific behaviors have been observed and that these behaviors indicate a drug problem. They should be informed that chemical dependency is treatable and provided a list of helping agencies. If the student is hurting other people or themselves, or damaging property, it may be necessary to require an immediate examination at the campus health service as a condition of remaining in the residence hall. Drug abusers are likely to deny that a problem exists and to refuse to seek treatment. It may be helpful to assist them in making an appointment or to accompany them to the health services.

Treatments for drug problems vary according to the type of drug and the severity of dependence. Usually medically supervised detoxification is necessary to control the withdrawal symptoms associated with stopping the drug. Psychotherapy or counseling helps the dependent person learn how to cope with the problems that have contributed to drug use, and self-help groups or family counseling provide a source of support so that the individual is not tempted to return to the use of drugs once the body is detoxified. In some cases, group homes and halfway houses become the new residence while the individual is recovering and reentering a more productive lifestyle.

Case Studies and Structured Group Experiences on Substance Abuse: Food, Alcohol, and Drugs

Case Studies: Eating Disorder

Instructions: Read the case studies and respond to the questions which follow. First work alone. When you are finished, share your answers with other RAs in small group discussions or as the basis for a classroom discussion.

Kelly's friends have come to you, seeking advice about her unusual behaviors. Since midterm exams she has been staying up all night and sleeping most of the daytime hours when she is not in classes. Even though she appears exhausted, Kelly says she must study late so she can earn no less than a 3.8 this semester, the grade-point she needs in order to be accepted to law school next year. She says her parents expect her to become an attorney, just like her older brother. Each morning when her friends arrive to walk with her to class, they have observed her trash can filled with empty containers of ice cream, frozen desserts, and doughnuts. They report that she frequently invites them to accompany her to the neighborhood fast food restaurants and that she usually orders two or three times as much as she used to because she is "nervous about final exams," which are still a month away. They say they are amazed that she does not seem to have gained any weight. One of her friends says she has noticed the smell of vomit in the restroom after Kelly has been there and that once she saw an empty bottle of ipecac in the trash can. Furthermore, Kelly has not been taking care of her appearance lately and seems to have lost her usual vitality and good humor.

Case Study Questions:

1. What are the behavioral, physical, and psychological symptoms of Kelly's problems? _____

_____

_____

_____

_____

_____

2. What are the probable sources of her stress? _____

_____

_____

_____

_____

_____

3. How will you handle the problem? _____

_____

_____

_____

_____

_____

_____

_____

_____

_____

Case Study: Alcohol Abuse

Rob, a freshman from a small, rural community, is living it up since he arrived at the largest university in the state. Almost every weekend night, he has arrived at the residence hall drunk. He never misses a chance to go out to the bars with the other guys on his floor and frequently invents a reason to "celebrate." He likes to brag about how much beer he drank on a given occasion, and his friends have dubbed him "Slosh." He has begun to miss classes in the morning because he feels too sick to get out of bed and says he has to drink a little bit in order to reduce the symptoms of his hangovers. Recently, his roommate requested to move out of the room because it always is cluttered with empty bottles and cans, which the roommate refuses to clean up, and the place continually smells like sour beer. When his roommate told Rob that his midterm grades indicated that he might flunk out of school if he didn't buckle down and study, Rob became angry, screamed that it was "none of his business," and threw an empty bottle out the door of the room.

Case Study Questions:

1. What behaviors indicate that Rob has a drinking problem? _____

2. What are the possible sources of Rob's problem, and what factors might encourage its continuance?

3. How will you handle the problem? _____

Case Study: Drug Abuse

Mark is a shy architecture student who spent his first year living in a single room. Because his parents were concerned that he was not integrating well with other students, they required him to share a room this year. They were relieved to discover that Mark's roommate included him in his social group immediately. When Mark visited his parents over the holidays, they noticed that he appeared to be extremely nervous, anxious, and irritable. They have telephoned to request that you determine if Mark is having any problems on campus and that you let them know as soon as possible. Although you have observed that Mark, once quiet and retiring, now is part of his roommate's "fast" crowd and that they "party" frequently, no unusual problems have been noticed.

This night, Mark's roommate rushes in to ask for your help. Mark is lying doubled up on the floor of their room. His breathing rate is accelerated, his pupils are dilated, and he is trembling and sweating profusely. He says he "feels like he's going to die." As you telephone for an ambulance, you notice a small mirror and straw lying on the desk.

Case Study Questions:

1. What are the physical symptoms of Mark's problem? _____
   _____
   _____
   _____
   _____

2. What are the probable cultural influences leading to his problem? _____
   _____
   _____
   _____
   _____

3. How will you handle the problem? _____
   _____
   _____
   _____
   _____
   _____
   _____
   _____

Exercise: Values Clarification

Goals:

1. To identify and publically admit values held regarding people with substance abuse problems;
2. To analyze how these values may help or hinder the resident assistant's assigned responsibilities.

Group Size: Small sub-groups of 3 to 5 people within the larger class of less than 40

Time required: Approximately 45 minutes

Materials: Pens and pencils; copies of "Beliefs about Substance Abuse"

Physical Setting: Desks placed in small circular groups to facilitate discussion

Process:

1. Individual members will complete the sentence stems provided on the questionnaire entitled "Beliefs about Substance Abuse."
2. Each sub-group member in turn will reveal to the others how each sentence was completed.
3. The small sub-group will discuss how these values will help or hinder their work with residents.

Beliefs about Substance Abuse

Directions: Complete each sentence stem with the first thought that comes to mind. Try to be honest about your feelings.

1. When I smell or see vomit, I feel _____

2. People who self-induce vomiting are _____

3. Dieting is _____

4. People who are successful dieters are _____

5. When dieting, I feel _____

   _____

6. When I think of someone gorging large quantities of food into her mouth as fast as she can, I feel

   _____

7. Obese people are _____

8. The smell of sweat makes me feel _____

9. Drunk people are _____

10. When I see someone out of control I feel _____

11. If someone fell to the floor, writhing and screaming in pain, I would feel _____

12. Using drugs for non-medical reasons is _____

13. A friend who introduces drugs to his roommate is _____

14. A college student who gives drugs to children is _____

15. People who harm others while under the influence of drugs should be _____

16. Thinking about finding a person who has overdosed on drugs makes me feel _____

17. People who cannot stop a bad habit are _____

18. Counselors who choose to work with drug addicts are _____

19. A person who breaks a promise is _____

20. People who turn to drugs to cope with life problems are _____

Exercise: Identifying Substance Abuse Problems

Goals:

1. To identify the symptoms of substance abuse
2. To compare and contrast symptoms of eating disorders, alcohol abuse, and drug abuse

Group Size: Small sub-groups of 3 to 5 people within the class of less than 40 members

Time Required: Approximately 45 to 60 minutes

Materials: 1. Pens or pencils; 2. "Identifying Substance Abuse" forms; 3. Chalkboard or large pad on an easel

Physical Setting: Desks, placed in small circular sub-groups to facilitate discussion

Process:

1. Group members discuss and fill in the chart "Identifying Substance Abuse."
2. After all groups have completed their charts, representatives report the results for placement on the chalkboard or overhead projector.
3. The class then discusses the similarities and differences among the different types of abuse.

Identifying Substance Abuse

Instructions: For each symptom in the chart below, rate its relative degree of association with each type of substance abuse by writing *U* if it is "usually present," *S* if it is "sometimes present," and by leaving blank those symptoms that are never present.

	Anorexia	Bulimia	Alcohol	Marijuana	Stimulants	Depressants	Hallucinogens	Opiates	Inhalants
INFLUENCES									
culture									
genetics									
personality									
familial pressure									
peer pressure									
environmental press									
BEHAVIORAL:									
social isolation									
social integration									
restrictive dieting									
binge eating									
normal eating									
excessive exercise									
diuretics, laxatives									
ipecac use									
vomiting									
substance preoccupation									
body size preoccupation									
secretive use									
frequent use									
intermittent use									
pattern of use									
compulsive use									
impulsive acts									

	Anorexia	Bulimia	Alcohol	Marijuana	Stimulants	Depressants	Hallucinogens	Opiates	Inhalants
BEHAVIORAL: *Continued*									
irresponsibility									
mood changes									
coping mechanism									
behavioral changes									
denial									
intoxication									
passes out									
blacks out									
social problems									
neglects hygiene and health									
violent, aggressive									
PHYSICAL:									
vomiting									
nausea									
dental decay									
amenorrhea									
loss of head hair									
loss of appetite									
weight loss									
normal weight									
underweight									
overweight									
dehydration									
malnutrition									

PHYSICAL: *Continued*	Anorexia	Bulimia	Alcohol	Marijuana	Stimulants	Depressants	Hallucinogens	Opiates	Inhalants
fatigue									
drowsiness, lethargy									
insomnia									
headache									
slurred speech									
rapid speech									
mental alertness									
euphoria									
laughter									
weeping									
restless, jittery									
trembling									
sweating									
rapid breathing									
depressed breathing									
rapid heartbeat									
depressed heartbeat									
flushed face									
impaired coordination									
sneezing or coughing									
nosebleeds, congested nose									
runny nose and eyes									
bloodshot eyes									
dilated pupils									
constricted pupils									
skin marks or abscesses									
infections									
organic disease									
mental confusion									

	Anorexia	Bulimia	Alcohol	Marijuana	Stimulants	Depressants	Hallucinogens	Opiates	Inhalants
PHYSICAL: *Continued*									
hallucinations									
physical collapse									
convulsions									
organic failure									
unconsciousness, coma									
death									
PSYCHOLOGICAL:									
lack of confidence									
lack of independence									
social isolation									
mood swings									
irritability									
extreme anger									
unhappiness, sadness									
elation, happiness									
anxiety, nervousness									
agitation									
suspiciousness									
fearful or worried									
mental confusion									
faulty judgment									
distorted perceptions									
loss of reality									
loss of memory									
unconsciousness									

Exercise: Counseling a Substance Abuser

Goals:

1. To identify methods of counseling people who have substance abuse problems to facilitate their treatment by professionals
2. To practice confrontation methods for possible future duplication in an emergency situation

Group Size: Small sub-groups of 5 to 7 people within the larger class of less than 40 members

Time Required: Approximately one hour

Resource: Invite a professional substance abuse counselor to serve as role model and a group facilitator.

Physical Setting: Chairs arranged in small groups; two chairs facing each other and the others behind or encircling the two for easy observation

Process:

1. One group member volunteers or is selected to be a student who exhibits a substance abuse problem. The professional counselor serves as a resident assistant who is to counsel the student to facilitate the appropriate professional treatment. The other group members serve as observers and, later, as analysts of the role play.
2. Role players will demonstrate actions and reactions typical of their various roles until the problem reaches a state of resolution:

   Resident Assistant: defines specific behaviors displayed by the substance abuser, various feelings experienced by the resident assistant and the abuser's peers, the need to seek appropriate treatment, the availability of college and community resources, and a plan of action to seek help.

   Substance Abuser: displays defensive behaviors such as making excuses and becoming angry, hostile, frustrated, or sad; gradually moves toward recognition and acceptance of the problem, and helps determine a plan of action to seek help.
3. Observers will point out specific behaviors exhibited by both players and will discuss strengths and weaknesses of the action.
4. The procedure is repeated again with two new volunteers demonstrating a different substance abuse problem.
5. The entire class, assisted by the professional counselor, discusses difficulties that occurred and possible means to resolve them in the future.

CHAPTER 13

Sexuality

Jan Miltenberger, R.N.,
Indiana State University

Dr. Lawrence J. Miltenberger,
Indiana State University

Sexuality is related to one's total personality since it involves all that one is in terms of femaleness or maleness. Sex roles, self-esteem, psychosocial development, family structure, schooling, dating experiences, and similar factors, are all intertwined in determining one's perception of sexuality. Probably the first issue to be discussed is the uniqueness of each individual's sexual preferences and differences. It is hard enough to get to know and understand yourself, let alone another person. We learn about ourselves and others by discussing and re-discussing issues, ideas, and problems. This is as true of sexuality as of any other topic.

Initially, it may appear that an RA would not have to deal with problems related to sexuality. However, as college students come into contact with the multitude of living and learning experiences, sexuality is bound to become an issue. One of the biggest lessons to learn is tolerance and acceptance of others and their choice of lifestyle. Living in a residence hall exposes one to living on a day-to-day basis with others quite different from the nuclear family and high school friends.

What does this have to do with sexuality? Many college students living away from home for the first time will be dating more, drinking, and becoming more intimate with the opposite sex. Since society has a more open attitude toward sexuality, each resident will have to make many adjustments and decisions. For example, a female student comes to you, the RA, because her roommate, who has a steady boyfriend, wants her to leave on weekends so he can stay in the room. Or, several students approach you, the male RA, because they are certain that one of the men on the floor is gay. As an RA, it is important for you to have a good understanding of your own attitudes, feelings, and values regarding various aspects of sexuality. You may need to assess your background. Did you take a sex education course in high school or college? Have you attended seminars dealing with sexual issues (e.g., rape awareness)? Do you take advantage of group sessions discussing controversial topics such as abortion, AIDS, or premarital sex? There is no way that anyone can have all of the answers, but it is your responsibility to be aware of your own history and how it influences your attitudes about sex.

As an RA, you should learn about the various resources available on the campus and in the community. You should be able to answer the following questions as they apply to your campus:

1. Is there a student health center on campus?

2. Are the health practitioners sensitive to the sexual problems of young adults?

3. What are the services available to you at the health center?

4. Can students get contraceptive information at the student health center?

5. Are contraceptives dispensed there?

6. Is there a family planning or Planned Parenthood clinic in close proximity?

7. What are the services offered by the family planning agency?

8. Is there a strong Pro-Life group in the community?

This chapter will discuss contraceptives, abortion, pregnancy, homosexuality, and two of the most recently publicized sexually transmitted diseases—chlamydia and AIDS. Then there is a section that includes a case study and two structured exercises.

Contraceptives

There have been many changes in contraceptive practices over the years. In 1984, 36 million American women were faced with preventing an unintended pregnancy. What is the role of the RA in dealing with contraceptive issues? Certainly the RA plays both a supportive and informative role on this issue. Some of the residents on your floor may be knowledgeable about this topic, while others will be almost ignorant. The most familiar methods of contraception are the IUD, sterilization, "the pill," condoms, the sponge, various spermicides, and the Vaginal Contraceptive Film, a new method.

For all practical purposes, IUDs are no longer a significant choice for women. This has come about due to fears, lawsuits, dissatisfaction and medical complications from its use. In 1986, the Progestasert-T IUD was the only one being produced in the United States, and most women were not responding to it positively because it must be replaced annually (Wilbur, 1986).

Sterilization, by means of tubal ligation and other surgical procedures, is the method of choice for women over 30, while "the pill," used by 10 million women, is the second most popular. The condom ranks next; it is depended upon by 4.5 million American women. That number may rise, because society is presently experiencing a major change of attitude about the purchase and use of condoms due to the fear of AIDS. Recent reports indicate that both men and women are buying more condoms. Ads for them are beginning to appear on some television stations and in major newspapers and magazines. The new openness is mandated by serious public health concern. It may well be that using the condom as a means of disease prevention may have the secondary advantage of preventing unwanted pregnancies (Ory, 1983).

A number of birth control techniques have come onto the market in recent years. Spermicides in the form of creams, jellies, suppositories and foams are used by at least 3 million women. Many women do not like the messiness and inconvenience. The "Today" Vaginal Contraceptive Sponge is a leading seller in the over-the-counter market. The sponge contains the spermicide nonoxynol-9, and fits loosely over the cervix. It is a fairly reliable method (10 to 20 percent failure rate) and is easy to buy and use. Clinical studies have shown the sponge to have almost no side effects; however, some women consider it inconvenient and bothersome.

Probably the newest contraceptive method is the Vaginal Contraceptive Film (VCF). This two inch by two inch, paper-thin film contains nonoxynol-9 spermicide. It is inserted into the vagina no less than five minutes and preferably fifteen minutes before intercourse. It remains effective for two hours and does not need to be removed because it dissolves in natural body fluids The most significant side effect has been minor vaginal irritation. The vaginal film is easy to use and is sold over the counter (Leon, 1986).

As RA, you will also have to deal with myths and half-truths. For instance, several articles have been published recently, alerting consumers to beware of using Coca-Cola as a contraceptive douche. A team of Harvard Medical School doctors tested Coca-Cola as a contraceptive and published the results in the *New England Journal of Medicine,* December, 1985. The results indicated that although Coca-Cola does have some spermicidal effects, those effects are limited, and in no way can the soft drink be considered an effective contraceptive (*Statement . . .,* 1985).

It is important for the RA to be aware of the basic information regarding birth control pills, spermicides, diaphragms or cervical caps, the vaginal sponge, condoms, and so on. Students are usually interested in this topic, regardless of their sexual activity. Much is written today about what to use, when, and why. Some college health centers require women students to view a videotape on the various contraceptive choices before discussing the best choice for the individual at specific times in her life. Most students are aware that there is no such thing as the perfect contraceptive with 100 percent effectiveness. The selection of the best contraceptive is a matter of individual choice.

There is always new information available about contraceptives. Programming this topic can be an excellent way of meeting resource people in your community. It is important that you seek knowledgeable, open-minded, sensitive people to be guest speakers for these types of programs. Sexuality and contraception are areas where some people are very opinionated and biased. Good speaker possibilities might include a family practice physician, a gynecologist, a nurse midwife, a sex therapist, a health educator, or a nurse practitioner, especially if the specialty is gynecology.

Pregnancy

As an RA, you may be approached by a female student (or her boyfriend) who "thinks" she might be pregnant. It is extremely important that she see a health professional for evaluation. Does your student health center perform pregnancy tests? If not, the student should go to a family planning clinic, Planned Parenthood, or a private physician. What about home pregnancy tests that you can buy over-the-counter in a drug store? Are they reliable? Answers to these questions require that you have a certain amount of knowledge about pregnancy and about campus and community resources.

Diagnosing a pregnancy is not as easy as you may think. All currently-used pregnancy tests indicate the presence of HCG (human chorionic gonadotropin), a hormone produced by the developing placenta and secreted in the urine. These hormone levels can vary greatly in different women and at different times of the pregnancy. Diagnosing a pregnancy involves both a laboratory test and a pelvic exam by a health professional, either a nurse practitioner or a physician.

The laboratory tests are said to be positive, negative or inconclusive. "False positive" means that the test is positive for pregnancy, even though the woman is not pregnant. This is rare, but it can occur, even with experienced laboratory personnel performing the test. False positives can be caused by drugs such as marijuana, methadone, large amounts of aspirin, birth control pills, and some tranquilizers (Boston Women's Health Collective, 1985). "False negative" means that the test shows that the woman is not pregnant, when in actuality, she is. False negatives are fairly common. There are a number of reasons for this, but among recent findings, researchers have found that if a woman has used marijuana in the last 48 hours, she may have a false negative test (Hatcher, 1984). (Given the effects of any drug use on a variety of tests, as well as other health matters, women students should not get upset when a health professional asks about drug use. The professional needs to have factual information when making these important health decisions.) All of this information regarding pregnancy tests should make most students question the reliability of home pregnancy kits. The test instructions must be followed precisely, and there is still room for error. Money and time are probably best spent by going to a professional health practitioner in the first place.

Once the pregnancy is confirmed, the student can proceed to the next step—deciding what to do. These are not easy decisions, and women need to be aware of their options to decide responsibly. As an RA you may be involved in helping the student think through some of the questions. What are the resources available in your area? What about the father of the child? Who are the support people for the pregnant student? Whom does she want to tell? If she decides to keep the child, what is involved in parenting? As an RA, you must support the person in the choice that is right for her. There is no room here for judgmental, opinionated, and moralistic responses. Be as genuine and compassionate as you can be in understanding her dilemma and her choice.

Abortion

Abortion is still a very emotional laden term, especially in the United States. Each year, American women have approximately 16 million abortions (Ory, 1983). Most students prefer relying on abstinence or contraceptives as their first choices in preventing an unwanted pregnancy. However, accidents do happen for a multitude of reasons, and college women have to make some very serious decisions when an unplanned and possibly unwanted pregnancy occurs.

The RA may be an early confidant of someone who thinks she is pregnant. The RA needs to assess the facts and discuss the situation within the limitations of his or her own experiences and knowledge. A relatively inexperienced RA may want to refer the student to the hall director to assist with beginning decision-making. You should consider these questions: Who should or should not be told? What medical services are necessary? What counseling services are necessary?

If the female student chooses to abort this pregnancy, the RA may again be sought out as a trusted friend and resource person, before, during, and/or after the abortion. The RA needs to carefully assess his or her own attitudes, knowledge, and values regarding abortion. It is important to remember that you only know what is right for you. Each unwanted pregnancy and potential abortion is so uniquely individualized that it is always a challenge to remain objective and support the student's choice. It is *almost never* an easy decision. If you have determined that you canot be totally objective regarding abortion, it may be best for you to refer the student immediately to a professional in the counseling center, the student health center, Planned Parenthood, or to a private physician. Many people believe professional counseling is always needed to assist a woman in makng the most responsible decision for herself and others close to her. Certainly every woman seeking an abortion will need certain types of professional assistance.

Although the abortion issue is too complex to discuss adequately in this chapter, rest assured that the subject is appropriate for programming, provided the topic is handled carefully, objectively, and with good taste. It is wise to confer with your hall director before programming in this area. And always remember, like many other life experiences, potential abortion is certainly easier to discuss and decide as a hypothetical situation than to live through the real thing.

Homosexuality

Homosexuality is probably a topic that will always be controversial and emotional. College age males seem to be extremely fearful, resentful, and reactive toward effeminate males, whom they stereotype as possible gays. Since many of these young males are struggling with identity, self-esteem, and developmental issues, it seems easier for some males to make fun, harrass, or intimidate possible gays than to take the time to learn and understand about differences in lifestyle choices. The RA may have difficulty with some residents, especially males, who discriminate against a possible gay student. The RA may have to be protective of a possible gay student if a group of "macho" males try to pull a prank or pick on someone they have stereotyped as a gay. In general, women students seem to be more accepting of gays and lesbians.

The AIDS epidemic has certainly influenced many opinions and attitudes regarding the homosexual population. Some heterosexuals feel like those who have chosen the gay lifestyle deserve this deadly disease. Others are challenged to accept differences in people and have reached out to help young gays who are having to cope with devastating illnesses, death, and dying. More about the AIDS issue will be considered in the next section of this chapter.

A student who is gay may be having some difficulty dealing with some aspects of his choice, and he may be interested in discussing counseling options. Whatever the situation, the RA is challenged to assess his or her own knowledge, attitudes, and beliefs about homosexuality. Do you feel you would still be accepting of your best friend if he or she decided to share with you his or her sexual preference for the same sex? Are you able to talk with a person who is homosexual and see many aspects of his or her personality without focusing on sexual choice? Are you judgmental and opinionated, whether overtly or covertly, when you see certain people who portray the stereotype of male or female homosexuals? Are you concerned about members of the gay population who have AIDS, ARC, or a positive HIV antibody test?

It is your responsibility as an RA to honestly examine your feelings and attitudes regarding the homosexual lifestyle. If you are very prejudiced about homosexuality, it would be wise to read about the subject and work hard at being a more accepting, tolerant individual. One of the greatest challenges in life is increasing one's tolerance and acceptance of others. As an RA, you are a role model for many of your residents, and you certainly have the responsibility to set a good example.

If your residents verbalize or demonstrate problems and concerns about understanding and accepting the issues of homosexuality, you may want to consider some of the following approaches:

1. Encourage the student to take a course in sexuality. On the college level, the course usually considers many controversial topics.

2. If you have a gay rights group on campus or in the community, you may want to schedule a member as a speaker. A word of caution—you should prepare your residents in advance, telling them that they should only attend if they are willing to listen and learn. Emphasize that the speaker is being invited to speak and is a guest. It may help to have questions written out in advance.

3. Invite someone from the counseling center to talk to your floor about appropriate aspects of homosexuality and/or tolerance of lifestyle differences.

The important point is to be willing to listen and learn. Many people believe myths and misconceived ideas regarding individuals much different from themselves. Watch special TV programs, read, and attend seminars, classes, and workshops to broaden your perspective. It is understandable that your world may have had a fairly narrow perspective during your high school years. The challenge in college and throughout your lifetime is to be willing to explore our world and broaden your outlook. You have an opportunity to listen and learn about many different topics in an effort to grow into a self-actualized person. Unfortunately, some people are locked into lower levels of thinking and do not reach out to learn about and accept others. Be challenged to reach out and learn about others quite different from yourself.

It is important to remember that you can learn about many differences in life without condoning the ideas or practices for yourself. AIDS has challenged many professionals, including physicians, nurses, and counselors, to closely re-examine their beliefs and values regarding human life and homosexuality. Everyone has to make many choices every day. These choices may be vastly different from yours, but each individual does have a right to be treated with kindness and respect as a human being.

Sexually Transmitted Diseases (STDs)

"STDs" is the new term for venereal diseases because there are many more diseases included in this term than syphilis and gonorrhea. There is much concern presently about the epidemic of STDs. People must be educated about prevention, diagnosis, and treatment of these serious communicable diseases. We can no longer hide behind feelings of shame and guilt. College students are definitely involved in the STDs epidemic. Since RAs and college students have access to information on most STDs, the focus of this section will be on chlamydia and AIDS.

Chlamydia

One of the largest problems is a disease called chlamydia (pronounced kla-mid-e-uh). A recent article indicates that chlamydia strikes between 3 to 10 million Americans each year. Chlamydia causes more infections than syphillis, gonorrhea and herpes combined. It causes infections in 10 percent of the college students and is often not diagnosed and treated properly (*Time,* 1985).

Why the mystery about chlamydia? There are many reasons.

1. The disease was not isolated and studied as a bacterium until 1965.
2. The signs are not easy to diagnose. Men have a burning sensation during urination and a mucus discharge, while women have genital itching and a vaginal discharge. These symptoms also resemble gonorrhea or a urinary tract infection.
3. 60 to 80 percent of the women and 10 percent of the men have no symptoms at all.
4. When seen by some doctors, individuals are treated with penicillin for possible gonorrhea or drugs used for urinary tract infections. Neither of these stop chlamydia (p. 67).

Physicians can help control the disease by better diagnostics, using newer laboratory tests, and treatment with certain antibiotics for 7 to 14 days. Both partners must be treated, and affected individuals should abstain from intercourse until a health professional tells them it is safe. It is estimated that 40 percent of women and 20 percent of men with gonorrhea also have chlamydia; therefore both diseases may require treatment.

Young adults are especially susceptible to chlamydia if they are sexually active and have multiple partners. Women taking oral contraceptives seem to be more at risk. But the main concern is that if chlamydia is not treated quickly it can cause very serious complications in men and women.

1. It can spread from the cervix to the lining of the uterus, causing endometritis.
2. It can spread to the fallopian tubes and cause scarring of the tubes, which could cause infertility and possibly a tubal pregnancy.
3. It can spread to the entire female reproductive organs and surrounding pelvic tissues causing PID (Pelvic Inflammatory Disease.)
4. It can even spread to the liver.
5. In men, the bacterial organisms can spread to the epididymis, which may cause sterility.
6. In both sexes chlamydia may cause conjunctivitis (infection of the eyes) and proctitis (infection of the rectum) (Bete, no date).

It is important to limit the number of sex partners and know as much as possible about your partner's sexual activities. When in doubt, a condom is recommended.

AIDS

AIDS (Acquired Immune Deficiency Syndrome) is characterized by a defect in the individual's natural immunity to fight disease, and this predisposes the person to serious opportunistic infections and malignancies. AIDS is a very complex disease process, and there are still many unanswered questions as of 1988. The scientific community has given different names to the AIDS virus:

HIV—Human Immunodeficiency Virus
HTLV-III—Human T-Lymphotopic Virus Type III
LAV—Lymphadenopathy Associated Virus
ARV—AIDS Related Virus

HIV is now becoming the preferred term for many scientists. In this chapter the term, "AIDS virus," will be used.

When the AIDS virus enters the blood stream, the infected person will begin to produce antibodies against the virus. These antibodies can be detected by a simple blood test 2 weeks to 3 months after the infection. Once the person is infected with the AIDS virus, several possibilities can occur:

1. Some people remain well but can infect others.
2. Some people may develop a less serious disease than AIDS called ARC (AIDS Related Complex).
3. Some people will develop AIDS, which means the virus does enough damage to the immune system that other severe infections and cancers will occur. It is these diseases that make the person with AIDS so ill.
4. Some people will have damage to the nervous system and brain several years after infection from the AIDS virus (Surgeon General's Report, 1986).

There is presently no cure for AIDS, and no vaccine to prevent it. The most important tactic against the disease is education. It is important to learn as much as possible about AIDS from reliable sources. There have been many seminars, workshops, and forums presented by hospital personnel, public health departments, student health centers, and health education departments. In this chapter the basic information will be presented to help you in your position as an RA to think about how you should respond if you learn a person with AIDS is living on your floor or in your building.

Certainly much of the public's concern about AIDS centers around its contagiousness. The U.S. Department of Health and Human Services and the Centers for Disease Control have studied the disease intensely since the first cases in 1981. These agencies state that casual contact with a person having AIDS does not place others at risk of getting the disease. In other words, there is no known risk of infection from casual situations that we encounter in our daily lives. Family members living with individuals who have AIDS do not become infected except through intimate sexual relations. There is no spread of the virus when family members share towels, cups, razors, toothbrushes, and even when they kiss each other (Facts about AIDS, 1985).

The AIDS virus has been found in various body fluids, including tears and saliva, but a person can only get the virus through one of three ways:

1. **Through intimate sexual contact.** The virus can be passed when an infected person exchanges blood or semen with a sexual partner during anal intercourse or vaginal intercourse. Oral-genital and oral-anal sex may also be ways the AIDS virus is spread. Anal intercourse can result in tears in the rectum, which allows the virus to enter the bloodstream.
2. **Exchange of blood.** The blood of an infected person coming into contact with the blood of another person primarily occurs when drug abusers share needles and syringes.
   Early in the 1980s the AIDS virus was transmitted through blood transfusions to a few people. Since 1985 all donated blood is screened for the AIDS antibodies. It is almost impossible to get AIDS through a blood transfusion, but some health professionals recommend that people inquire about donating their own blood to be used in certain situations.
3. **Mother to Child.** Only a few children acquire AIDS from an infected mother during pregnancy or childbirth. The virus may be spread through breast milk. The woman with a positive antibody test should postpone pregnancy and should not breastfeed her child (Yarber, 1987).

If a person with AIDS was to attend your university, it might be advisable for him or her to be in a single room—not to protect other residents but to decrease the individual's exposure to infections. Personal items, such as razors and toothbrushes, that could become contaminated with blood should not be shared. AIDS is not spread by the casual contact of touching, talking, sitting near, or using the same restroom facilities as a person who has the disease. Casual social contact, such as shaking hands, hugging, social kissing, coughing, or sneezing, will not spread the AIDS virus. AIDS has not been contracted from swimming pools, hot tubs, or from eating in restaurants. You cannot get AIDS from toilets, doorknobs, telephones, office equipment, or furniture. You cannot get AIDS from body massages or any non-sexual contact (Surgeon General's Report . . ., 1986).

Who is at highest risk of getting AIDS?

1. Homosexual and bisexual men. About 70 percent of the people who have AIDS are in this group. Some of these are also IV drug abusers.
2. Heterosexual IV drug abusers. About 17 percent of the people with AIDS are in this group.
3. Heterosexual sex partners of persons with AIDS are at high risk of AIDS. About 4 percent of the persons with AIDS are in this group.
4. Recipients of blood transfusions prior to 1985. About 3 percent of the people with AIDS are in this group.

The Surgeon General's Report on AIDS estimated that about 1.5 million persons in the U.S. are infected with the AIDS virus. It is difficult to predict how many will get AIDS or ARC because the symptoms can take as long as nine years to appear. If a resident has a positive HIV antibody test, it is unknown whether the person will become ill or not. Since the test results are confidential, it is likely that the RA would know such personal information unless the resident chooses to share it for some reason. Most likely the information will be known only to physicians.

There is much concern about how responsible some AIDS carriers or HIV positive individuals are. Hopefully, there would have been a great deal of pre- and post-counseling if a student tests positive. Anyone who is at high risk should have the testing done so there can be some peace of mind in knowing the facts.

Anyone who is HIV positive must understand that he or she is capable of spreading the virus, even though AIDS itself is not present. HIV positive carriers should also know that they should never donate blood or organs. The key to preventing the spread of the virus is education, counseling, safer sexual behaviors, and avoidance of sharing IV drug equipment.

What can you as an RA do to cope with AIDS? Since new information and concerns about AIDS is released on almost a daily basis, it is important that you try to stay fairly current with factual information. There are a lot of myths and misinformation that need to be corrected. You may want to provide some programming on AIDS, either through a videotape, speaker, or discussion of pamphlets, newspaper or magazine articles, or recent books. It is important to realize that AIDS is a multi-disciplinary topic, affecting several university departments and community agencies. And it is important to realize that the whole approach to AIDS could change drastically with the invention of an effective treatment, vaccine, or cure.

Colleges must be concerned about providing accurate information and education to prevent further spread of the disease. The American College Health Association has been a leader in studying the impact of the disease on college campuses. This association has published two resources: "AIDS—What Everyone Should Know," and "AIDS on the College Campus." You may obtain these materials by writing to the American College Health Association, 15879 Crabbs Branch Way, Rockville, MD 20855. Additional information on AIDS is available from:

U.S. Public Health Service—AIDS Hotline—1-800-342-AIDS
National Gay Task Force—AIDS Crisis Line—1-800-221-7044
Gay Men's Health Crisis—1-212-807-6655

Conclusion

This chapter has touched just a few of the topics related to sexuality that may be discussed with the RA. There are always going to be relationship problems and concerns about intimacy, fair fighting, love, communication, and sharing. It is important for the RA to realize that he or she knows a little bit about a lot of things. You need to carefully examine and try to understand your "inner" self as you deal with others and their problems. Be aware of campus and community resources in terms of materials and people, and be ready to refer a student to other sources when you lack experience, knowledge—or attitude.

Case Studies and Structured Group Experiences about Sexuality

Case Studies: Mary

Instructions: Read the case studies and respond to the questions which follow. First work alone. When you are finished, share your answers with other RAs in small group discussions or as the basis for a classroom discussion.

Case Study: Mary

Louise is the RA for the east wing. Mary L. comes down to talk to her. She thinks she may be pregnant because she is 10 days late with her period, is sexually active, and has always been as regular as a clock.

1. Has she seen a health practitioner? _____
   _____

2. How early can a pregnancy test be done? _____
   _____

Mary is pregnant. She definitely does not want to marry Jeff. She has been a fairly regular church-goer, and she has said she doesn't believe in abortion. However, now she doesn't know what she believes in or what she wants to do. Her parents are divorced, and she never has related very well to her Mom.

3. As an RA, how can you help Mary? _____
   _____
   _____
   _____
   _____

4. Where on campus or in the community could you refer Mary? _____
   _____
   _____
   _____
   _____
   _____

5. Should you help Mary explore all the options available to her?
   a. Advantages/disadvantages of an abortion _____
   _____
   _____
   _____
   _____
   _____

   b. Advantages/disadvantages of keeping the baby and staying single _____
   _____
   _____
   _____
   _____
   _____

   c. Advantages/disadvantages of keeping the baby and getting married _____
   _____
   _____
   _____
   _____
   _____

   d. Advantages/disadvantages of giving the baby up for adoption _____
   _____
   _____
   _____
   _____
   _____

6. If you are adamantly pro-choice or pro-life on the issue of abortion, should you influence Mary in making her decision? _____
   _____
   _____
   _____
   _____

Case Study: Susan and Chuck

Mary and Susan are roommates in a coed hall. Susan is very popular and several times has come back to the hall with her boyfriend Chuck. She pleads with Mary to please leave the room so that she and Chuck can be together for the night. This is the third time Mary has had to leave the room. She has tried to be firm with Susan and tell her no, but she gets all upset and starts crying, so Mary gives in to keep the peace. Mary can always sleep in a friend's room, which is a single. Mary has tried to discuss the situation with Susan but she is fed up and comes to you, her RA.

Case Study Questions:

1. Will getting the two together to discuss the matter be of any help at this stage? _____

_____

_____

_____

_____

2. Is a room change in order? If so who should move? _____

_____

_____

_____

_____

3. Are there any other possibilities? _____

_____

_____

_____

_____

Case Study: Sam and Sara

Sam and Sara have been going together during their two years at college. They have intercourse frequently. Sara is faithful to Sam, but everyone knows that Sam occasionally has relationships with others. Sara is very concerned about AIDS. She thinks Sam may be considered to be in the high risk group, since she knows some of his previous sexual partners. Sara comes to see you, the RA on her floor. Sara says she trusts you and wants your advice.

Case Study Questions:

1. Sara wants to know if Sam should have the AIDS test. She wants to know where he should go for the test. She also wonders if she should take the test too. _____

_____

_____

_____

_____

_____

2. Should Sam and Sara be tested? Why? Where? _____

_____

_____

_____

_____

_____

_____

3. What advice can you give? _____

_____

_____

_____

_____

_____

_____

4. Although Sara indicates she takes the pill, should you discuss the concept of safe sex with her? ____

_____

_____

_____

_____

_____

Case Study: Lester

Several of the men on your floor are talking about Lester, who is a junior Speech and Theatre major. Lester is a very talented actor, who has been in several campus plays. Lester seems to be ill a lot and goes to the health center frequently. He says he is always tired, has a sore throat and has lost about fifteen pounds in the last two months. Three of your residents come in to talk to you.

Case Study Questions:

1. The residents think that Lester has AIDS. They feel that he should be tested and that they have a right to know the results. _____

_____

_____

_____

_____

2. The residents say that if Lester does have AIDS, they want him removed from the hall so they will not get the virus. They feel all AIDS victims should have to live off campus. How will you respond?

_____

_____

_____

_____

_____

_____

Case Study: Mark

Mark, one of the most popular residents on your floor, comes to talk to you in a very troubled mood. In addition to being well liked, Mark is a good athlete and has excelled in intramurals in certain sports. Mark asks if he can confide in you, and upon receiving a positive response he proceeds to tell you that he is homosexual. He has kept this fact hidden until now, but he believes he should "come out of the closet" and announce the truth to the rest of the floor. He believes he is well liked enough that the truth will have a positive impact on how people view homosexuality. He believes he will be doing a service to everyone. He wants your opinion.

Case Study Questions:

1. What are the pros and cons of Mark's proposed course of action on your particular campus? _____

2. What is your feeling about his proposal? _____

3. How would you personally feel about Mark if he were on your floor? _____

Exercise: It Bugs Me When. . . .

Goal: To increase awareness of the feelings we have toward certain behaviors of the opposite sex.

Group Size: Small groups of 5 or 6 of the same sex.

Time required: 20 to 30 minutes

Materials: 1. Newsprint; 2. Marker for each group

Physical Setting:

Process:

1. The females will write at the top of their sheet: "It Bugs Me When Men . . . They will then list the concerns.

2. The males will write at the top of their sheet: "It Bugs Me When Women . . ." They will then list their concerns.

3. After 10 minutes, the two groups will read their concerns to the rest of the group. It is best to *alternate* male and female responses.

Exercise: College "Friends"

Goals: To identify, verbalize and clarify personal values.
To increase awareness of judgments and decisions.

Group Size: Divide the group into 5 to 6 members per group.

Time required: 30 to 40 minutes.

Materials: 1. Paper and pencil; 2. Transparency of the cast of players

Physical Setting:

Process:

1. Use the transparency to introduce the story. Instruct the class members to read through the story.
2. Have each person rank the five people in the story. Number 1 is the person best liked, and #5 is the person least liked.
3. Each group of 5 or 6 should compare their papers and try to come up with one list.
4. Discuss the main issues presented in this story.

Cast of Characters:

> John: Mary's fiance
> Mary: John's fiance
> Jim: Mary's classmate
> Susan: Mary's best friend
> Frank: Mary's new friend

Story:

John and Mary are engaged to be married in six months. John is going to college at a school in the East. Mary lives in Indiana, where she is employed and attends college. Mary and Jim have a college class together on Tuesday evenings. They start going out for a drink after class. This leads to a few overnights, during which Mary and Jim have intercourse. Mary decides this isn't right, and she stops going out with Jim.

A couple of months later, Jim tells Mary he's going out East for a long weekend. Mary asks if she can ride along, and she'll spend the weekend with John. Jim says she's welcome to go along, if she'll go to bed with him.

Mary doesn't know what to do. She talks the situation over with Susan. Susan says she wouldn't do it, but Mary will have to make her own decision. Mary decides to go to bed with Jim.

Jim drives Mary out East to see John. Mary decides to tell John about her relationship with Jim. John breaks the engagement because he has been seeing another gal at school. They also discuss the fact that neither is ready to get married.

Mary returns to Indiana. She meets Frank at work, and they start dating. One month later Mary moves in with Frank.

CHAPTER 14

Suicide: Prevention, Intervention and Postvention

Dr. Myron G. Mohr
Baton Rouge Crises Intervention Center

During the 1970s and first half of the 1980s the suicide rate for American young people, ages 15 to 24, was three times higher than was the case for the preceding 25 years. Suicide now ranks as one of the leading causes of death for adolescents, exceeded only by accidents. The largest number of suicides in this age group occur in people 20 to 24. In American culture this period is referred to as late adolescence, and the statistics indicate that most college-age students, therefore, are in a higher-risk group for suicide than the general population.

Suicide is a complex and often frightening phenomena that has been surrounded by myths and taboos. It is a subject that many people do not like to think about, let alone talk about. Unfortunately, it is just such fear and ignorance that create the biggest obstacle to suicide prevention. Most suicide deaths are unnecessary, because suicidal behavior can be prevented. But for prevention to become a reality, someone must see the signs of impending danger and act intelligently to obtain qualified assistance.

It has been said that if suicide prevention activities are left only to mental health professionals we will never effect the suicide rate in a positive way. Suicide prevention is an appropriate activity for everyone. Just as we expect the general public to have some knowledge and skills in first-aid, from preventing drowning and choking to saving the life of a heart-attack victim, we could expect the same for suicide prevention. Training is valuable for all, but it is especially important for "gatekeepers," those whose activities bring them into contact with people who may have problems or be at high risk for suicide. Resident assistants are significant gatekeepers for university students, and knowledgeable and skilled gatekeepers can facilitate a troubled student's entry into the helping system. For many students, this system may appear a forboding, never-ending maze requiring more energy to navigate than they can muster. However, through understanding and support of significant others, most students are able to cope effectively and benefit from such help. On the other hand, a well-meaning, but untrained "gatekeeper" may unintentionally close the gate on someone seeking help, regardless of how obvious or disguised that seeking process may be.

This chapter is written to provide resident assistants with the basic knowledge and skills to be effective gatekeepers with students who may be suicidal. The chapter is divided into three sections: prevention, intervention, and post-vention. These sections define the areas into which structured responses to suicide can be delineated. While all the suggestions and recommendations in this chapter are written for resident assistants in general, it should be understood that each university will have its unique characteristics and students are encouraged to be as familiar as possible with their own university's policies and procedures, support services, and appropriate personnel. The size of a campus population, either too big or too small, should not be an excuse for failing to develop a positive psychological atmosphere in student living quarters.

This chapter will not make you an expert on suicide or enable you to be the sole source of counsel and treatment for suicidal people. The advice and expert knowledge of a qualified professional are needed whenever there is a serious risk of suicide. The informed resident assistant, however, is a key factor—often of life-saving importance—in knowing that a problem exists, in getting help, and in understanding how to support the work of the professional.

Prevention

As noted earlier, a greater number of suicides occur in the college age group than in the high school age group. Berkovitz (1985) gives several possible reasons for this fact, including increased anonymity, absence of familiar support groups, superficial relating, and aggravated feelings of failure. Being aware of such factors has led many universities to try to lessen the amount of social alienation and isolation by developing campus social support systems. Such activities range from a "buddy system" for entering freshmen, social mixers, and dormitory discussion groups to more structured programs designed to impact particular social and health problems (e.g., weight control, alcohol and drugs, sexual behavior, and suicide) faced by many students. It is through a well-developed social support system that a university can provide a positive psychological atmosphere for students. With the opportunities for validation, growth, and training in a supportive and challenging environment most students are able to meet the demands of college life.

The value of social support systems cannot be underestimated. However, regardless of how effective this system is, not all students will accept or use the support offered. These students become higher-risk for suicide when they are confronted with a crisis, especially a life crisis that they have not experienced previously, i.e., death of a family member or financial insecurity. There is also the unfortunate possibility that this support system, because it mirrors the community or society surrounding the university, will not attend to issues that are controversial or taboo, such as birth control, problem pregnancies, and suicide.

Overcoming Old Attitudes

Suicidal behavior has been documented since the earliest of times, but societal attitudes toward suicide have varied widely. Religions and governments have used shame, disgrace, and punishment as means to deter suicide. These never have been shown to be effective. Instead, from such practices grew social taboos and myths that, to some extent, still surround self-destructive behavior and thoughts. The terms that people use when they talk about people who commit suicide reveal a number of preconceived attitudes. The attitudes and feelings of faculty, staff, resident assistants, and other students will determine the type of response a troubled student receives when he or she seeks help.

Many commonly used descriptive words or phrases used to describe suicide are extremely judgemental and biased attitudes impede the helping process. Further, many of these words or phrases also reflect false beliefs that still exist about suicide. Some of the most common myths are these (Hoff, 1984 and Shneidman, 1981):

Myth: People who commit suicide are mentally ill or "crazy."
Fact: People who commit suicide are usually in emotional turmoil but not necessarily mentally ill.

Myth: Good circumstances—wealthy parents or making good grades—prevent suicide.
Fact: Suicide is very "democratic" and is seen in all socio-economic classes, races, ages, and achievement levels, though its frequency varies among different groups in society.

Myth: Suicide is inherited or "runs in families."
Fact: Suicide does not run in families. It is an individual pattern.

Myth: People who talk about suicide won't commit suicide. They are just trying to get attention.
Fact: People who die by suicide almost invariably talk about suicide or give clues and warnings about their intention through their behavior, even though the clues may not be recognized at the time. Further, attention is important, and think about how desperate a means suicide is of getting attention.

Myth:	People who attempt suicide with low-lethal methods (e.g., wrist cutting, non-prescription medication) and don't succeed are not a risk for suicide. It was just a "gesture."
Fact:	Many people who kill themselves have made at least one previous attempt. Any self-injury, even those in which the chances of death are slight, should be taken seriously. Not to do so may precipitate another attempt, possibly of higher lethality.
Myth:	People who are deeply depressed don't have the energy to commit suicide.
Fact:	The "energy level" of another person is subjective and difficult to assess. People may kill themselves when depressed or following improvement. Frequent and repeated assessment is therefore indicated.
Myth:	People who are upset or depressed are so "weak" and "suggestible" that talking about suicide will put the idea in their heads.
Fact:	Suicide is much too complex a process to occur as a result of a caring person asking a question about suicidal intent.
Myth:	Once a person is suicidal, he/she is suicidal forever.
Fact:	Individuals who wish to kill themselves are "suicidal" only for a limited period of time.

The facts listed above are based on recent research with self-destructive persons. Societal values do not change quickly, and suicide prevention education is needed through all levels of our society. Educational activities that provide the facts in a non-sensational manner increase the probability that suicide warning signs will be recognized before it is too late.

Suicide Warning Signs

Suicide does not happen without warning. Of any ten persons who kill themselves, eight have given definite indications of their suicidal intentions (Shneidman and Farberow, 1961). Probably the most costly, in terms of lost lives, of the previously noted myths is "People who talk about suicide won't commit suicide." This is simply not true. More often than not, people who kill themselves have verbally expressed their intention prior to the action. Sometimes such statements are direct and specific, while others may verbalize their desire to be dead in more disguised ways, with remarks such as "Well, you won't see me here next semester," "That's the last *F* I will ever receive," or "My parents won't have to shell out anymore money on me after next week." Such statements should always be taken seriously. This does not necessarily mean a "call to action" but rather a "call to attention."

Not all people who kill themselves are depressed. However, depression is seen often enough in those with suicidal ideation that it is a significant indicator for possible suicide behavior. Everyone experiences occasional depression without being suicidal. However, when such feelings persist over time and are associated with such symptoms as sleeplessness, weight loss, crying, restlessness, withdrawal, and hopelessness among others, the probability for suicide increases.

Sudden, unexplained changes in behavior or personality may also be a reason for concern. Examples include missing classes by a student who previously was conscientious about attendance, or loud and boisterous behavior by the usually reserved student, or vice versa. Such changes are not "just natural" and should not be ignored.

Making final arrangements can also be a warning that a student is preparing to commit suicide. Such behavior might not be as obvious as making a will. Instead, the individual could give away prized possessions, officially drop all classes for no obvious reason, or say good-byes to friends and other residents at times when others are not leaving.

All of the above warning signs become even more significant when they are exhibited by a student who has experienced a recent loss, real or imagined. Losses are the most common precipitating events for crisis periods. These are times in people's life when their usual coping behavior is not effective in reducing feelings of anxiety and pain. The probability for suicide risk is increased further when the student has a history of past suicide attempts. Among college students it is estimated that there are probably fifty attempts to every completed suicide. Obviously, most of these attempters are able, usually with supportive counseling, to regain a sense of equilibrium and often learn new constructive coping skills they did not have prior to the attempt. But for a few, especially those who do not accept help or utilize the social support system, suicide becomes a viable option in their next crisis period.

There are, of course, other indicators of suicide risk, but these four are significant: verbal suicide threats or similar statements, prolonged depression, marked changes in behavior or personality, and making final arrangements. These warning signs take on added significance when associated with a recent loss and a previous suicide attempt.

Fear is not an uncommon response for people when confronted with signs of suicide. It is not possible to combat fear when the subject remains hidden. Bringing suicide "out of the closet" and presenting it factually decreases the probability that helpers will be frightened into believing there is nothing they can do. Through such education efforts we also destigmatize suicide. People who have suicide thoughts often feel limited in sharing their fantasies for fear of the response they will receive. People judged as "crazy," "weak," or "attention-seeking" are rarely listened to and are often "put away." The stigma of suicide inhibits people from directly asking for help and is probably one of the reasons "cries for help" are often disguised. Education is our primary preventative tool.

Intervention

As the resident assistant, you may be the person to whom a suicidal student turns to for help. However, he or she will probably not discuss suicide directly. With the knowledge of warning signs and probably some degree of familiarity with the student, you have a good basis from which to begin the helping process. For many people in your position, this type of beginning is comfortable because the student initiated the contact. But given what we discussed earlier, the suicidal student may be reluctant to seek assistance so directly. It is probable that the responsibility for initiating contact with such a student will rest with you. The student may come to your attention from your own observations or from the concerns of roommates or fellow residents who identify you as the appropriate person to intervene. When the latter situation occurs, obtain all pertinent information that the concerned resident has that led him or her to come to you.

One purpose of this process is to review the student's observations and determine if these observations warrant further action. It is better to err on the side of safety and intervene when there is the slightest doubt. It would be appropriate to check whether or not the student has attemped to intervene. If he or she has and was rejected, this does not mean you should not try. Rather, it tells you about possible resistance or hostility to your own intervention. A high degree of resistance and hostility to intervention when suicidal signs are evident heightens the risk, and it would be appropriate for you to consult with the head resident or other appropriate authority in such circumstances.

Whether you are initiating contact or the student seeks you out, it is important to know what your time limits are. If your time is limited and the situation is not an emergency, plan to see the student at your earliest opportunity. Although students who initiate contact do not like to be put off, it is appropriate for you to determine briefly the student's needs and then set an appointment time. If the student's needs are a priority, arrange for him or her to see someone at that time.

Confidentiality vs. Responsibility

This may be the appropriate time to address the issue of confidentiality. This is an ethical standard you accepted when you took the RA position. Trusting is not always easy for people living in a large group setting, and it becomes more difficult when a person feels helpless and worthless. Your ability to respect the rights of another serves as an excellent role model and increases the probability that a troubled student will seek your counsel. There is one exception to the rule of confidentiality when you are working with someone who is suicidal. It is now accepted that if you are aware of a student who you believe is a high-risk for suicide, and if this student will not cooperate in talking with you or meeting with an appropriate professional, it is not a breech of confidentiality for you to inform someone of higher authority about the situation. In fact, it is expected of you. Each resident assistant should know to whom they should report if there were such a need.

Understanding and accepting your own feelings is the first step in understanding and accepting the feelings of others. Accepting someone's feelings does not necessarily mean that you agree with a conclusion that they hold. I can understand that a student could feel hopeless and worthless, but not agree that suicide is the best solution for resolving such pain. The ability to be empathic is of prime importance in communicating with a suicidal person.

Before we discuss some specific steps of the intervention process there are two important things to know that may help relieve some tension for you when you are required to invervene. The first is that suicidal people are not fragile. By this I mean the best approach is simple, direct communication that tells the student that you are not frightened of talking about suicide. It is your responsibility to determine the meaning of suicidal behavior and to identify the clues from words and attitudes of the self-destructive person. You do not do this by inferring the person's meaning, but by asking. Through direct open questioning—"What do you mean you won't be around next semester . . . Are you thinking of suicide?" or "What did you hope would happen when you took the pills?"—you communicate your care and interest in ways others have avoided out of fear or lack of knowledge. Through assertive responding, you begin to help the person feel reconnected to someone. This process also provides you with information you need for assessing current risk and making plans of action. I am not suggesting you would begin a contact with these questions, but that throughout the interaction your caring and sense of confidence are reassuring to someone who feels hopeless. Accepting that the suicidal person is not fragile also helps you avoid agreeing with his or her belief that he or she is helpless. Allow the person time to make decisions with your support and encouragement.

The second point is that suicidal people are usually struggling with two irreconcilable wants: the want to live and, at the same time, the want to die. This is known as ambivalence. The concept is basic to intervention. The person's words are saying "I want to die," but by interacting with you his or her behavior is saying "I want to live." This ambivalence is true, even though the person may not be consciously aware of it. As long as the person has ambivalent wants and feelings, it is possible to help the person consider choices. Persons who are no longer ambivalent do not make themselves available for intervention.

Model Intervention

The following outline of intervention steps is a model, an ideal representation of an interaction. Each interaction is unique, but a model provides direction for you, the gatekeeper.

First, accept the possibility that the person may really be suicidal and listen actively. This means verbally let the person know you heard, not only what he or she said, but also how he or she feels.

As rapport is established, talk openly, candidly, and calmly. If someone hints about suicide or comes right out and says it, it is important not be judgemental. Ask questions about the person's thoughts and feelings, including "Have you thought about how or when you would do it?" or "Have you made a specific plan?" The more specific a person's plan, the higher the risk for carrying it out. "Specific" means when, where, what method, and the availability of the method. Remember, you may be the first person who is actually allowing this person to ventilate what are usually frightening thoughts that he or she has been keeping only to himself or herself. Ventilating and sharing may be the most important part of the whole process. If you are not appalled, and if you care enough to listen, this conveys the message that he or she is not worthless and that possibly there is a glimmer of light at the end of what previously was a never-ending, dark tunnel.

If the suicidal person can move in this direction, you will also begin to hear clues or statements indicating that part of him or her that desires to live. Through this process you may be able to determine what may have triggered the suicidal crisis, and with some reduction in tension and anxiety the person may begin to look at options that were not apparent before. There is no need to give advice or glib reassurance.

Rather, be appropriately supportive and affirming by recognizing the person's strengths that are observable to you. Remember, for this individual this interaction with you represents a big risk—trusting you enough to let you know what he or she is thinking and feeling.

Most suicidal people experience a reduction of tension through this process and will choose to cope in different ways. However, this does not mean the crisis is over, and discussion about seeing a mental health professional is an appropriate part of determining the next step. Many students are initially hesitant to make such a decision. Remind them of their initial hesitancy with you. With support and realistic responses to possible concerns about such a move, facilitate the follow-through on your referral.

At this point, your knowledge and familiarity with appropriate services such as the campus or community crisis intervention center, the number of the 24-hour crisis line, or the way to make an appointment at the campus counseling center are most important. Your knowledge and support of such services illustrates your belief that change can occur in this person's life. Finally, make plans for recontact within the next 12 to 24 hours, depending on the person's ability to cope at that time. This is a supportive function, and it also allows you to check on his or her follow-through on your referral.

Actually, most interactions do end this way. Given a safe atmosphere (a non-judgemental listener) in which to ventilate, most suicidal people choose to live. When you are confronted with persons who resist your help and remain highly charged, do not leave them alone, and request assistance from within your support system. Knowing when to ask for help and consultation is a strength, not a weakness.

Post-vention

The suicide death can have devastating effects on survivors. Shneidman (1975) coined the term "suicide survivor" to refer to the individuals surrounding the suicide victim. These people are vulnerable to guilt, regret, and grief that is significantly different from the grief one experiences in response to a natural death and have a statistically greater risk of suicide themselves (Albert, et al, 1973 and Cain, 1972). One of the effects of suicide in the high-school age group is the "cluster phenomena," multiple suicides or attempts within a short period of time in the same school. Also included in the network of suicide survivors are helpers, people who may have been working with the person prior to his or her self-destructive act.

The group environment of a university residence hall increases the number of survivors in the event of a suicide of a resident and creates a population who are often in need of especially designed responses. "Post-vention" refers to the activities or helpful acts of care for the bereaved that reduce the after-effects of trauma in the survivors' lives. As you can see, these activities have a broader effect than just grief resolution. Since suicide survivors are thrust into a higher-risk group for suicide, post-vention activities also become prevention activities.

Because of the crisis created by a student suicide, it is strongly recommended that all colleges and universities prepare written guidelines for use in the event of suicides on their campus. Prior preparation and orientation of staff members, including resident assistants, will greatly assist those expected to assume leadership roles following a student's suicide. Such preparation also assures the professional residence hall staff of a support system for dealing with their own special survivor issues, e.g., "Did I do enough?" "I should have known." Resident hall personnel, especially those who may have been actively involved with any intervention activities with the deceased, should have opportunities to meet with consultants or support persons to debrief their own reactions and to evaluate actions they took. This is important to avoid "de-skilling"—underestimating or devaluating one's own skills—that may occur for those gatekeepers who were involved with the suicide victim.

Unfortunately, in a recent study by Webb (1978) it was found that probably less than 20 percent of colleges and universities have such written guidelines. This means that most university personnel are left to improvise in such situations. Most commonly, nothing is done to attend directly to the various survivor needs. Denial of the grief associated with the suicide, while common, only creates problems for the future.

Following the suicide death of a resident, other residents need to be given the facts and have opportunities to discuss their feelings and ask questions in an open, honest environment. This process offers individuals an opportunity to share their grief and also reduces the probability of rumor-spreading and blaming, which are not uncommon reactions following a suicide. Resident hall personnel should also be attentive to the needs of particular individuals, such as roommates of the suicide victim or special friends or enemies of the suicide victim, who may have difficulty in dealing with the death. Increased drinking and drug use and withdrawal have been observed in college student suicide survivors. Note that there are also warning signs for possible suicidal thoughts, and such students need counseling assistance to prevent negative or destructive coping with grief. "How-to responses" for resident assistants confronted with this occurrence are the same as we discussed under intervention.

Conclusion

Suicide has become a leading cause of death for college-age students, and yet, in many settings, it still remains a behavior people do not want to address. Avoidance as a response to suicide has shown to reap negative effects.

Destigmatizing suicide does not mean holding suicide as an accepted coping behavior; rather it makes suicide a topic that can be dealt with openly and honestly. Openness increases the probability that students who are suicidal will be identified earlier in the suicide crisis period and receive the type of help that we know can prevent the person from following through with self-destructive behavior. Resident assistants are on the front-lines of college campuses and can, with training and support, be the effective first link in the process of suicide prevention.

Case Studies and Structured Group Experiences for Suicide: Prevention, Intervention and Post-vention

Instructions: Read the case studies and respond to the questions which follow. First work alone. When you are finished, share your answers with other RAs in small group discussions or as the basis for a classroom discussion.

Case Study: Ted and Jack

Ted, a resident of your dormitory informs you that his roommate Jack, a second semester freshman, is expressing a lot of anxiety over his failure to get straight A's, even though he is doing much better than average. Ted continues to tell you that last week Jack broke up with his girlfriend and was drunk this past weekend. (Ted had never seen Jack drunk before.) Today Jack skipped class and asked Ted to drive him to a pawn shop where supposedly he was going to buy a pistol to give his father as a gift. Ted refused to skip class do do this, and Jack got angry and laid down on his bed, where he still is two hours later. Ted doesn't know what to do.

Case Study Questions:

1. What do you think is happening and why? _____

_____

_____

_____

_____

_____

_____

_____

_____

2. What is your plan of action with Ted? _____

_____

_____

_____

_____

_____

_____

_____

3. What is your plan—if any—with Jack? _____

_____

_____

_____

_____

_____

_____

_____

Comments

Case studies can be used as homework, giving individuals time to consider and formulate their responses. At the next training session these cases can be reviewed and compared in small groups. During these group sessions it is important that the facilitator utilize effective consultation skills, especially in helping someone reconsider his or her response. This consultation process is also an excellent role-modeling process.

Case Study: Jane

In the days following the suicide death of her roommate, you observe Jane spending most of her time in the lounge watching TV, even at 3 A.M. When you have attempted to be friendly, you have received little to no response. This is unlike Jane's previous behavior. When mentioning this to several of your co-resident assistants, they tell you "not to worry," "that is a common reaction to grief" and then change the subject.

Case Study Questions:

1. Discuss what is possibly happening here to those involved, including yourself. _____

_____

_____

_____

_____

_____

_____

_____

_____

2. Define the several courses of action or nonaction you could take. _____

_____

_____

_____

_____

_____

_____

_____

_____

3. Predict the outcome of the actions you noted above. _____

_____

_____

_____

_____

_____

_____

_____

4. What would you do for yourself in this situation? _____

_____

_____

_____

_____

_____

_____

_____

Comments

Case studies can be used as "homework," giving individuals time to consider and formulate their responses. At the next training session these cases can be reviewed and compared in small groups. During these group sessions it is important that the facilitator utilize effective consultation skills, especially in helping someone reconsider his or her response. This consultation process is also an excellent role-modeling process.

Exercise: Defining Your Institution's Support System

Goals: To help you identify various supportive resources available on your campus and in your surrounding community.

Group Size: Small groups of 5–9 with any number of groups.

Time Required: One to two hours.

Materials: Exercise sheet and pencils.

Physical Setting: Room with movable chairs.

Process:

Social support systems are what bind individuals and groups together. Practically, social supports are the people (or groups, organizations, agencies) who support an individual through crises and calm and with whom feelings can be shared without fear of condemnation. By providing emotional sustenance, supportive others help individuals master their own emotional problems by mobilizing their psychological resources. Additionally, by providing these people with tangible aids, resources, information, and cognitive guidance, the supporters further enhance the individual's ability to cope with stressful situations.

Each university and college has a social support system. Residence hall living quarters are a component of that system, and resident assistants are the operators of that component. To provide positive psychological atmospheres in which students can live, we must be familiar with the various components of the social support system within which we live and work and know how these components relate or communicate with each other.

The following exercise is designed to challenge you to identify the various supportive resources available on your campus and in your surrounding community. In your work as a resident assistant, making referrals and seeking consultation are important skills.

1. Individually, in writing,
    a. list the various social support resources available to students.
    b. note with a check (✓) those resources about which you want more information and a plus (+) next to those on which you can advise others.
2. Answer the study questions at the end of this exercise.
3. In small groups (5–9)
    a. compare lists
    b. discuss and share information regarding resources
    c. which resources are identified as needing further investigation for best understanding?
    d. which resources would be most appropriate for referral of someone who is suicidal and why?

Remember, the purpose is to generate as much resource data as you can. There is probably not just one best resource for each problem. Discuss reasons for choices for referral.

Study Questions

1. List the various social support resources available to students.

    1. _____
    2. _____
    3. _____
    4. _____
    5. _____
    6. _____

7. _____

8. _____

9. _____

10. _____

11. _____

12. _____

13. _____

14. _____

15. _____

2. Note with a check (✓) those resources about which you want more information and a plus (+) next to those on which you can advise others.

Study Question

1. Does your college or university have written guidelines for post-vention activities following the suicide death of a student? _____

   _____

   _____

   _____

   _____

   _____

   _____

   _____

   _____

2. If so, what is the defined role for resident assistants? _____

   _____

   _____

   _____

   _____

   _____

   _____

   _____

3. If not, what would you do in the aftermath of a suicide death of a resident? _____

_____

_____

_____

_____

_____

_____

_____

Exercise: Attitudes Toward Suicide

Goal: To illustrate the effects of attitudes toward suicide.

Group size: No limit

Time required: Approximately 30 to 45 minutes

Materials: 1. Paper; 2. Pencil or pen

Physical Setting: Room with movable chairs for arranging small groups of 5 to 7 persons in each group.

Process:

1. List, in writing, words or phrases you have heard people use to describe suicide or people who have killed themselves. Allow 5 to 10 minutes.
2. Then form groups of 5 to 7 persons. Each group should compare their lists and discuss the types or forms of response behavior you would expect to see from people using these words when interacting with a student who had expressed the desire to commit suicide.
3. At the conclusion of the small group discussion, one member of each small group is to summarize verbally what their group discovered or discussed in front of the total group.

List the words or phrases you have heard people use to describe suicide or people killing themselves.

1. _____
2. _____
3. _____
4. _____
5. _____
6. _____
7. _____
8. _____
9. _____
10. _____
11. _____
12. _____
13. _____
14. _____
15. _____

Exercise: Group Role Play in Suicide Prevention

Goals:
1. To practice intervention skills.
2. To illustrate that there is not just one way to intervene effectively.

Group Size: Up to 15

Time Required: As much time as available.

Materials: 1. Props or set, but not necessary: 2. Paper, pen or pencil

Physical Setting: Large enough room so that 5 groups of 3 persons have their own space to work, without interfering with other trios.

Process:

1. The group is divided into trios.
2. Each person of the trio selects a role.
   a. Resident assistant
   b. Troubled student
   c. Observer
3. Briefly set the scene, e.g., the troubled student, who is quiet, reserved, homesick, and having suicidal thoughts, knocks on the resident assistant's door. When the door opens, the student hesitates and then asks "how much refund will my father get if I move out of the dorm this week?" The rest of the scene is improvised by the two actors.
4. The observer watches and notes in writing the specific skills or approach utilized by the RA. Note especially, the positive skills.
5. At the conclusion of the scene, the trio discusses what happened. Specifically, identify feelings experienced by the role players while in their respective roles and review the feedback from the observer. The scene may not be concluded within 30 minutes. If not, debrief what has happened to that point, and discuss what would happen based on the direction the action was going.

Comments

This is an example role play. Participants could also simply be asked to develop their own scenes or play a situation that actually happened to them. Depending on time, participants should get an opportunity to experience all three roles.

Notes to the Facilitator:

Role-play exercises often trigger a degree of anxiety for most participants; therefore, it is helpful to do some warm-up exercises prior to the actual scenes in which you want to practice intervention skills. Less-threatening role plays assist participants in feeling comfortable with the group and illustrate that role-playing can be done.

Trainers also choose to model a role-play before the class before asking the participants to do so. One caution here: some participants may simply try to imitate the trainers rather than risk drawing upon themselves. One way to avoid this is have the trainers model several interventions, including ones that we would consider poor, and then have participants discuss what they observed, noting differences, their own reactions to the differences, etc.

Role Play

Paul has been depressed recently. He appears at your door one evening, hesitates and then says "how much refund will my father get if I move out of the dorm this week?"

Bibliography

Chapter One

Blimling, G. S., & Miltenberger, L. J. (1981). *The resident assistant: Working with college students in residence halls.* Dubuque, IA: Kendall/Hunt Publishing Company.

Case, F. D. (1981). Dormitory architecture influences patterns of student social relations over time. *Environment and Behavior, 13*(7), 23–41.

Ender, K., Kane, N., Mable, P., & Strohm, M. (1980). *Creating community in residence halls.* Cincinnati, OH: ACPA.

Hennessy, T. J. (1981). A philosophy of community development for residence halls. In G. S. Blimling & J. S. Schuh (Eds.), *Increasing the educational role of residence halls* (pp. 13–21). San Francisco: Jossey Bass.

Mable, P., Terry, M. J., & Duvall, W. H. (1980). Student development through community development. In D. A. DeCoster & P. Mable (Eds.), *Personal education and community development in college residence halls* (pp. 103–113). Cincinnati, OH: ACPA.

McKaig, R., & Policello, S. (1984). Student advising—defined, described and examined. In J. H. Schuh (Ed.), *A handbook for student group advisers* (pp. 45–69). Carbondale, IL: ACPA.

Menne, J. M. C., and Stinnett, F. R. (1971). Proximity and social interaction in residence halls. *Journal of College Student Personnel, 12,* 26–31.

Miller, T. K., & Prince, J. S. (1976). *The future of student affairs.* San Francisco: Jossey-Bass.

Schroeder, C. C. (1981). Student development through environmental management. In G. S. Blimling & J. H. Schuh (Eds.), *Increasing the educational role of residence halls.* San Francisco: Jossey-Bass.

Schuh, J. H., Kuh, G. C., Gable, A., Friedman, K., Stipanovich, M., & Wegryn, L. (1981). The RA role revisited: Differences in perspectives of RA responsibilities. *The College Student Affairs Journal, 4*(1), 13–22.

Werring, C. J., Winston, R. B., Jr., & McCaffrey, R. J. (1981). How paint projects affect residents' perceptions of their living environments. *The Journal of College and University Student Housing, 11*(2), 3–7.

Zander, A. (1985). *The purpose of groups and organizations.* San Francisco: Jossey-Bass.

Chapter Two

Bandura, A. (1977). *Social Learning Theory.* Englewood Cliffs, NJ: Prentice-Hall.

Davis, T. R. V., and Luthans, F. (1980). A social learning approach to organizational behavior. *Academy of Management Review, 5,* 281–290.

Deal, T. R., and Kennedy, A. K. (1982). *Corporate Cultures: The rites and rituals of corporate life.* Reading, Mass: Addison-Wesley.

Feldman, D. C. (1981). The multiple socialization of organization members. *Academy of Management Review, 6,* 309–318.

Peters, T. J., and Waterman, Jr., R. H. (1982). *In search of excellence.* New York: Warner Books.

Kerr, S. (1975). On the Folly of Rewarding A, While Hoping for B. *Academy of Management Journal, 18,* 769–783.

Manz, C. C., and Sims, H. P., Jr. (1981). Vicarious learning: The influence of modeling on organizational behavior. *Academy of Management Review, 6.* 105–113.

Schein, E. H. (1985). *Organizational Culture and Leadership.* San Francisco, CA: Jossey-Bass.

Wanous, J. P. (1980). *Organizational entry: Recruitment, selection, and socialization of newcomers.* Reading, Mass: Addison-Wesley.

Wanous, J. P., Reichers, A. E. and Malik, S. D. (1984). Organizational socialization and group development: Toward an integrative perspective. *Academy of Management Review, 9,* 670–683.

Chapter Three

Allen, W. (1982). *National study of black college students,* Department of Sociology, The University of Michigan.

Allport, G. (1979). *The nature of prejudice.* Reading, Mass.: Addison-Wesley.

Amir, Y. (1976). The role of intergroup contact on change of prejudice and ethnic relations. In P. H. Katz (Ed.), *Towards Elimination of Racism,* New York: Pergamon.

Banks, J. A. (1984). *Teaching strategies for ethnic studies,* 3rd Ed. Boston: Allyn and Bacon.

Bennett, C. (1986). *Comprehensive multicultural education: Theory and practice.* Boston: Allyn and Bacon.

———. (1986) Teaching intercultural competence and informed citizenship. Paper presented at the Annual Conference of the National Council of the Social Studies in New York, November 1986.

———. (1984) Interracial contact experience and attrition among black undergraduates at a predominantly white university. *Theory and Research in Social Education, 9,* 2 (Summer).

Bennett, C. and Bean, J. (1984). A conceptual model of black student attrition in predominantly white institutions. *The Journal of Educational Equity and Leadership, 4* (Fall).

Birdwhistel, R. (1970). *Kinesics in context.* Philadelphia: University of Pennsylvania Press.

Byrne, D. (1961). The influence of propinquity and opportunities for interaction on classroom relationships. *Human Relations, 14.*

Cohen, E. (1979). Status Equalization in the Desegregated Schools. Paper presented at the Annual Meeting of the American Educational Research Association, San Francisco (April).

Cross, W. (1979). The negro-to-black conversion experience: toward a psychology of black liberation. *Black World, 20* (July).

Dennis, R. M. (1981). Socialization and racism: The white experience. In B. P. Bowser and R. G. Hunt, Eds., *Impacts of racism on white Americans.* Beverly Hills, Calif.: Sage Publications.

Devries, D. and Edwards, K. (1974). Student teams and learning games: Their effects on cross-race and cross-sex interaction. *Journal of Educational Psychology, 66.*

Fleming, J. (1985). *Black College Students.* Jossey Bass.

Ford, M. L. (1979). The Development on an Instrument for Assessing Levels of Ethnicity in Public School Teachers. Unpublished Ph.D. dissertation, University of Houston.

Hall, E. T. (1959). *The silent language,* New York: Doubleday.

———. (1966) *The hidden dimension,* New York: Doubleday.

———. (1976) *Beyond Culture.* New York: Doubleday.

———. (1983) *The dance of life.* New York: Doubleday.

———. (1972) Proxemics: The study of man's spatial relations. In Larry A. Samouar and Richard E. Porter (Eds.) *Intercultural Communication: A Reader.* Belmont, Calif.: Wadsworth, 172–180.

Hilliard, A. (1976). Alternatives to IQ testing: An approach to the identification of gifted minority children. Final Report to the California State Department of Education.

Johnson, K. R. (1972). Black Kinesics and Cultural Anthropology. In Larry A. Samouar and Richard E. Porter (Eds.) *Intercultural Communication: A Reader*. Belmont, Calif.: Wadsworth, 181–189.

Jones, J. M. (1981). The Concept of Racism and Its Changing Reality. In Ed. Benjamin D. Bowser and Raymond G. Hunt, Eds. *Impacts of Racism on White Americans*. Beverly Hills, Calif.: Sage.

Keefe, J. W. and Languis, M. (1983). *Learning Styles Network Newsletter* (New York) *4,* (Summer).

LaBarre, W. (1972). Paralinguistics, kinesics, and cultural anthropology. In Larry A. Samouar and Richard E. Porter (Eds.) *Intercultural communication: A reader*. Belmont, Calif.: Wadsworth, 172–180.

Longstreet, W. (1976). *Aspects of ethnicity: Understanding differences in pluralistic classrooms*. New York: Teachers College Press.

Montagu, A. (1974). *Man's most dangerous myth: The fallacy of race,* 5th ed. New York: Oxford University Press.

Milleones, J. (1976). The Pittsburg project—Part II, Construction of a black consciousness measure. Reprinted from W. E. Cross, Jr., Ed., *Third Conference on Empirical Research in Black Psychology*. Washington, D.C.: Department of Health, Education and Welfare, NIE (December).

Nettles, M. and Johnson J. (1986). "Race and gender distinctions in the determinants of student socialization in the college environment." Educational Testing Service. Paper presented at the Annual Conference of the American Educational Research Association in San Francisco (April).

Nora, A. (1986). Determinants of retention among Chicano college students: A structural model. Paper presented at the Annual Conference of the American Educational Research Association. San Francisco (April).

Pettigrew, T. (1973). The case for the racial integration of the schools. In O. Duff (Ed.), *Report on the Future of School Desegregation in the United States*. Pittsburgh: University of Pittsburgh, Consultative Resource Center on School Desegregation and Conflict.

Rokeach, M. (1969). *Beliefs, attitudes and values*. San Francisco: Jossey-Bass.

Schofield, J. W. (1978). School desegregaton and intergroup relations. In D. Bar-Tal and L. Saze (Eds.), *The Social Psychology of Education*. New York, Halstead Press.

Shade, B. J. (1982). "Afro-American cognitive style: A variable in school success?" *Review of Educational Research, 52,* no. 2 (Summer).

Stereotypes, distortions and omissions in U.S. history textbooks (1977). New York: Council on Interracial Books for Children.

Chapter Four

Ardrey, R. (1966) *The territorial imperative*. New York: Atheneum.

Barker, R. & Gump, P. (1964). *Big school, snall school*. Stanford, CA: Stanford University Press.

Chickering, A. (1969). *Education and identity*. San Francisco, CA Jossey-Bass.

Fowler, J. (1981). *Stages of faith*. San Francisco: Harper & Row.

Kalsbeek, D., Rodgers, R., (1982) Marshall, D., Denny, D. and Nicholls, G. Balancing challenge and support: a study of degrees of similarity in suitemate personality type and perceived differences in challenge and support in a residence hall environment. *Journal of College Student Personnal, 23,* 434–442.

Kegan, R. (1982) *The evolving self*. Cambridge, MA: Harvard University Press.

Knefelkamp, L., Widick, C., and Parker, C. A. (Eds.) (1978). *Applying new developmental findings*. San Francisco, CA: Jossey-Bass.

Kohlberg, L. (1984). *The psychology of moral development: Volume two of essays on moral development*. San Francisco: Harper & Row.

Loevinger, J. (1976). *Ego development*. San Francisco, CA: Jossey-Bass.

Perry, W., Jr. (1970). *Intellectual and ethical development in the college years: A scheme.* New York: Holt, Rinehart & Winston.

Rodgers, R. F. (1980). Theories underlying student development. In D. G. Creamer (Ed.), *Student development in higher education: theories, practices and future directions.* Washington, D.C.: American College Personnel Association.

Rodgers, R. F. (1983). Using theory in practice. In T. K. Miller, R. B. Winston, Jr., and W. R. Mendenhall (Eds.) *Administration and leadership in student affairs.* Muncie, IN: Accelerated Development.

Schroeder, C. C. (1985). *Campus ecology: theory and application.* Fort Collins, CO.: Campus Ecology Symposium, Colorado State University.

Schroeder, C, C. (1980). Student development through environmental management. In F. B. Newton and K. L. Ender (Eds.), *Student development practices: strategies for making a difference.* Springfield, IL: Charles C. Thomas.

Chapter Five

Carkhuff, R. R. (1969). *Helping and human relations. Vol. I. Selection and training.* New York: Holt, Rinehart and Winston.

Davis, J. R. (1977). *Going to college: The study of students and the student experience.* Boulder, CO: Westview Press.

Ellis, A. (1973). *Humanistic psychotherapy.* New York: Julian Press.

Rogers, C. R. (1951). *Client-centered therapy.* Boston: Houghton Mifflin.

Sydnor, G. L. and Parkhill, N. L. (1978). *Systematic human relations training: A manual for trainers.* West Monroe, LA: Human Resources Development Training Institute.

Chapter Six

Blimling, G. S. and Miltenberger, L. J. (1984). *The Resident Assistant: Working with College Students in Residence Halls, 2nd Ed.* Dubuque, Iowa: Kendall/Hunt Publishing Company.

Brown, R. D. (1972). *Student development in tomorrow's higher education: a return to the academy.* Washington, DC: American College Personnel Association.

Carkhuff, R. R., and Truax, C. B. (1965). Training in Counseling and Psychotherapy. *Journal of Consulting Psychology, 29,* 333–336.

Feldman, K. A., and Newcomb, T. M. (1969). *The impact of college on students: an analysis of four decades of research.* Vol 1. San Francisco: Jossey-Bass.

Newcomb, T. M., and Wilson, E. K., eds. (1966). *College peer groups: Problems and Prospects for research.* Chicago: Aldine.

Powell, J., Plyler, S., Dickson, B., and McClellan, S. (1969). *The personnel assistant in college residence halls.* Boston: Houghton Mifflin Company.

Upcraft, M. L. (1982). *Residence hall assistants in college.* San Francisco: Jossey-Bass.

Chapter Seven

Chickering, Arthur W. (1971). *Education and identity.* San Francisco, Jossey-Bass.

Hall, C. S., and Lindzey, Co. (1950). *Theories of personality.* New York: John Wiley & Sons. Inc.

Hoelting, F. B. (1973). *How to do it in residence halls: 1001 ways to program.* Macomb, Illinois.

Keller, B. Y. (1985). Alcohol Abuse: Programming for the Solution. *The Aglaia of Phi Mu, 80* (Fall).

Moos, R. H. (1979). *Evaluating Educational Environments.* San Francisco: Jossey-Bass.

Residential Services (1986). *Residence hall staff manual.* Unpublished, Bowling Green State University, Bowling Green, Ohio.

Student life programs (1983). *Wellness ISU* unpublished, Indiana State University, Terre Haute, Indiana.

Walsh, W. Bruce, (1973). *Monograph Ten: The theories of personality environment interaction: Implications for the college student.* The American Testing Program.

Walter, P., Acerra, K., Epperly K., Malaska, A., McGough, K., Sherman, S., Giampetro, M. A. (1985). *The Ashley challenge . . . WE DARE YOU!* unpublished paper, Bowling Green State University, Bowling Green, Ohio.

Wellness Committee (1983). *Wellness Resource Book,* unpublished handbook, Student Residential Programs, Western Illinois State University, Macomb, Illinois.

Chapter Eight

Astin, A. W. (1977). *Four critical years.* San Francisco: Jossey-Bass.

Chickering, A. W. (1974). *Commuting versus residence students.* San Francisco: Jossey-Bass.

Chickering, A. W. (1977). *Education and identity.* San Francisco: Jossey-Bass.

Erickson, E. H. (1968). *Identity: Youth and crisis.* New York: W. W. Norton.

Kohlberg, L. (1971). Stages of moral development. In C. M. Beck, B. S. Crittenden, and E. V. Sullivan (Eds.), *Moral Education.* Toronto: University of Toronto Press.

Kohlberg, L. (1975). The Cognitive-Developmental Approach to Moral Education. *Phi Delta Kappan, 56*(1), 670–677.

Perry, W. G., Jr. (1970). *Forms of intellectual and ethical development in the college years.* New York: Holt, Rinehart and Winston.

Smith, A. F. (1978). Developmental Issues and Themes in the Discipline Setting—Suggestions for Educational Practice. Unpublished doctoral dissertation, Ohio State University, a.

Smith, A. F. (1978). Lawrence Kohlberg's cognitive stage theory of the development of moral judgment. In L. Knefelkamp, C. Wideck, C. Parker (Eds.), *Applying Developmental Findings.* San Francisco: Jossey-Bass, b.

Turiel, E. (1974). Conflict and Transition in Adolescent Moral Development. *Child Development, 45*(1), 14–19.

Chapter Nine

American Behavioral Scientist (Nov/Dec 1983). *27* (2). (Issue devoted to Negotiation: Behavioral Perspectives.)

Brown, B. R. (1968). The effects of need to maintain face on interpersonal bargaining. *Journal of Experimental Social Psychology, 4,* 107–122.

Deutsch, M. (1973). *The Resolution of Conflict.* New York: Yale University Press.

Engram, B. (1985). *Roommate Negotiation Workbook.* Frederick, MD: Hood College.

Fisher, R. and Ury, W. (1983). *Getting to Yes.* New York: Penguin Books.

Kelly, J. B. (1983). Mediation and psychotherapy: Distinguishing the differences. *Mediation Quarterly, 27,* 33–44.

Chapter Ten

Ardell, D. B. (1984). The history and future of wellness. *Wellness Perspectives: Journal of Individual Family and Community Wellness, 1,* 3–23.

Ardell, D. B., and Tager, M. J. (1982). *Planning for wellness: A guidebook for achieving optimal health* (2nd ed.) Dubuque, IA: Kendall/Hunt Publishing Company.

Archer, Jr., J., Probert, B. S., and Gage, L. (1985, March). College student attitudes toward wellness: Testing the face validity of a wellness model. Paper presented at American College Personnel Association, Boston.

Beeler, K. D. (1985). Wellness promotion in higher education and college student affairs. *College Student Affairs Journal, 3,* 10–22.

Beeler, K. D. (in press). Personal and personnel wellness: A primer for college student affairs. *National Association of Student Personnel Administrators Journal.*

Cohen, M. S. (1980). The student wellness resource center: A holistic approach to student health. *Health Values: Achieving High Level Wellness, 4,* 209–212.

Cooper, K. (1982). *The aerobics program for total well-being.* New York: M. Evans and Co.

Dunn, H. A. (1961). *High-level wellness.* Arlington, VA: R. W. Beatty.

Elsenrath, D. E. (1984, July/August). The role of the counseling center in the promotion of wellness. *Health Values: Achieving High Level Wellness, 8,* 30–34.

Fitness: The facts (undated). Daly City, CA: Krames Communications.

Healthy people: The Surgeon General's report on health promotion and disease prevention (1979). Washington, DC: Department of Health and Human Services, Public Health Service, Office of Disease Prevention and Health Promotion.

Hettler, W. (1980). Wellness promotion on a university campus. *Family and Community Health: The Journal of Health Promotion and Maintenance, 3,* 77–92.

Johnson, G. (Chair) (1984). Unpublished report of Education Program Research and Information Committees, ACUHO-I. Macomb, IL: Western Illinois University.

Knapp, S., and Magee, R. (1979). The relationship between life events to grade point averages of college students. *Journal of College Student Personnel, 20,* 497–502.

Knefelkamp, L., Widick, C., and Parker, C. A. (1978). Editors' notes: Why bother with theory? In L. Knefelkamp, C. Widick and C. A. Parker (Eds.), Applying new developmental findings. *New Directions for Student Services* (p. VIII). San Francisco: Jossey-Bass.

Krivoski, J. F., and Warner, M. J. (1986). Implementing strategies for high-level wellness programs in student housing. In F. Leafgren (Ed.). Developing campus recreation and wellness programs. *New Directions for Student Services* (53–66). San Francisco: Jossey-Bass.

Leafgren, F. (1984, July/August). Coordinating student life services to enhance wellness opportunities. *Health Values: Achieving High Level Wellness, 8,* 4.

Leafgren, F., and Elsenrath, D. E. (1986). The role of campus recreation programs in institutions of higher education. In F. Leafgren (Ed.). Developing campus recreation and wellness programs. *New Directions for Student Services* (3–17). San Francisco: Jossey-Bass.

Levin, L. S. (1979). Self-care: New challenges to individual health. *Journal of American College Health Association, 28,* 117–120.

McDonald, K. (1983, May 11). Physical education extending beyond the gym and around the track. *Chronicle of Higher Education,* pp. 17–18.

McMillan (1986, February 19). Bran muffins at faculty meetings and 5-mile runs at lunch: This college is mecca for fitness buffs. *Chronicle of Higher Education,* p. 23.

Monagham, P. (1984, October 17). Athletics for the fun of it: Big boon on campuses. *Chronicle of Higher Education,* p. 26.

National Wellness Institute (1984). *Lifestyle assessment questionnaire* (4th ed.). Stevens Point, WI: University of Wisconsin—Stevens Point.

Newsweek on campus: Food, tolerable food (1987, March), *Newsweek on Campus,* p. 19.

On Campus Poll: Drugs and health (1987, April), *Newsweek on Campus,* p. 23.

Opatz, J. J. (1985). *A primer of health promotion: Creating healthy organizational cultures.* Washington, DC: Oryn.

Pelletier, K. R. (1979). *Holistic medicine: From stress to optimum health.* New York: Dell.

Phys. ed. shapes up (1985, March). *Newsweek on Campus,* pp. 32–33.

Proxmire, W. R. (1973). *You can do it! Senator Proxmire's exercise, diet and relaxation plan.* New York: Simon and Schuster.

Seffrin, J. R., and Torabi, M. R. (1984). *Education in healthy lifestyles: Curricular implications.* Bloomington, IN: Phi Delta Kappa.

Tager, M. J., and Harris, J. S. (undated). *Improving your odds: A planning guide for high-level wellness.* Chicago: Great Performance, Inc.

Taking stock of your health: A self-scoring questionnaire (1986, February 19). *Chronicle of Higher Education,* p. 22.

Ten leading causes of death in the United States (1975). Atlanta: U.S. Department of Health, Education, and Welfare, Public Health Service, Centers for Disease Control.

Travis, J. (1977). In D. B. Ardell, *High-level wellness: An alternative to doctors, drugs, and disease* (p. 13). Emmaus, PA: Rodale Press.

Travis, J. (1981). *Wellness workbook for helping professionals.* Mill Valley, CA: Wellness Associates.

Tubesing, N. L., and Tubesing, D. A. (Eds.). (1988a). *Structured Exercises in wellness promotion* (Vol. 4). Duluth, MN: Whole Person Press.

Tubesing, N. L., and Tubesing, D. A. (Eds.). (1988b). *Structured exercises in stress management* (Vol. 4). Duluth, MN: Whole Person Press.

Warner, M. J. (1985). Wellness: A developmental programming model for residence halls. *Journal of College and University Student Housing, 15,* 31–34.

Warner, M. J. (1984). Wellness promotion in higher education. *National Association of Student Personnel Administrators Journal, 21,* 3, 32–38.

Well now! (Undated). Appleton, WI: Aid Association for Lutherans.

Well on your way (1985). West Columbia, SC: Palmetto Health Systems.

Chapter Eleven

Benson, H. (1975). *The relaxation response.* New York: Morrow.

Borysenko, J. (1984). Stress, coping, and the immune system. In J. D. Matarazzo, S. M. Weis, J. A. Herd, N. E. Miller, and S. M. Weis (Eds.), *Behavioral health: A handbook of health enhancement and disease prevention* (pp. 248–260). New York: John Wiley and Sons.

Cooper, A. H. (1977). *The aerobics way.* New York: Bantam Books.

Ellis, A., and Grieger, R. (1977). *Handbook of rational-emotive therapy.* New York: Springer.

Lazarus, R. S. and Folkman, S. (1984). *Stress, appraisal, and coping.* New York: Springer Publishing Co.

Marlatt, G. A. and Gordon, J. R. (1985). *Relapse prevention: Maintenance strategies for behavior change.* New York: Guilford Press.

Marx, M. B., Garrity, T. F., and Bowers, F. R. (1975). The influence of recent life experience on the health of college freshmen. *Journal of Psychosomatic Research, 19,* 87–98.

Meichenbaum, D. H. (1977). *Cognitive behavior modification: An integrative approach.* New York: Plenum.

Pelletier, K. R. (1984). *Healthy people in unhealthy places: Stress and fitness at work.* New York, N.Y.: Delacorte Press/Seymour Lawrence.

Rahe, R. H., and Arthur, R. J. (1978). Life change and illness studies: Past history and future directions. *Journal of Human Stress, 4,* 3–15.

Selye, H. (1975). *Stress without distress.* Philadelphia: Lippincott.

Sime, W. E. (1984). Psychological benefits of exercise training in the healthy individual. In J. D. Matarazzo, S. M. Weis, J. A. Herd, N. E. Miller, and S. M. Weis (Eds.), *Behavioral health: A handbook of health enhancement and disease prevention* (pp. 488–508). New York: John Wiley and Sons.

Woolfolk, R. L., and Richardson, F. C. (1978). *Stress, sanity, and survival.* New York: Signet.

Chapter Twelve

Alcohol, Drug Abuse, and Mental Health Administration (ADAMHA, 1986, April). Cocaine use in the United States. Rockville, Maryland: Dept. of Health and Human Services.

American College Health Association (ACHA, 1984). Eating disorders. *Health Information Series.* Rockville, Maryland: ACHA.

American Council on Alcoholism (ACA, no date). *The most frequently asked questions about alcoholism.* Baltimore: ACA

American Psychiatric Association (APA, 1980). *Diagnostic and Statistical Manual of Mental Disorders* (3rd ed.). Washington, D.C.: APA.

Blimling, G. S., and Miltengerger, L. J. (1984). *The Resident Assistant* (2nd ed.). Dubuque, Iowa: Kendall/Hunt Publishing Company.

Dennison, D., Prevet, T., and Affleck, M. (1980). *Alcohol and behavior: An activated education approach.* St. Louis: Mosby.

Gadaleto, A. F., and Anderson, D. S. (1986). Continued progress: The 1979, 1982, and 1985 college alcohol surveys. *Journal of College Student Personnel, 27*(6), 499–509.

Gormally, J. (1984). The obese binge eater. In Hawkins, R. C., Fremouw, W. J., and Clement, F. F. (Eds.), *The binge-purge syndrome: Diagnosis, treatment, and research* (pp. 47–73). New York: Springer.

Halmi, K. A. (1983). Classification of eating disorders. *International Journal of Eating Disorders, 2*(4), 21–26.

Holmgren, S., Humble, K., Norrig, C., Roos, B. E., Rosmark, B., and Solberg, S. (1983). The anorectic bulimic conflict. *International Journal of Eating Disorders, 2*(3), 3–14.

Kreipe, R. E., and Carafos, M. A. (1985). The identification of anorexia nervosa and bulimia on student health forms. *Journal of American College Health, 34*(1), 11–17.

Leigh, G. (1985). Psychosocial factors in the etiology of substance abuse. In Bratter, T. E., and Forrest, G. G. *Alcoholism and substance abuse: Strategies for clinical intervention* (pp. 3–48). New York: Free Press.

Mills, K. C., Neal, E. M., and Peed-Neal, I. (1983). *A handbook for alcohol education: The community approach.* Cambridge, Massachusetts: Ballinger.

Mitchell, J. E., and Pyle, R. L. (1982). The bulimic syndrome in normal weight individuals: A review. *International Journal of Eating Disorders, 1*(2), 61–73.

Myers, J. K., Weissman, M. M., Tischler, G. L., Holzer, C. E., Leaf, P. J., Orvaschel, H., Anthony, J. C., Boyd, J. H., Burke, J. D., Kramer, M., and Stoltzman, R. (1984). Six-month prevalence of psychiatric disorders in three communities. *Archives of General Psychiatry, 41,* 959–967.

National Institute on Alcohol Abuse and Alcoholism (NIAAA, 1980). *Facts about alcohol and alcoholism.* Rockville, Maryland: Dept. of Health and Human Services.

National Institute on Alcohol Abuse and Alcoholism (NIAAA, 1982). *Treating alcoholism: The illness, the symptoms, the treatment.* Rockville, Maryland: Dept. of Health and Human Services.

National Institute of Child Health and Human Development (NICHHD, no date). *Anorexia nervosa.* Rockville, Maryland: Dept. of Health and Human Services.

National Institute on Drug Abuse (NIDA, 1983). *Drugs and American high school students, 1975–1983.* Rockville, Maryland: Dept. of Health and Human Services.

National Institute on Drug Abuse (NIDA, 1984). *Just say no* series (Marijuana, Hallucinogens and PCP, Sedative-Hypnotics, Opiates, Inhalants, Stimulants and Cocaine). Rockville, Maryland: Dept. of Health and Human Services.

Norman, D. K., and Herzog, D. B. (1983). Bulimia, anorexia nervosa, and anorexia nervosa with bulimia. *International Journal of Eating Disorders, 2*(2), 43–52.

Oetting, E. R., and Beuvais, F. (1986). Peer cluster theory: Drugs and the adolescent. *Journal of Counseling and Development, 65*(1), 17–22.

Robins, L. N., Helzer, J. E. Weissman, M. M., Orvaschel, H., Gruenberg, E., Burke, J. D., and Regier, D. A. (1984). *Archives of General Psychiatry, 41,* 49–958.

Schwartz, D. M., Thompson, M. G., and Johnson, C. L. (1982). Anorexia nervosa and bulimia: The socio-cultural context. *International Journal of Eating Disorders, 1*(3), 20–36.

Solomon, J., and Keeley, K. A. (1982). *Perspectives in alcohol and drug abuse: Similarities and differences.* Boston: Wright.

Wright, L. S., and Moore, R. (1982). Correlates of reported drug abuse problems among college undergraduates. *Journal of Drug Education, 12*(1), 65–73.

Chapter Thirteen

Boston Women's Health Collective (1985). *The new our bodies ourselves.* New York: Simon and Schuster.

Bete, C. L. (no date). What Everyone Should Know about Chlamydia. Pamphlet, Channing L. Bete Publications.

Chlamydia: The Silent Epidemic (February 4, 1985). *Time* 67.

Facts about AIDS. (1985). Pamphlet, U.S. Department of Health and Human Services (August).

Hatcher, R. A., Guest, F., Stewart, F., Stewart, G., Trussel, J., and Frank E, (1984). *Contraceptive technology—1984–85,* 12th ed. New York: Irvington Publishers.

Leon, S. (1986). *Contraceptive Technology Update.*

Ory, H. W. (1983). *Making Choices.* New York: Alan Guttmacher Institute.

Planned Parenthood Federation of America (1985, November). *Statement on Coca-Cola as a contraceptive.* News release.

Surgeon General's Report on AIDS (1986). U. S. Department of Health and Human Services.

Wilbur, A. E. (1986). The Contraceptive Crisis. *Science Digest* (September), 84–85.

Yarby, W. L. (1987). "Aids: What Young Adults Should Know." Pamphlet, Indiana State Board of Health.

Chapter Fourteen

Albert, G., Forman, N. and Masik, L. (1973). Attacking the college suicide problem. *Journal of Contemporary Psychotherapy. 6*(1).

Berkovitz, I. H. (1985). The role of schools in child, adolescent, and youth suicide prevention. In *Youth suicide,* Peck, M. L., Farberow, N. L., and Litman, R. E. (Eds.). New York: Springer Publishing Co.

Cain, A. E., Ed. (1972). *Survivors of Suicide.* Springfield, IL: Charles S. Thomas.

Hoff, L. A. (1984). *People in crisis understanding and helping,* 2nd Ed. Boston: Addison-Wesley Publishing Co.

Shneidman, E. and Farberow, N. L. (1961). *Some facts about suicide.* PHS Publication No. 852, U.S. Government Printing Office, Washington, D.C.

Shneidman, E. (1975). Postvention: The care of the bereaved. In *Consultation-liaison Psychiatry.* Pasnau, R. O. (Ed.) New York: Grune and Stratton.

Shneidman, E. (1981). Suicide. *Suicide and Life Threatening Behavior, 11*(4).

Webb, N. B. (1986). Before and after suicide: A prevention outreach program for colleges. *Suicide and Life Threatening Behavior. 16*(4).